Writing Fiction
FOR
DUMMIES®

by Randy Ingermanson
and
Peter Economy

WILEY

Wiley Publishing, Inc.

Writing Fiction For Dummies®

Published by
Wiley Publishing, Inc.
111 River St.
Hoboken, NJ 07030-5774
www.wiley.com

Copyright © 2010 by Wiley Publishing, Inc., Indianapolis, Indiana

Published by Wiley Publishing, Inc., Indianapolis, Indiana

Published simultaneously in Canada

For general information on our other products and services, please contact our Customer Care Department within the U.S. at 877-762-2974, outside the U.S. at 317-572-3993, or fax 317-572-4002.

For technical support, please visit www.wiley.com/techsupport.

Wiley also publishes its books in a variety of electronic formats. Some content that appears in print may not be available in electronic books.

Library of Congress Control Number: 2009939355

ISBN: 978-0-470-53070-2

Manufactured in the United States of America

15 14 13

WILEY

About the Authors

Randy Ingermanson is the award-winning author of six novels. He is known around the world as "the Snowflake Guy," thanks to his Web site article on the Snowflake method, which has been viewed more than a million times. Before venturing into fiction, Randy earned a Ph.D. in theoretical physics from the University of California at Berkeley and published a number of articles on superstring theory. He has spent a number of years working as a computational physicist developing scientific software for high-technology companies in San Diego, California.

Randy has taught fiction at numerous writing conferences across the country and sits on the advisory board of American Christian Fiction Writers. He also publishes *The Advanced Fiction Writing E-zine,* the world's largest e-zine on how to write fiction. Randy's first two novels won Christy Awards, and his second novel, *Oxygen,* coauthored with John B. Olson, earned a spot on the New York Public Library's *Books for the Teen Age* list. Visit Randy's personal Web site at www.ingermanson.com and his Web site for fiction writers at *www.AdvancedFictionWriting.com.*

Peter Economy of La Jolla, California, is a best-selling author with 11 *For Dummies* titles under his belt, including two 2nd editions and one 3rd edition. Peter is coauthor of *Writing Children's Books For Dummies, Home-Based Business For Dummies, Consulting For Dummies, Why Aren't You Your Own Boss?,* and many more books. Peter also serves as Associate Editor of *Leader to Leader,* the Apex Award–winning journal of the Leader to Leader Institute. Check out Peter's Web site at www.petereconomy.com.

Dedication

To my loyal blog readers on the Advanced Fiction Writing Blog. You've taught me more in your questions than I could possibly teach you in my answers.

— Randy Ingermanson

Authors' Acknowledgments

We would like to thank the many people who took time to provide their advice and input to us as we created the book you now hold in your hands. Specifically, we would like to thank the folks at Wiley who cared enough to make this book the best it could be, including Tracy Boggier, Natalie Harris, Danielle Voirol, and Christy Pingleton. Thanks also to our talented technical editor David Hassler.

Randy would like to thank his coauthor Peter Economy for guidance in learning the *Dummies* way and for many strategic and tactical conversations during the writing of this book. He also thanks his wife, Eunice, for being there always and his daughters, Carolyn, Gracie, and Amy, for many hundreds of hours of reading-out-loud time.

Peter would like to thank his coauthor Randy Ingermanson for his hard work and dedication to this project and for showing him that there is much more to the world of writing than nonfiction. He would also like to thank his wife, Jan, and kids, Peter, Skylar, and Jackson, for their ongoing love and support.

Publisher's Acknowledgments

We're proud of this book; please send us your comments at http://dummies.custhelp.com. For other comments, please contact our Customer Care Department within the U.S. at 877-762-2974, outside the U.S. at 317-572-3993, or fax 317-572-4002.

Some of the people who helped bring this book to market include the following:

Acquisitions, Editorial, and Media Development

Project Editor: Natalie Faye Harris

Acquisitions Editor: Tracy Boggier

Senior Copy Editor: Danielle Voirol

Assistant Editor: Erin Calligan Mooney

Editorial Program Coordinator: Joe Niesen

General Reviewer: David Hassler

Editorial Manager: Christine Meloy Beck

Editorial Assistants: Jennette ElNaggar, David Lutton

Art Coordinator: Alicia B. South

Cover Photos: © Gerard Fritz

Cartoons: Rich Tennant (www.the5thwave.com)

Composition Services

Project Coordinator: Sheree Montgomery

Layout and Graphics: Carl Byers, Joyce Haughey, Melissa K. Jester, Christine Williams

Proofreader: Shannon Ramsey

Indexer: Christine Karpeles

Special Help: Christine Pingleton

Publishing and Editorial for Consumer Dummies

Diane Graves Steele, Vice President and Publisher, Consumer Dummies

Kristin Ferguson-Wagstaffe, Product Development Director, Consumer Dummies

Ensley Eikenburg, Associate Publisher, Travel

Kelly Regan, Editorial Director, Travel

Publishing for Technology Dummies

Andy Cummings, Vice President and Publisher, Dummies Technology/General User

Composition Services

Debbie Stailey, Director of Composition Services

Contents at a Glance

Table of Contents

Part II: Creating Compelling Fiction 85

Chapter 10: Action, Dialogue, and More: The Lowest Layer of Your Plot 177

Chapter 11: Thinking Through Your Theme 203

Introduction

· ·

So, you want to write a novel? Great! Writing a novel is a worthwhile goal. It'll challenge you, stretch you, and change you. Getting it published will gain you respect from your family and friends, and it may even earn you a bit of fame and money.

But respect, fame, and money aren't the only reasons for writing a novel. The only reason you need to give for writing a novel is that you want to write a novel. Don't let anyone bully you by demanding some better reason; there isn't one.

Whatever your reason, *Writing Fiction For Dummies* can help you make the leap from writer to author. You can write a powerful novel. You can get it published. And you can be the author you've always wanted to be.

About This Book

Writers like to think of themselves as artists, and rightly so; writing fiction is an art form. But artistic talent is not enough. Writing fiction is also a *craft* — a set of practical skills you can learn. This book is about teaching you the craft of writing fiction so that your art can shine through. So if you're a budding novelist, then we wrote this book specifically for you. This book teaches you the craft you need, shows you how to edit yourself, and takes you through the process of getting published.

If you're more advanced than a beginning writer, that's great! You'll find some parts of this book obvious. We hope to surprise you with some fresh insights, though, so stay alert. We've found that even published novelists are sometimes weak in certain areas. Our aim is to give you a solid foundation in every aspect of writing fiction.

We focus on novel-writing, but if you're a screenwriter or you want to write short stories, you'll find virtually all the material here useful to you; however, we don't try to cover the specialized things you need to know to write screenplays or short stories. Again, our goal is to give you the foundation that every fiction writer must have in order to write strong stories.

As you build your craft, remember that *every* rule we mention in this book can be broken. Every rule. If we sometimes sound horribly dogmatic on some of the rules, it's because they're almost always true. When we sound less certain with a rule, it's because it's true more often than not. The one unbreakable rule of fiction writing is that no rule is unbreakable — you should use whatever works.

Conventions Used In This Book

We use the following conventions throughout the text to make everything consistent and easy-to-understand:

- ✔ All Web addresses appear in `monofont`.
- ✔ New terms appear in *italics* and are closely followed by an easy-to-understand definition.
- ✔ **Bold** text indicates keywords in bulleted lists or highlights the action parts of numbered steps.

The English-speaking world is still trying to sort out how to deal with generic pronouns. In the bad old days, *he* was understood to refer to both men and women, which never made sense, but it was the standard. Now there is no standard. Replacing *he* with *they* is awkward, so in most cases, we try to use *he* and *she* in roughly equal numbers.

Because more fiction readers are women than men, we often tilt toward using *she* when referring to the reader. Because a great many editors are women, we often use *she* for editors and *he* for agents, but we're not consistent. We try to mix up the *he* and *she* usage when referring to characters. Forgive us if we don't get our pronouns quite even. We tried, and anyway we know you're smart enough not to be confused.

What You're Not to Read

We've written this book so you can easily find information and readily understand what you find. We also simplify the presentation so you can identify "skippable" material. *Sidebars* are the shaded boxes that appear here and there. They share useful facts, but they aren't essential for you to read.

Foolish Assumptions

Every author writes with an ideal reader in mind. Here are some things we assume about you:

- ✔ **You want to get published.** You're a creative person, but you intend to act like a professional right from the start. You're willing to do unglamorous tasks, like researching your category and target audience, because you know that fiction writing is a business, not just an art.

- ✔ **You want to write a novel.** This book focuses on writing novels, which typically run 60,000 words or more. If you prefer to write short fiction, the information on craft applies, but you'll create a simpler plot and use fewer characters. If you want to write a screenplay, you'll find all the information on story world, characters, structure, plot, and theme valuable, but we don't discuss the formatting you need to know for screenwriting, and we don't tell you how to sell your screenplay (you can find that kind of info in *Screenwriting For Dummies,* by Laura Schellhardt [Wiley]).

- ✔ **You recognize that fiction is a big tent with many different opinions on what's good and what isn't.** In this book, we give you broad guidelines that apply to most kinds of fiction, but there are no rules that apply everywhere and always for all writers. You'll strongly disagree with us sometimes, but you're smart enough to take the advice that works for you and ignore the rest. You know that many other writers will find the advice you reject useful.

- ✔ **You want to figure out how to tell a great story rather than how to fix grammar and punctuation.** You already have a good handle on grammar, or you know where to find the help you need (perhaps you plan to enlist your grammar-guru friends, consult Geraldine Woods's *English Grammar For Dummies* [Wiley], or hire a freelance proofreader). When you do break grammar rules, you claim artistic license and do it on purpose.

How This Book Is Organized

This book is divided into five parts. Dive in wherever you like. This section describes what's in this book and where we put it.

Part I: Getting Ready to Write Fiction

A little planning can go a long way. We believe strongly in strategic thinking — setting goals, defining *story,* choosing a category, developing a creative style, researching your novel, and getting the right tools. If you need help in strategic planning for your next novel, check out this part and see whether you can find some ideas you've never seen anywhere else.

Part II: Creating Compelling Fiction

Writing fiction is about giving your reader a powerful emotional experience. To do this, you need to master several main aspects of fiction, including creating a great story world, constructing believable characters, building a well-structured plot, and overlaying it all with a theme. These are your core skills, and this part gives you step-by-step guides for developing them. After you've mastered this part, you'll have all the tools you need to write the first draft of your novel.

Part III: Editing and Polishing Your Story and Characters

After you have a first draft, you need to edit it to a high polish. Editing isn't hard, but you need a strategic and tactical plan to help you analyze your characters and your plot. This part shows you how to ask the right questions of your manuscript and how to use your answers to rework your story. We give you many practical tips for editing your manuscript from top to bottom.

Part IV: Getting Published

With an excellent manuscript in hand, you're ready to take it out to the world and knock 'em dead with your story. You'll want to get a second opinion, of course, but after you've been through that, you're ready to find out about editors and agents. Don't be terrified of these folks — they're looking for writers (like you) with great stories. If you have what they need, they'll become your instant lifelong friends.

This part shows you how to research and identify the agents or editors who are most interested in your kind of fiction. You discover how to pitch your work to agents and editors who are looking for exactly what you have.

Part V: The Part of Tens

This part contains some quick resources on two subjects of undying interest: Ten steps to designing your story and ten reasons people in the publishing business reject novels.

Icons Used in This Book

To make this book easier to read and simpler to use, we include some icons in the margins that can help you find and fathom key ideas and information.

Tips provide advice that's short and easy to remember that you can use right away.

This icon marks a writing exercise that you should do to move forward on your novel.

Remember icons flag advice you'll come back to again and again over the years.

This icon indicates a warning note about some special hazard that you should avoid.

The True Story icon marks anecdotes that illustrate what we're talking about.

Where to Go from Here

The great thing about this book is that you decide where to start and what to read. It's a reference you can jump into and out of at will. Just wander over to the table of contents or the index to find the information you want.

If you're new to writing fiction, you may want to start at the beginning of this book and read through to the end. If you're more experienced, then you can find a topic that interests you and turn right to it. If you're interested in character development, check out Chapter 7. If you've already written a story and want to analyze the plot, flip to Chapter 13. And if you want advice on finding an agent, try Chapter 17. Whatever the case, you'll find a wealth of information and practical advice. Ready? Set. Go!

Part I
Getting Ready to Write Fiction

The 5th Wave

By Rich Tennant

FOR WALTER, THE COMPONENTS FOR WRITING GOOD FICTION WERE ALWAYS PLOT, CHARACTER, SETTING, AND MARTINI.

In this part . . .

We know you're excited to start writing, but before you begin, you need to do some strategic thinking. In this part, we consider exactly what makes a great story and how to find the fiction category that works best for you and your reading audience. Next, we take a look at four common methods writers use to write a novel. Finally, we delve deeply into the important subject of managing your time — and yourself.

Chapter 1

Fiction Writing Basics

- -

In This Chapter

▶ Setting your sights on publication

▶ Getting your head ready to write

▶ Writing great fiction and editing your story

- -

So you want to write a novel? Great! But is that all you want to do? After all, anybody can type a bunch of words and call it a novel. The trick is writing one that's good enough to get published. This book is for fiction writers who want to write an excellent novel and get it published. That's a tough, demanding goal, but it's entirely doable if you tackle it intelligently.

If you're going to write a novel, you need to get your head fully into the game. That means making a game plan that's a proven winner and then executing your game plan. After you have a plan, you need writing (and rewriting) skills — lots of them. Writing fiction means developing a raft of technical skills, both strategic and tactical. None of these steps are hard, but they're a lot easier to pick up when you have some guidance.

After you've written a great novel, whether you choose to get an agent or make the deal yourself, selling a strong story is about making the right connections with the right people at the right time.

Our goal in this book is to take you from being a *writer* to being an *author*. We have every confidence that you can do it, and this chapter explains how. It can happen — and it will happen — if you have the talent and persistence to do what you need to do.

Five urban legends that can hurt you

As soon as you admit to your family and friends that you're working on a novel, they'll start feeding you all kinds of urban legends about writing. These are things that "everybody knows," and yet they're dead wrong. Wrong or not, they can kill your career before it gets rolling. Here are some of the urban legends we've heard, along with answers you should have ready:

✔ **Legend 1: You're not smart enough to write a novel.** How smart do you have to be to write a novel? How do you know? What does IQ have to do with writing fiction? The fact is that the main thing any novelist needs is the ability to tap into her own emotional wellsprings and create a story that can move her readers. We know plenty of novelists, and they run the gamut on intelligence from average to ultra-high. But every one of them is a person we'd be happy to be stranded with on a desert island for long periods of time. Fiction writers are exceptionally honest people who don't balk at telling their own inner truths. If you can do that, you can write fiction.

✔ **Legend 2: You're not talented enough to write a novel.** What is talent? Does anybody know how to measure talent? What if talent is something you grow, not something you inherit? The fact is that writing fiction requires quite a few skills. We've never met anyone who had all those skills when they started writing. Every single published novelist we know spent long hours learning the craft of fiction. They all had one thing in common: persistence. We have no idea what talent may be, but we do know persistence when we see it. If you have persistence, you have as good of a chance of getting published as anyone else.

✔ **Legend 3: You have nothing to write about.** Is there only one kind of novel that you can write? Do all novelists have to come from New York City? Do they all have to be trendy and cool? Why? If you've lived long enough to be able to type, you have something to write about. If you've ever known fear, joy, rejection, love, rage, pleasure, pain, feast, or famine, then you have *plenty* to write about. If you've survived a miserable childhood or a wretched middle school or a toxic relationship — if you've been to hell and back — then you have enough material to write about for your whole career. If your life has been one long happy stream of nicey nirvana from beginning to end, then you'll need to work a little harder, but you should still be able to scrape a story out of that.

✔ **Legend 4: You have to know people to get a novel published.** Who knew Stephen King before he got published? Who knew Tom Clancy? Who knew J. K. Rowling? If you have great writing in your pocket, you'll get to know people quick enough. All you have to do is show around what you have, and the right people will find you. Yes, really. Great writing trumps great connections every time.

✔ **Legend 5: You'll forget your friends when you're famous.** Which famous writers ever forgot their real friends when they hit the limelight? Why would they do that? If you become famous, you'll be besieged with people posing as friends who are looking for a piece of your fame. Soon enough, you'll find out that the friends who knew-you-when are the *only* friends that you know for sure love you for yourself. You won't forget your real friends — you'll value them more than ever.

Setting Your Ultimate Goal As a Writer

If you're writing a novel, don't be modest about your goals. First of all, you want to write a really good novel, right? You aren't in this game to write a piece of schlock. You have some talent, and you have a story, and you want to write it well.

Second, you want to get the darned thing published. Don't hang your head and say, "I'll be happy just to get it written." Write to get published. Humility is a fine thing, but false humility can keep you from doing the one thing you really want to do.

Do this right now:

1. **Take a piece of paper and write down these words:**

   "I'm going to write a novel and get it published. I'm going to do it because writing a novel is worthwhile and because I have the talent to do it. I'm going to do it because I have something important to say to the world. I refuse to let anything get in my way."

2. **Put today's date at the top and your signature at the bottom.**

   Hang it where you can see it every day, and tell your family and friends about it.

As of this moment, you're a *writer*. Don't be ashamed to say so. On the happy day when you get your novel published, you'll be an *author*.

It's all too common for a writer to say (hanging head in shame), "I'm an unpublished writer." Banish that word *unpublished* from your vocabulary. You are a writer. Call yourself a writer, whether you've been published or not.

Randy's path to publication

Back in 1988, Randy decided that he was going to write a novel and get it published someday. Never mind why — just because. He started writing that novel, and about a year later, he'd written enough that he felt ready to go to a writing conference. He met some other writers there, got some great training, and joined a critique group.

(continued)

(continued)

Another year passed, and Randy's skills were developing. At a certain point, he realized that the novel he'd been working on for more than two years was fatally flawed. He put it in the drawer and never looked at it again, but he didn't abandon the vision. The goal was not to get *that* novel published; the goal was to get *some* novel published. Randy kept writing, worked hard, and after a couple of more years, he finished a novel.

He then began looking for an agent. Meanwhile, he began writing the next book. Within a year or so, he met an agent at a writing conference and within a few months signed an agreement for literary representation with him. The agent submitted the manuscript to a number of likely publishers. Randy kept writing.

One by one, every publisher on the list rejected Randy's manuscript. The agent submitted it to more publishers and resubmitted it to some publishers who'd rejected it but seemed interested. One of the publishing houses eventually rejected it three times. Randy kept writing.

The last publisher on the list saw some merit in Randy's work. The publishing committee looked at the manuscript for several months — and then rejected it. However, they took the time to point out three major problems that prevented them from buying the work. Randy's agent called him with the news that the novel was dead. He also explained to Randy the publisher's three concerns.

That day, Randy began working on a new novel, one that didn't have any of those problems. This time, he felt sure, he had a winner. This one would be the novel that got published. His agent liked the idea and told him to pursue it. Randy kept writing.

Three months later, the agent died. Randy was devastated. He'd now been writing for eight years. He'd completed a novel, done his best to sell it, had it rejected everywhere, and then lost his champion. He kept writing.

Shortly thereafter, Randy went to a writing conference and made an appointment to talk with an editor he'd never met before. He stumbled through his pitch, making a perfect hash of it. Finally, the editor asked to see a writing sample. Randy pushed five pages across the table, and the editor skimmed over them. "You write pretty well," he said. "Here's my card. Send me a proposal and 100 pages."

A year and a half later, without an agent, Randy sold that novel to that editor's publishing house. The novel appeared in the spring of 2000, 12 years after he started writing. At last, he was an author. That novel, *Transgression,* went on to win a Christy Award, and Randy went on to write several more award-winning novels. He became well-known enough that conferences began asking him to teach.

Fast-forward another nine years. Randy has taught hundreds of writers. He's mentored a number of them to become authors. He's seen his students hit the bestseller list. And he's now seeing them as finalists for major awards. In this book, he's distilling what he's learned over the last 21 years on the art and craft of writing fiction.

Pinpointing Where You Are As a Writer

Now that you've set your goal — to write a novel good enough to get published — we can talk strategically about how to get there. It won't be easy, but it will be straightforward, so long as you do things in the right order.

We've identified four stages in the life of most writers on the road to publication. They're analogous to the four years of college, so we like to call these stages *freshman*, *sophomore*, *junior*, and *senior*.

Please note that these stages may take more or less than a year to work through. We've seen a writer go from sophomore to senior in less than a year. Randy is pretty sure he was stuck as a junior for about eight years. If he'd had a coach, he could've zipped through that painful junior stage in about a year. That's why he takes such joy in coaching writers.

This section looks at those four stages and explains how you can advance to the next level.

Freshmen: Concentrating on craft

Freshman writers are new to the game, and that's okay. Every Ph.D. was a freshman in college at one time, and every author was a freshman writer at one time. It's one step along the path. Typically, *freshman writers* have been reading fiction all their lives, and at last they've decided to start writing a novel. They write a few chapters and then discover an unpleasant truth: This fiction-writing game is harder than it looks.

Some freshmen give up at that point, but those who persist decide to get some training in the craft of writing fiction. They read books, take courses, join critique groups, and maybe go to a writing conference. Most importantly, they keep writing.

Nobody ever got good at writing by talking about it. Or hearing about it. Or reading about it. You get good at writing by doing it. Then you get your work critiqued, figure out what's not up to par, and try it again. And again. And again.

At first, freshmen writers feel like nothing is happening — those miserable critique partners never seem to be satisfied, and new flaws seem to pop up before they solve the old ones. But persistence pays off. Eventually, after months of hard work, freshmen writers wake up one day to a surprising truth: They've gotten better. They've gotten a whole lot better.

A freshman advances by writing and by getting it critiqued and by studying the craft of fiction and by writing some more.

Sophomores: Tackling the proposal

Sophomore writers have been writing for a good while, and they're no longer rank newbies. The other writers in their critique group are telling them, "That's pretty good. You've made a lot of progress."

A sophomore has generally taken at least one course on writing or has read several books on writing. A sophomore has almost always gone to at least one writing conference. He or she is starting to feel pretty confident. This writing game no longer seems hopeless. The craft of fiction is no longer a mystery.

But one thing is still an enigma: By now, a sophomore has heard how hard it is to break into publishing. There's a thing called a *book proposal* that needs to get written, but who knows what that's supposed to look like? And it requires a dreaded *synopsis,* and that sounds too ghastly for words. And how are these things related to a *query letter?* Typically, a sophomore feels a mix of confidence and terror: A growing confidence in craft, a rising terror of marketing. (If you're curious about query letters, synopses, and proposals, see Chapter 16.)

Retreating into defeatism here is easy, but that way lie dragons. The winning strategy is to keep writing — advancing in craft — but now to begin figuring out how to market yourself effectively. Writing marketing materials like a query, a synopsis, and a proposal is a skill that no novelist can afford to ignore.

If you're a sophomore, it's high time to go to a good writing conference armed with a proposal (and a finished chapter or two) and show it to somebody — maybe a writer. Maybe an agent. Maybe an editor. The proposal will likely need a lot of work. Go with that attitude and ask for a critique of your proposal. Make it clear that you're not pitching the project yet; you're just learning how to pitch. You'll get all the critique you can handle. (If you're uncertain about the difference between an agent, an editor, and a publisher, see Chapter 17.)

Can't wait! Practicing your proposal

Does a novel need a nice, long proposal to be sold to a publisher, or is a short synopsis good enough? Most writers Randy knows always prepare and submit full proposals, even to publishers that they've worked with frequently. The agents Randy knows all insist on receiving a proposal before agreeing to represent an author, and most of them use proposals in submitting potential novels to publishers. One editor says that she loves proposals because they help her get ready to take a project to her committee.

Randy insists that figuring out how to write a proposal is a highly valuable exercise for any writer. Many writers of commercial fiction need them, and this is becoming even more true as publishers find the economic screws tightening — they need to know that the project has a good chance to sell well.

Please note that the fiction proposal is substantially different from the nonfiction proposal. A query letter is often part of the process (all of which we explain in Chapter 16). However, proposals are very important for a great many novelists, and it's unwise to remove them from the table. If you meet an agent and he's interested in your work after reading your query, he'll ask for more — either a manuscript or a proposal with sample chapters. It's far too late at that point to suddenly realize you have to learn to write a proposal. Even agents who don't want a proposal will be asking all the same questions that a proposal answers.

Go home and rework that proposal. And then do it again. And again. Sooner or later, you'll find that by some magic, you have a terrific proposal to go along with your excellent writing. You'll be a junior.

A sophomore advances by writing, by studying how to write a proposal, by writing that first practice proposal, and then by testing the proposal at writing conferences.

Juniors: Perfecting their pitches

Juniors are excellent writers. They've mastered most of the skills they need to get published. Their critique partners are saying, "Why aren't you published yet?"

A junior has typically taken a proposal or a sample chapter to a conference, showed it to an editor or an agent, and heard the magic words, "Send that to me." The junior has also heard back a few months later with the news, "Your work isn't right for me."

The junior year can be frustrating, humiliating, and depressing. It can be exhilarating beyond words at the same time. The junior period carries great highs and great lows, but you get through it if you persist.

If you're a junior, then you need to be writing, writing, writing — perfecting your craft. You also need to be polishing proposals and pitching them, preferably in person at writing conferences.

It's quite possible that you'll find an agent late in your junior year. Or you may hear from an editor that your book is under review by the publishing committee. Or a published author may read some of your work and tell you that you're almost there. If any of these things happen, you can be quite confident that you've become a senior.

A junior advances by striving for perfection in craft, by polishing proposals, and by pitching projects to live agents or editors.

Seniors: Preparing to become authors

Seniors are those chosen few who are destined to get published. This is clear to everyone — their critique buddies, their family, their friends, their agent. But it doesn't always feel that way to the senior.

Your senior period can be supreme agony. You are *that close* to getting published. You know in your gut that you write better than many published authors. In a just universe, you ought to be published. So why aren't you?

The answer is that you just haven't found the right publisher with the right project at the right time. Making that connection takes time: the time you spend as a senior. Any senior could be published at any time.

Your action plan as a senior is simply to follow the process. By this time, you must have a very polished complete manuscript and a strong proposal. Get your work out to editors (or better yet, have your agent get your work out). Keep getting it out, ignoring the rejections. It only takes one yes to get published. Keep looking for that yes.

And keep writing. You may one day wake up with a brilliant idea for a novel. You know instantly that this is The One — this novel will be your ticket. If this happens, follow your instinct. Write that novel in a white fury. You now have all the skills to write an excellent novel, and you'll find that you can write it far more easily than you can revise that old worn-out thing you started as a freshman writer.

Someday — this usually happens on a miserable day when the car's had a flat tire, or when the washing machine has leaked soapy water all over the floor, or your 3-year-old son has decided to iron the cat — on a day like that, the phone rings. It's your agent, calling to tell you that a publisher has made an offer on your novel. On that day, you suddenly forget all those years of striving, rejection, and heartache. On that day, you're an author.

A senior advances by ignoring rejections and continuing to submit a polished project until a publisher buys it.

Getting Yourself Organized

Most writers hate organization. We do, too. We probably hate it twice as much as you do, because there are two of us. However, we've found that we're a whale of a lot more productive when we do a bit of organization first. It isn't fun, but it makes the fun stuff easier.

It helps to know exactly what that fun stuff is, so in this book we begin (in Chapter 2) with a high-level look at why fiction is fun and why your reader wants to read your novel. What keeps your reader turning pages at 3 a.m. when the alarm is set for 6? We show you that secret and what you need to do to keep that reader up all night.

In Chapter 3, we discuss your niche and your genre. You can't appeal to every reader ever born. But the good news is this: Neither can any other author. Some readers walking this planet may find you the best author they've ever read. You need to figure out what those readers look like and how you can best meet their needs. When you know that, you're ready to write the perfect book for them.

You're unique. That means that you'll probably use methods different from your friends' for getting the first draft of your story down on the page. Some authors (Peter, for example) love outlines. Most authors hate them. Our job is not to tell you the one best process to write your novel. Our job is to show you (and we do so in Chapter 4) a variety of roads to completion and to let you choose one that works for you — or better yet, to find a unique road that fits you perfectly.

You have only a few resources that you can use to write your novel: time, energy, and money. Manage those effectively, and writing fiction will be a joy. Fail to manage them well, and writing will be a grind. In Chapter 5, we share some ideas we've found helpful.

Mastering Characterization, Plotting, and Other Skills

Novice writers have great ideas. Great writers have great ideas *and* great craft. Your first task is to understand the craft you need to turn your great ideas into great stories. Here's what you need:

- ✔ **Story world:** Your novel doesn't happen in a vacuum. It's set somewhere. That *somewhere* is usually called the *setting* or *milieu,* but we prefer the term *story world* because it's the world in which your story takes place.

   In Chapter 6, we show you what goes into constructing a great story world. It's harder than it looks, but we give you a checklist of key concepts you need to nail down to have a fully defined story world. We also show you the most common backdrops that make a story world cry out for a story to fill it up with meaning.

- ✔ **Characters:** Your characters have a past, a present, and a future, and you need to know each of these. In Chapter 7, we show the ideas that go into building a believable backstory for each character. And we show why backstory is essential for knowing the possible futures of your characters. Finally, we show you how the past and the future intersect in the present — right now — to create a compelling story that moves (and moves your reader).

- ✔ **Plot:** The typical modern novel has a plot that contains six layers of structure, ranging from the 100,000-foot view all the way down to the up-close-and-personal view. As a novelist, you need to master each of these six layers and put them together into a harmonious story. In Chapters 8 through 10, we coach you through each level.

- ✔ **Theme:** Every novel has a core idea — a *theme.* The twin hazards of theme are to put in either too little or too much. Go to Chapter 11 to see how to find your theme by listening to your characters. We also show you what to do to fix the most common problems.

Editing Your Fiction

Great writing never happens in the first draft. It happens when you edit your work — keeping what works, chucking what doesn't, and polishing it all till it gleams.

You can't depend on your editor to fix your novel. Modern editors are vastly overworked and underpaid. When you hand them your masterpiece, it needs to be burnished to a brilliant shine already.

Editing your fiction is hard work, but it's not a hard idea. It comes down to two primary tasks:

- ✔ Reworking your characters so that they come fully alive
- ✔ Revising your storyline at all six layers of plot

In Part III of this book, we tell you what you need to do and show you how to do it. In Chapter 12, you find out about character bibles, backstory, values, ambitions, story goals, and most importantly, the subtleties of point of view (POV). And in Chapter 13, we show you how to create a hook for your story that will be the number one sales tool at every link in the seven-point sales chain that comes between you and your masses of readers. We teach you Aristotle's three-act structure, but we add to it a three-disaster structure that Aristotle never dreamed about.

Your scenes are critical to making your story work, so in Chapter 14, you find out how to triage a scene — when to kill a scene, when to leave it alone, and how to fix it when it needs fixing. In Chapter 15, we show you how to analyze your story paragraph by paragraph to put your reader right inside the skin of your characters.

Chapter 2

What Makes a Great Story?

*Y*our readers desperately want one thing from you when they pick up your novel: a powerful emotional experience. Readers want to feel something, and they want to feel it deeply and fully. If you fail to deliver that emotional punch, you lose, no matter how clever your story or charming your characters.

But assuming you deliver what readers want, you also have the freedom to give them more — possibly much more. It's up to you to decide what else you want to give, if anything.

The art of writing fiction is built around five key tasks, which we like to call the *five pillars of fiction*. You must construct a believable setting, fill it with interesting characters, create a strong plot, develop a meaningful theme, and do it all with style. Most writers excel at only one or two of these, but you must become reasonably competent at all of them before you're likely to get your novel published. You also have seven tactical tools to use in your writing: action, dialogue, interior monologue, interior emotion, description, flashback, and narrative summary. When you use these effectively, you give your readers that all-important powerful emotional experience.

Choosing What to Give Your Readers

Why do you write? We've asked many writers over the years what drives them to write fiction. We've heard zillions of different answers. Here are six of them:

- ✔ To see my name on a book cover
- ✔ To be a famous author
- ✔ To make lots of money
- ✔ To educate people
- ✔ To entertain my readers
- ✔ To persuade people to accept my views on politics or religion

These are all fine reasons to write a novel. Your reasons for writing are your reasons for writing. You don't have to justify them to anybody. But it's important to know what they are. Otherwise, how will you know whether you're succeeding?

Take a few minutes right now and write down why you want to write fiction. What do you hope to get out of it? What do you want to do for your readers? On the same sheet of paper, write down the reasons you read. Circle the one that's most important to you. If you're like most readers, the main reason you read is to have fun — to be entertained.

In this section, we discuss how novels can educate, persuade, and, above all, entertain readers.

Creating a powerful emotional experience: What your readers desperately want

What is entertainment? After writing and teaching fiction for many years, we're convinced that *entertainment* can be boiled down to one thing: giving the reader a powerful emotional experience. Here we unpack this concept a little:

- ✔ **Why emotions matter:** Emotion is common to all fiction. Think about any of the major genres of fiction, and you see that each of them packs some sort of emotive punch:

    - Romance novels and erotica deliver some combination of love and lust, as does any novel with a romantic thread.

- Suspense novels, thrillers, action-adventure novels, and horror fiction all deliver various flavors of fear.

- Mysteries arouse a strong sense of curiosity and usually deliver a healthy dose of fear.

- Historical novels, fantasy, and science fiction all give the reader an experience of being "elsewhere."

- General fiction and literary fiction can deliver any of the preceding emotions, along with a strong sense of feeling understood.

✔ **Why emotions must be powerful:** Think about that for five seconds. Do you know anyone who ever bought a novel in the hopes that it would deliver an insipid emotional experience? Of course not! Powerful emotions make stories more enjoyable and memorable. Most people want excitement when they read a novel. They want a *lot* of excitement. Boatloads of it. If your readers want it, that's all the reason you need for giving it.

✔ **Why the experience is critical:** Your readers don't want to read about somebody else having powerful emotions. That's actually rather dull. Imagine spending hours of your life watching somebody you don't know crying or shivering in terror or kissing somebody you've never heard of. That's boring.

Your readers want to *become somebody else* for a few hours, to live an exciting life, to find true love, to face down unimaginable terrors, to solve impossible puzzles, to feel a lightning jolt of adrenaline. Give them that, and you'll earn fans for life. Give your readers anything else, and you'll lose them forever.

The rest of this book has one goal only: to teach you — as simply and as quickly as possible — how to give your reader a powerful emotional experience. Nothing matters more.

Educating your reader

Some novels educate readers, allowing them to explore other cultures, speculate on scientific discoveries, build up their stores of trivia, or just understand a bit more about how the system (or the world) works. English professors would add that great fiction explores what it means to be human, but don't feel pressured to explain the meaning of life — plenty of readers just want a little mental exercise.

Virtually all historical fiction has some educational value if the author has done his research well. James Michener is famous for fact-packed novels that let his readers painlessly discover vast amounts of historical information. Jean Auel's *Clan of the Cave Bear* series comes loaded with lore about life in Ice Age Europe. Likewise, many science fiction novels teach all sorts of things about science and engineering. If you really want to know about Mars, one easy way to find out about it is to read Kim Stanley Robinson's brilliant series *Red Mars, Green Mars,* and *Blue Mars.*

Readers who love military suspense and technothrillers enjoy finding out about the latest military hardware and technology. Those who read Amish novels are intrigued by the Amish subculture. Fans of legal thrillers enjoy learning about the law. Police procedural buffs thrive on understanding how cops think. Educating your readers is perfectly fine, as long as you're writing the kind of book where readers expect to learn something.

Don't bore your reader. If you want to work in some information that you find fascinating, make sure it's also fascinating to your reader. You do that by making it essential to the story. If your characters can't survive unless they know the details of quark theory, then your reader will want all the quantum details. Remember, though, that you're not writing a research paper.

Practicing the gentle art of persuasion

Many writers don't merely want to teach their readers; they want to persuade them of something — often an economic or political or religious or ethical opinion. Many novels carry a strong message of some kind. For example

- ✔ Ayn Rand's novels, such as *Atlas Shrugged* and *The Fountainhead,* make her case that a strong and unchecked capitalism is the finest economic system.

- ✔ Tom Clancy's early military technothrillers show his conviction that the Soviet system was corrupt and would soon collapse under the weight of its own incompetence.

- ✔ The *Left Behind* series by Jerry Jenkins and Tim LaHaye presents a detailed and adrenaline-laced roadmap for the authors' beliefs about Biblical end-times prophecy.

- ✔ Michael Crichton's novel *Next* explores the ethics of unchecked genetic manipulation in modern biotechnology.

Each of these authors found many readers who agreed strongly with their messages. Each of them has been criticized for preaching their messages too fervently. Yet each of them succeeded in persuading numbers of "nonbelievers" to change their minds.

A novel can persuade some readers if it's also entertaining, but it's most likely to find its main audience among those who already believe and who enjoy having their beliefs reinforced. Nobody ever bought a novel because they wanted to change their economic theories, switch political parties, or convert to a new religion. Nobody.

Respect your readers by first meeting their need for a powerful emotional experience. You can never persuade readers unless you first entertain them.

Decide what your goals are for your fiction. Besides entertaining your reader, what else do you want to achieve? Does your mission include educating readers? Persuading them? Something else? Will these goals undercut the reader's powerful emotional experience?

Making Life Hard on Your Characters: Conflict Plus Change Equals Story

A *story* consists of characters in conflict. Your characters want some sort of change in their lives, a change that (for most of the novel) they can't have. The change may be

- ✔ A change in the relationships of the characters
- ✔ A change within a single character
- ✔ A change in the story world (setting)

In *The Lord of the Rings*, for example, Frodo the hobbit sets out on a quest to destroy the Ring of Power. If he succeeds, Middle Earth will be radically changed — forever freed from the dark lord Sauron. If he fails, Middle Earth will also be radically changed — forever under Sauron's vicious boot. The stakes are extraordinarily high. Change is coming, one way or another. It's up to Frodo to change things for the better.

Always, always, always make your characters want something to change in their lives. The desire for change is what makes your reader invest emotionally in your story. Readers would love to change their own lives, so they respect anyone willing to risk making a change. But you can't make things easy on your characters. The minute they try to change things, conflict sets in. That's bad for the characters, but it's good for your story. The more conflict your characters face, the more emotion your reader invests into them. Your story is an account of how your characters deal with conflict in pursuing change.

If your lead characters get the change they want by the end of the story, that's usually a happy ending. If they don't get the change they want by the end of the story, that's usually an unhappy ending. (We say *usually* because in either case, your characters may realize at the end of the story that they didn't really want what they thought they wanted. But that, too, is a change — a change in mental attitude.)

What makes a great story great? That's a complex question, but part of a story's greatness comes from the depth of the change your character is pursuing. The power of Frodo's story comes from the high stakes. If he wins, all the free races win; if he loses, so do they. The higher the stakes of the change, the more powerful your story.

The Five Pillars of Fiction

Fiction has five main elements, each of which helps you create a powerful emotional experience for your readers:

- ✔ Story world (often called *setting* or *milieu*)
- ✔ Characters
- ✔ Plot (which includes structure)
- ✔ Theme
- ✔ Style

We use each of these *pillars of fiction* as technical terms throughout this book. You use each of these story aspects in different ways to move your readers. In this section, we look at each pillar in turn to see the meaning it carries.

Setting the stage: Your story world

We prefer the term *story world* to other common terms, such as *setting* or *milieu*. These other words are excellent words, but we want a term that captures the vastness of the stage for your novel. Your story world is all of the following and more:

- ✔ The universe or world where the story takes place

- ✔ The geography, including national boundaries

- ✔ The races of people, other intelligent beings, plants, and animals

- ✔ The historical context

- ✔ Political, economic, religious, and social structures

- ✔ Foods, drinks, and drugs

- ✔ Languages, entertainment methods, and sexual rules and roles

Some genres require enormously complex story worlds; others simply assume the story world of the reader. In either case, the author should know the story world inside out, because it determines what kind of story is possible. In this respect, story world sets constraints on what kind of powerful emotional experiences you can give your reader. A great story world greatly increases your chances of writing a great story.

Here are some examples of story worlds:

- ✔ *The Lord of the Rings,* by J. R. R. Tolkien, has Middle Earth as its story world. You could argue that Middle Earth is Tolkien's finest creation.

- ✔ *River God,* by Wilbur Smith, takes place in 18th-century B.C.E. Egypt. Smith appears to have taken a lot of liberties with the actual history, but no matter. His story world is complete and dazzling.

- ✔ *The Chosen,* by Chaim Potok, is set in Brooklyn in the 1940s in a Hasidic Jewish neighborhood. Potok's story world is close in space and time to modern America and yet worlds apart culturally.

- ✔ The *Harry Potter* series, by J. K. Rowling, is set in modern England but with one important change — some humans are genetically capable of magic. This single change enables Rowling to paint an epic battle between good and evil.

- ✔ *The Da Vinci Code,* by Dan Brown, is set in modern Europe and features numerous tourist attractions, including the Louvre and Westminster Abbey. Brown overlays on this an alleged secret society, the Priory of Sion, and he weaves its tentacles back through centuries of Western civilization, reinterpreting a number of famous historical figures.

Creating characters

Characters are the players on the stage of your story. Each character comes into the story with a long and detailed past (known as a *backstory*). And each character is driven in some direction — he or she has abstract ambitions and concrete goals.

You can't have conflict until you have characters. More importantly, your reader can't have a powerful emotional experience without at least one character. That powerful emotional experience comes when you weave such a convincing account of a character that your reader actually *becomes* that character. Your characters exist so that your reader can get inside the skin of one of them and do battle with the others.

Check out some examples of characters and their essential conflicts:

- Lizzie Bennet, in Jane Austen's novel *Pride and Prejudice,* wants desperately to find a man of character with whom she can fall in love. But is that possible when her family seems determined to play the fool?

- Jack Ryan, the leading man in a number of Tom Clancy's novels, is a CIA agent trying to do an excellent job in a world of bureaucrats. Can Jack win against foreign agents and terrorists, or will he be winged by his own side?

- Scarlett O'Hara, in Margaret Mitchell's *Gone With the Wind,* wants to be the belle of the ball forever in a disappearing world of Southern gentility. Can Scarlett find her place when her world is changing in unspeakably horrible ways?

- Ender Wiggin is a young boy in Orson Scott Card's novel, *Ender's Game.* Ender hopes to be chosen as the military leader who will save humanity from the coming alien "buggers." But can he survive the jealousy and hatred of his fellow students in Battle School?

Constructing the plot

Plot is the series of actions your characters take to move the story forward. You have to choose these actions carefully. In real life, things often appear to just happen. In your novel, nothing "just happens"; everything that you show must mean something to at least one of your characters. That meaning is what gives your reader a powerful emotional experience. Therefore, your plot must ignore all events that have no meaning.

Plot has several different layers, which we detail in Chapters 8 through 10. Each layer of plot is designed to elicit your reader's emotions. Here, we give examples of four layers of plot and the emotions they evoke (two other layers are the synopsis and scene list):

- ✔ **The highest layer of plot is a single-sentence summary of the story.** In *The Hunt for Red October,* by Tom Clancy, a Soviet sub captain tries to defect to the United States — bringing the latest low-noise submarine along with him. This one-sentence summary is designed to stir strong feelings of nationalistic pride in Americans.

- ✔ **The next layer of plot is the famous *three-act structure,* which normally contains a major disaster at the end of the first act, forcing the lead character to commit to the rest of the story.** In *Outlander,* by Diana Gabaldon, a recently married English nurse accidentally time-travels from 1945 back to 1743 Scotland. Her goal to return to the future hits a huge roadblock when she's forced to marry a charismatic and extremely attractive Scottish outlaw. This disaster commits the lead character into a stormy romance and is designed to make the reader feel maximum conflict between a woman's love for her two very different husbands.

- ✔ **One of the middle layers of plot is the *scene,* several pages of action that takes place at a single place and time.** In a scene in *The Pillars of the Earth,* by Ken Follett, bandits steal a 12th-century English stonemason's pig. The mason, Tom, pursues and fights the bandits, but they get away with his pig — the winter's food supply for his family. This disastrous ending to the scene is designed to arouse in the reader a feeling of desperation in the face of starvation.

- ✔ **The lowest layer of plot is the paragraph.** In a fight sequence in Irwin Shaw's novel *Rich Man, Poor Man,* a soldier punches a 16-year-old boy in a street brawl. The boy pretends pain from the ineffective blow and then responds with a devastating combination of jabs and punches. This action sequence covers just a few paragraphs and is designed to create in the reader a lurid fascination with a likeable young punk who loves to fight.

You must create your plot in all six layers, with each layer designed to give your reader a powerful emotional experience of your choosing. Most paragraphs should try to deliver some emotive punch. Absolutely every scene needs to deliver some emotive content, although not all scenes have the same intensity — that'd be boring. The scenes should work together to deliver powerful emotional experiences at the high points of the novel. And when the book is over, the reader needs to be left with an overall emotive response to the work as a whole.

Formulating a theme

Every novel means something beyond the bare story that it tells. We call that deep meaning of your story the *theme*. Your theme does not have to be profound (by which we mean intellectually deep). It's hard to pull profundity out of your ear, so don't make that your special burden in life. Your theme can be as simple as "everybody needs to be loved" or "life stinks" or "crime doesn't pay."

Your burden is to tell a great story, which means nothing more nor less than giving your reader a powerful emotional experience. You can and should try to make your theme *emotionally* deep. If it also happens to be intellectually deep, then that's a plus.

Great novels typically probe emotionally deep themes. Consider two examples:

- ✔ In *A Tale of Two Cities*, Charles Dickens builds a powerful theme of redemption via self-sacrifice. Sydney Carton, a low-living lawyer, loves a woman married to another man. Carton redeems a long life of selfishness by finding a way to save the life of the woman's husband — at an extraordinary cost to himself. The reader is left with a powerful emotional experience that combines fear, love, rage, and joy.

- ✔ Chaim Potok's novel, *My Name is Asher Lev,* examines the dark theme of what makes art great. Asher Lev is an Orthodox Jew in a community that condemns the painting of nudes. When Asher creates his masterpiece, it separates him from his community and his family, giving the reader a powerful emotional experience of triumph mixed with bitter sorrow.

Many authors begin their novels by choosing some theme that they want to illustrate. All too often, they believe that this means they don't have to work hard at building a great story world, three-dimensional characters, and a convincing plot. The result is a sermon masquerading as a story. Beware! Sermons hardly ever give a reader a powerful emotional experience, other than the powerful urge to fall asleep. If you build your story to fit your theme, it'll feel artificial. Write a great story first, and trust your inner artist to find the deep theme hiding within it. If necessary, you can strengthen your theme during the editing stage.

Expressing your style

As a novelist, you'll develop a unique way of expressing yourself — a mix of your personality, voice, tone, intellect, sense of humor, and a whole lot more. We call this mix your *style*. Your style may be complex or simple, flat or flowery, emotive or intellectual.

You'll find your personal style over time. It's another tool that lets you give your reader a powerful emotional experience — one that captures your essential being.

Don't try to mimic the style of some other author. Study those other authors, of course. Decide what you like in Austen, Twain, Hemingway, Faulkner, and a thousand others. But at the end of the day, realize that you can't be any of them. You have to be yourself. If you can't be yourself, who will?

Style is an advanced topic. Developing your personal style takes years, and you'll probably still be tweaking it long after you first get published. Because this is a book on the fundamentals of fiction writing, we don't cover style in detail.

Build a strong foundation for your writing by studying story world, characters, plot, and theme. Then write and write and write. Eventually, you'll find a style all your own. When you're well-advanced in the craft of fiction, you may find it helpful to get some coaching on style.

Seven Ways to Deliver the Goods

As a novelist, you have seven key tactical tools for giving your reader a powerful emotional experience. These all enter in at the very lowest level of plot — where your story unfolds paragraph by paragraph. You'll use some of these tools more than others, but you'll probably use all seven to some extent in every novel you write. A lot depends on your personal taste and on the sort of novel you're writing. Here are the tools:

- ✔ Action
- ✔ Dialogue
- ✔ Interior monologue (thoughts)
- ✔ Interior emotion

> ✔ Description
> ✔ Flashback
> ✔ Narrative summary

When do you use each of these? How should you mix them? Your yardstick for deciding should always be the same: Use whichever combination gives your reader the biggest, baddest, boldest powerful emotional experience possible.

This section shows you what these tools are all about. For more info on these tools, flip to Part II, which covers writing, and Part III, which covers editing.

The here and now: Action

Action is what's happening *right now*. Action is Scarlett kissing Rhett. The T-Rex eating the lawyer. The CSI tech finding the murderer's fingerprint. The marathoner collapsing at the finish line. The sniper pulling the trigger.

Action is key to your fiction, but you have to get one thing right: You must always show action happening now. Something that happened two years or two seconds ago is not action. Something that might happen in the future is not action. Something that's dragging out over minutes or months or millennia is not action. Action happens instant by instant. (Of course, you may be telling your story using past-tense verbs; most novels are narrated in the past tense. But even so, these stories detail action instant by instant.)

Look at two examples. The first shows actions happening in sequence; the second gives some narrative summary with no actions in it, without the visual detail.

> ✔ **Example of action:** George dropped to the ground, rolled to his left, aimed his Glock at the assassin, and squeezed off a shot. The hired killer screamed and collapsed.
>
> ✔ **Example that's not action:** George evaded the assassin for several minutes before finally shooting him.

Action is sensory. You can see, hear, smell, taste, or feel it. You can photograph it or record it.

Editors are always telling writers, "Show, don't tell." If they're talking about an action sequence, they mean that the actions are summarizing something that happened in the past, will happen in the future, or is dragging on over a period of time, or the action can't be seen, heard, smelled, tasted, or felt.

Showing absolutely everything, however, can slow the story down. See the later section, "Supplying narrative summary," for info on when writers may not need to show things blow-by-blow.

Giving your characters a voice: Dialogue

Dialogue is a special kind of action in which somebody's talking. Just like any other action, dialogue must be happening right now. The reader wants to hear it exactly the way it's said, without summary or judgment by the author.

Dialogue tells the reader the exact words of the speaker. When editors complain that your dialogue is "telling," they usually mean that you're summarizing the words instead of quoting them exactly. At times, you do want to summarize the words — when you want to pass along information quickly. But when you do so, you aren't writing dialogue; you're writing narrative summary, which we discuss later in this chapter.

Dialogue helps give your reader a powerful emotional experience because it connects directly to a voice. The human voice is primal. The reader can hear each character's voice and feel its power.

Revealing thoughts: Interior monologue

As a novelist, you have an enormous advantage over the screenwriter: You can show the reader your character's exact thoughts. The screenwriter is forced to make the viewer guess by showing a closeup of an actor's face or by using a voiceover (which many moviegoers regard as cheesy).

Interior monologue shows the reader what a character is thinking. You can choose from several levels of interior monologue:

- ✔ Quote the thoughts exactly.
- ✔ Summarize them.
- ✔ Give the overall flavor of the thoughts.

You get to decide which form to use — they're all legitimate.

Interior monologue plugs the reader directly into the character's brain. You can't get more intimate than that. And intimacy is essential if you want to give your reader a powerful emotional experience.

Feeling with your character: Interior emotion

Interior emotion plugs the reader directly into a character's feelings. This is the second major advantage the novelist has over the screenwriter. Use it wisely. You have two levels of interior emotion to choose from:

- **Showing your reader the exact physiological responses the character is feeling:** This technique is powerful, but a little goes a long way, so don't overuse it.

- **Telling the reader what emotions the character is having:** This is less powerful, but you can use this more often without wearing out your reader. Oftentimes, naming an emotion can weaken it.

Seeing what your character sees: Description

Description means plugging the reader into the character's senses. The character sees it, hears it, smells it, tastes it, touches it — and the reader does, too. (Be aware that you can summarize description, just as you can summarize action or dialogue. When you do so, you're using narrative summary, which isn't what we're talking about here.) Here's an example that mixes together a bit of action and several sentences of description:

Jack focuses his binoculars on the trees at the edge of the forest. An orange and black-striped form swims into view — 400 pounds of muscle and rage. The tiger's yellow eyes gleam with the last rays of the sun. It opens its mouth and roars, the sound hitting Jack like a hammer half a second later.

In this snippet, the reader becomes Jack, doing what Jack does, seeing what he sees, then hearing what he hears. That's what we mean by description. Many writers overuse description or water it down in narrative summary, but it's a powerful tool when you use it to put your reader directly inside your character's skin.

Description lets your reader see, hear, smell, taste, and touch what your character sees, hears, smells, tastes, and touches. Don't confuse this with description that's disconnected from your characters — that's part of narrative summary.

Taking a trip to the past: Flashback

A *flashback* is a nearly instantaneous transition backward in time to show the reader something that happened in a character's past.

Technically, a flashback is a different sort of beast than action, dialogue, interior monologue, interior emotion, and description, because a flashback *contains* all those things. So we're almost cheating here by classifying flashback alongside them, but there isn't any other place to put it, so we chose to put it here and not worry about whether our classification scheme is perfect.

A flashback has two oddball parts. At the beginning of the flashback, you have to give the reader some sort of cue that you're changing the time frame. At the end of the flashback, you need to give another cue that you're returning to the previous point in the story. Between these oddball points, you just proceed normally, as if the past were now.

A flashback is a container for action, dialogue, interior monologue, interior emotion, and description that happened at some earlier point in the story.

Supplying narrative summary

Narrative summary is exactly what it sounds like: a summary of things that happen some time other than right now. They may have happened in the past. They may be planned for the future. They may be happening sorta kinda now but all dragged out. Narrative summary may be a still-life description of something that exists right now but that isn't changing in any way.

Narrative summary isn't vivid or immediate, but it's very efficient. You can quickly cover a lot of ground using narrative summary.

The problem with narrative summary is that it isn't an experience. Your characters can't see, hear, smell, taste, or feel it. All they can do is remember, plan, summarize, or describe it, and those aren't nearly as good as experiencing it.

In the right time and place, narrative summary can be exceptionally potent. However, beginners often overuse this tool. As a rough rule of thumb, use narrative summary for the less emotive parts of your story, and use action, dialogue, interior monologue, interior emotion, and description for the more emotive parts.

Don't let anyone tell you that you must always "show, don't tell." It'd be exhausting to show all the minute details of a character's life using action, dialogue, interior monologue, interior emotion, description, and flashback. Use narrative summary as the glue that holds all these elements together; you don't need much glue, but you can't live without it altogether.

Chapter 3

Finding Your Audience and Category

There's no such thing as a one-size-fits-all novel. Your novel must be targeted toward a specific kind of reader (your *audience*), and it'll be shelved accordingly in the bookstore with similar books (your *category*).

You have to identify your audience and category before you can sell your book. Agents and publishers don't want to figure out your target audience and category — they expect you to tell them. If you don't know, or if you can't give an intelligible answer, your work may be rejected, no matter how good it is.

Professional novelists know their audience and their category. If you want to write professionally, you need to define both of these well enough to enable your publisher to create a marketing plan. We highly recommend that you think about audience and category before you even begin writing. That way, you won't spend months or years writing a book and only then discover that it's unmarketable.

In this chapter, you explore what you love to read and write, get to understand your ideal audience, and choose and research a category.

Identifying Your Ideal Novel

You can write the sort of book you most like to read, or you can write the sort of book you're best suited to write. These aren't always the same, although many writers and editors believe that they should be. We don't necessarily agree.

Plenty of successful commercial novelists love to read literary fiction but don't have the voice or lyrical style that a literary writer must have. Likewise, the world is full of romance writers who secretly enjoy reading science fiction, mystery writers who love romances, and suspense novelists who thrive on historical fiction. No law says you have to write exactly the kind of book you most like to read. The only real requirement is that you read enough of your chosen category to write it well.

Write the kind of book that you're best suited to *write*. Reading and writing are related, but they aren't the same thing. So don't feel guilty if your reading and writing tastes are somewhat different.

On the other hand, if you choose to write the kind of book you like to read, then you'll be three steps ahead, because you already know the conventions of the category — the do's and don'ts — and you know what gets readers excited and what turns them off.

What if you're not sure what kind of novel you're best suited to write? This section includes some exercises that may help you decide.

Looking at what you love to read

Although knowing what kind of book you love to read isn't a prerequisite to determining which kind of book you should write, it can help you get in touch with where your strengths lie. Here's how to analyze your reading:

1. **Take an inventory of your reading habits.**

   Make a list of the following:

   - The ten novels you love the most

   - The ten novels you've read most recently

   - The ten novels that have affected you most profoundly

You don't have to be rigid with these lists. If each list doesn't consist of exactly ten novels, don't worry. The point is to see what your reading patterns are.

2. **Analyze what these books have in common.**

   Are they all a similar genre (all mysteries, for example, or all romance, fantasy, or suspense)? This gives you a clue about the category that may suit you best.

   Do they all have a similar setting? A similar kind of lead character? A similar type of plot? A similar theme? Are they all written in a powerful style? Your answers give you clues about what your greatest strengths may be as a writer — story world, character, plot, theme, or style. (For details on these elements, see Chapter 2.)

3. **Make a list of the ten books you've hated the most and think about the ways in which these novels differ from the ones you listed in Step 1.**

   Does this list suggest any genres that you definitely don't want to write? Any kinds of plots you dislike? Themes you don't ever want to explore? Styles that would shame you to tears? Knowing what you don't want to write can help you narrow your list of what you do.

4. **Complete this sentence: "The kind of book that I love to read most in all the world is _____."**

   This may not be the kind of book that you want to write, but you'll probably want to incorporate some elements of the books you like to read into your own work.

Thinking about what you love to write

After you have some idea of the kind of book you want to write, you need to spell it out for yourself in some detail. You're going to have to explain it to your agent and editor someday.

You will not have to give any reasons for what you want to write. You want to write your book because you want to write it. That's all the reason you ever have to give. All you have to be able to do is *describe* what you want to write.

Take a sheet of paper and answer the following questions. Don't settle for merely thinking your answers through — write them down. You aren't committing to anything just yet; you're simply thinking on paper so you'll have a record of your thoughts.

✔ **Which authors would you most like to write like?** You aren't going to copy anyone's writing style; your style will be unique, but it'll be more like that of some authors than others. Write down the names of two or three authors whose style is close to what you envision yours being.

✔ **What categories interest you most?** We talk more about categories later in this chapter. For now, just list one or more that you think you'd like to write for. Typical categories include romance, suspense, mystery, historical, science fiction, fantasy, horror, western, literary, inspirational, children's, young adult, and so forth. You're allowed to mix categories, but one of them has to be dominant.

✔ **What story elements interest you most?** Do you want to write a story with a complex story world? Deep characters? A fast-paced, twisty plot? A powerful theme? A unique and captivating style? You can choose more than one of these, but remember that no author in the world is fantastic at all story elements. *Remember:* Choose what you want to write, not what you think you should write or what you think people expect you to write.

✔ **Where and when would you like to set your stories?** Name a particular place and a particular time period.

✔ **What special background or life experiences can you tie into your novel?** If you grew up in Afghanistan, for example, then a novel set there would ring especially true. But if you're from Alabama, Southern fiction may be far easier for you to write and sell.

✔ **What length of book would you most like to write?** A short novel runs around 60,000 words. A medium-length book is 80,000 to 90,000 words. A long book is anything over 120,000 words. You probably won't be able to nail down a particular length, but you probably gravitate toward novellas or massive epic sagas or mid-length novels.

There are no wrong answers to the preceding questions; however, some kinds of books may be much easier to sell than others. If you want to write a book that doesn't have much of an audience, then write it. But be aware that marketing it to an agent or publisher — and ultimately, to readers — will be an uphill battle.

Defining Your Ideal Reader

Enough about you. Now it's time to think about your reader (that's *reader* in the abstract sense — you'll have more than one in real life). You're going to find a publisher willing to invest in your book only if you can persuade that publisher that there are readers who'll want to buy and read it.

Many writers think that to get published, they need to appeal to a huge, broad target audience. Ultimately, yes, you'd like to have a lot of readers. But at the beginning of your career, you need to think narrow rather than broad. The early marketing has to focus on *somebody*. A marketing plan that targets everybody is going to be incredibly expensive, and it's also likely to dilute the message.

Your book's overall appeal will depend on how well you write your story, not on the size of your target audience. What small niche of readers can you interest better than any other author in the world? These few readers will burn hottest when you light your marketing flame. If you can find them, they'll help you find a broader audience.

This section helps you envision your ideal reader. If your ideal reader is a lot like you, you'll understand your reader's mindset well as you write. If your ideal reader looks nothing like you, that's fine — as long as you do your homework and figure out how your target reader thinks.

Considering worldview and interests

These questions may be the most critical ones you consider: How do your ideal readers think about the world? What captures their interest? Are your ideal readers

- ✔ Religious or not particularly so? If religious, are they Christian, Jewish, Muslim, or Buddhist, for example? If not religious, are they agnostic, atheist, or just not interested?

- ✔ Political or not especially so? If political, what party are they affiliated with? Are they conservative or liberal? Militarist or pacifist?

- ✔ Well-educated, or not inclined to consider education a priority?

- ✔ Interested in auto racing? Molecular biology? Parenting? Immigration issues? Submarine technology? Erotic liaisons? Hegelian philosophy? Gambling? Camel milking?

You have a profound opportunity to define your ideal reader in a way that excites your publisher. If you can show that you've identified some core group of readers who will love your novel, then you've found an audience worthy of a focused marketing plan. Here are some novels with well-defined target audiences:

- ✔ Dan Brown's *The Da Vinci Code* was targeted at readers skeptical of the official history of early Christianity. The novel combined lightning action with a series of intellectual puzzles that captured the imagination of the target audience and led to incredible word-of-mouth publicity.

✔ William P. Young's *The Shack* took aim at conservative Christian readers wanting answers to the tough theological question "How can a good and all-powerful God allow evil?" The novel touched the hearts and minds of these readers, leading to explosive sales.

Note that these two novels target completely separate audiences. The marketing campaign of each one was designed to appeal to a core audience, not to some vague "everybody." Both campaigns were far more effective because they were focused.

These next two novels also appeal to polar opposite audiences. Both have succeeded because of their sharply defined niches, not in spite of them.

✔ Tom Clancy's *The Hunt For Red October* created a new subgenre, the military technothriller. Designed to appeal to military men and political conservatives, the novel gained traction when people discovered that "everybody in Washington" was reading the book, including Pentagon top brass and even (according to rumors) then-President Ronald Reagan.

✔ Margaret Atwood's *The Handmaid's Tale* created a post-nuclear apocalyptic world with a female protagonist required to serve as a childbearing vessel for a couple rendered infertile by radiation. The novel targeted pro-choice women, but its powerful message took it to a far larger audience.

Looking at gender

We bet you're not surprised to hear this: Men and women think differently. They read different kinds of books. They tend to like different kinds of things (though we all know plenty of people who cross those pesky gender lines). Now answer this quickly: Are you writing mainly for men or women?

If you said either "men" or "women," then your target audience is likely to be sharply focused along gender lines. That's neither good nor bad; it's simply the way it is, and knowing the answer can help you appeal to your audience and help your publisher define your marketing plans.

What if you just aren't sure? In that case, your book probably won't be very gender-specific. Again, this is neither good nor bad; it's just a fact that will guide your publisher in marketing your book.

Writing for readers of a certain age

When you envision your typical readers, how old are they? Children? Early teens? Later teens? Twenty-somethings? Thirty to fifty? Fifty-plus? Each of these age groups has different reading habits. Each age group responds differently to cover art, titles, and back-cover copy. Your publisher will build your marketing plan around the age group of your target readers.

The most successful novel series in publishing history has been the *Harry Potter* series. Who was the target audience? Young adults! Not exactly "everybody," was it? But those kids talked it up, and before you could say "Alohamora!" everybody was reading the magical tales of the boy wizard.

Defining your niche

Word of mouth is the best thing going in marketing a novel. Therefore, your publisher will want a sharply focused niche group that it can target when your book launches. If your novel is strong, that niche group will talk . . . and talk. Then word of mouth will carry the message far outside that niche.

Don't worry too much about making your book more marketable. If your book appeals to a small segment of readers, you'll probably face less competition, and you may be able to dominate your niche more easily. Being a big fish in a small bowl is easier, and big fish often move on to bigger bowls.

Write a paragraph describing your ideal reader as precisely as you can — age, gender, political and religious affiliation, hobbies, thought patterns, likes, dislikes. Slam it down on paper as fast as you can. Edit it tomorrow. Save it for later. Your marketing director will love you for it someday.

Understanding Your Category

When the bookstore employees unpack your book from the cardboard box in which it was delivered, which shelf are they going to put it on?

Take a mental walk through the fiction section of your favorite bookstore. You probably see sections with different labels — fiction (or literature), romance, thrillers (or suspense), mystery, true crime, historical, western, science fiction, fantasy, horror, children, young adults (or teens), inspirational fiction (or religious fiction or Christian fiction), and more. If you wander through a dozen stores, you'll probably find that they all label their sections a little differently. You may see certain combinations of labels, such as "mysteries and thrillers" or "fiction and literature." Sometimes true crime is a subsection of mystery.

Labels make two kinds of distinctions. Most of them define a *genre,* or common class of books, such as romance, mystery, or thriller. But several of these labels define a target audience — for example, children, young adults, or religious people. To confound things, the sections that target particular audiences each contain books from most of the genres. So you can find mysteries not only in the main mystery section but also in the children, young adults, and Christian sections.

Confusing, isn't it? Because bookstores define categories in different ways, we're going to stick pretty closely to the set of categories defined by *Publisher's Weekly,* the trade journal of the publishing industry. Here are the categories we discuss in this section:

- ✔ Romance
- ✔ Thriller
- ✔ Mystery/crime
- ✔ Science fiction and fantasy
- ✔ Horror
- ✔ General/literary
- ✔ Inspirational
- ✔ Women's fiction
- ✔ Children
- ✔ Young adult

You have to choose one primary category for your novel. You can mix categories, but if you do, one category must still be dominant. The dominant category usually determines where the bookstore employees choose to shelve your book, so an inspirational romance will (almost always) go on the Inspirational shelves. Likewise, a literary mystery will (probably) end up in the Literary section. A young adult fantasy will go with the Young Adult novels. The bookstore staff has the ultimate say on where to shelve books, of course, so you may be surprised.

Join the club: Writing associations for your category

Joining a professional writing association can be a good way to understand more about your category, network with other writers, discover more about publishing, and compete for awards for published and unpublished works. Here are some major writing associations and the awards they offer. Some associations require that you have a novel or several short stories in that category published before you can join; others are open to anyone with an interest. Check their Web sites for details.

✔ **American Christian Fiction Writers (ACFW):** ACFW sponsors the Book of the Year Awards for published novels and novellas, along with the Genesis Awards for unpublished manuscripts. Visit www.acfw.com.

✔ **Horror Writers Association (HWA):** HWA sponsors the Bram Stoker Awards. You can find the HWA online at www.horror.org.

✔ **Mystery Writers of America (MWA):** MWA sponsors the Edgar Awards for published mystery novels. Go to www.mysterywriters.org.

✔ **Romance Writers of America (RWA):** RWA sponsors the prestigious RITA Awards for published romance novels and the Golden Heart Awards for unpublished manuscripts. You can find the organization at www.rwanational.org.

✔ **Science Fiction & Fantasy Writers of America (SFWA):** SFWA sponsors the Nebula Awards, the Andre Norton Award, and the Ray Bradbury Award. Find the SFWA online at www.sfwa.org.

✔ **Society of Children's Book Writers & Illustrators (SCBWI):** SCBWI sponsors the Golden Kite Awards and several other awards. If you write children's or young adult literature, check out the SCBWI at www.scbwi.org.

Genres: Surveying categories based on content

When a category or subcategory has a set of well-defined rules that determine the broad parameters of the story, it's called a *genre*. Typical genres include romance, thrillers, mysteries, science fiction, fantasy, and horror. We discuss those categories and others in this section. (Historical fiction is a special genre with special issues, which we talk about in the sidebar titled "What happened to historical novels?")

Romance

If you want to break into fiction writing, there may be no better avenue than to write a romance novel. Smirk all you want, but the romance novelists are taking it to the bank. More than 40 percent of all novels sold these days fit the romance category. The market for it is huge, and romance fans are voracious readers.

Romance novels almost always tell the story of an unmarried man and woman getting together, and they almost always have happy endings. The typical reader is female (we hope this isn't too much of a surprise), and the genre spans all age groups. Romance includes a bewildering variety of sub-genres, ranging from the wildest erotica to the tamest sweet romances.

The world of romance fiction is a world of narrowly defined niches. You must know your niche well, because there isn't much slack here. Romance novels tend to focus on the character and story world elements rather than on plot and theme, although the rule isn't ironclad.

Most publishers of romances list their exact requirements on their Web sites — and we aren't kidding when we use the word *exact.* Typical requirements specify a precise word count, the ages of the hero and heroine, how early in the book they must meet, and many other details.

For more advice on writing romance, check out *Writing a Romance Novel For Dummies,* by Leslie Wainger (Wiley).

Thrillers

The terms *thriller* and *suspense novel* are used interchangeably in the industry. Thrillers come in many varieties, including action-adventure, techno-thriller, legal thriller, war novel, and spy novel. These stories typically have a strong plot and may also shine in story world or characters. Theme is rarely a central aspect of a thriller.

Readers of all ages, both men and women, love this genre. Some thrillers, such as military technothrillers, tilt more toward men, whereas others, such as romantic suspense, are aimed more at women. Overall, however, the genre is reasonably gender-balanced. The appropriate level of violence in your story depends on the age and gender of your target reader.

The thrillers category is broad, so you need to choose your niche within the genre carefully to define your audience. You have tremendous freedom to create a new subgenre or make an existing one your own, as Tom Clancy did with technothrillers and John Grisham did with legal thrillers.

This genre is highly marketable, so if you love thrillers, don't hesitate to commit to it. The bestseller lists are packed with books in this category. However, the genre is competitive, so breaking in may not be easy for new novelists.

Mystery/crime

The mystery/crime genre is closely related to thrillers, but it always includes an intellectual puzzle to be solved, usually a murder but occasionally some other crime. The genre requires that the perpetrator be found and brought to justice, so the reader must not know who the bad guy is until the end of the book. (If you violate this rule, you're not writing a mystery; you're writing a thriller.) Mysteries are almost always shelved in the mystery section of the bookstore; one exception seems to be the serial-killer novel, which may end up shelved with thrillers.

Both men and women enjoy the mystery genre, which crosses all age lines, so the category is very broad. It has many subgenres, including police procedurals, private investigator novels, and cozy mysteries featuring amateur detectives. Many bookstores also include a shelf of _true crime_ books (although these aren't exactly novels, they use the storytelling techniques of the fiction writer, so classing them here is appropriate). As with thrillers, you have quite a bit of freedom to define your own special kind of mystery.

Mysteries are intellectual puzzles first, but you have plenty of options on which story element comes second — plot (which has an emotive element) or character is a common choice, but a unique story world can also make your book stand out in the crowd. The requirements of the mystery genre may be tightly defined by some publishing houses and loosely defined by others.

Like readers of the romance genre, mystery lovers read voraciously, so the market demands a constant stream of new titles. The mystery genre is a strong choice, and it gives you a lot of options. You must study the genre carefully before you try to write your mystery, but an unknown novelist has a good shot at breaking into this category.

Science fiction and fantasy

Science fiction and fantasy (SF&F) novels inspire fanatical readers who may avidly follow an author through a long series. Several of the best-selling fiction works of all time have been fantasies, including _The Lord of the Rings_ and the _Harry Potter_ series.

Within science fiction, you have numerous options, ranging from hard-science novels to space opera set in a galaxy far away. Likewise, fantasy has many subgenres. This category seems to be wide open to wildly new and inventive ideas, so if you have something truly weird, it may be the Next Big Thing. As always, the quality of your writing will determine whether you succeed.

In both science fiction and fantasy, constructing your story world is enormously important. This process, called *world-building,* is a requirement for any serious writer in this genre.

Science fiction and fantasy is not the largest genre, but its readers are exceptionally loyal. Study the genre before you write. Even unknown writers have a reasonable hope of getting published in SF&F. Certain publishers specialize in SF&F, so go over their current listings and their Web sites closely to track which sorts of projects they may be interested in.

Horror

The purpose of horror fiction is to inspire mind-bending, gut-wrenching fear in your readers and then resolve that fear in some way. The horror section of your bookstore is probably smaller than most of the other sections, but if horror's your thing, pursue it. One of the most successful writers of our time, Stephen King, has seen enormous success in this genre.

In horror fiction, either character or plot typically plays the major role, although you can make story world or theme the star. The rules of horror seem to be a bit less restrictive than those of some of the other genres, so you have quite a bit of freedom to define what a horror novel should be.

Horror is a small genre, so it may be more difficult to break into than some of the others. In this genre, possibly more than in any other, your ability to create a powerful emotional experience determines your success.

General/literary

The general/literary category applies to fiction that doesn't fit within any of the preceding genres. A novel is *literary* if it's language- and character-driven; otherwise, it's *general fiction.* Usually, literary fiction is written with a unique and beautiful style and is more intellectually demanding than general fiction.

Any of the genres we've listed earlier can be a literary novel. You can write a literary romance, thriller, or mystery, for example. In that case, the book usually goes in the literary section, but the decision is really up to the bookstore, and a lot depends on how your publisher markets you. The classification of fiction is complicated, and we can't give you a general rule for it.

The general/literary category is very competitive, and breaking into it is hard for new writers. Very few rules exist regarding what you can write about or how you should proceed. You can be as strongly oriented toward story world, character, plot, theme, or style as you like. The main requirement is that your fiction be truly excellent. Many fine novelists are trying to sell their work, so you can't sell a mediocre manuscript or even a pretty good one.

Many other novels will be fighting for shelf space with yours, so a published novel in the general/literary category may not sell very well. But even if the royalties for your novel make your accountant weep, you'll likely find this category artistically satisfying to write. Of course, some authors do extremely well in this category, so write your best novel and see where it takes you.

Absolute excellence in your craft is the main requirement for selling your novel in the general/literary category. "Good enough" is not good enough. You may never be able to quit your day job by writing in this category, but you'll very likely respect the person you see in the mirror every morning.

What happened to historical novels?

A *historical novel* is a novel set in a time period significantly earlier than the date of publication. For example, if you write a novel set in World War I, that'd be considered a historical novel; however, a novel written in 1918 and set in that year wouldn't. The line between a recent contemporary novel and a historical is a bit fuzzy, but "more than 50 years ago" is probably close to the mark.

If you love historical novels, be aware that few bookstores have a shelf for historicals, so you'll need to adopt some other category and add the word *historical* in front of it. You can do this with most of the genres. Take a look at some of the many examples of historical novels that have done well in each of the major categories.

Historical romance novels:

✔ *Gone With the Wind,* by Margaret Mitchell, captures the South during the Civil War era in exquisite detail.

✔ *Outlander,* by Diana Gabaldon, details the time of the Jacobite Rising in 18th-century Scotland.

Historical thrillers:

✔ *River God*, by Wilbur Smith, is a riveting suspense novel set in 18th-century B.C.E. Egypt at the time of the Hyksos invasion.

✔ *The Pillars of the Earth,* by Ken Follett, recounts the building of a cathedral in 12th-century England.

(continued)

(continued)

Historical mysteries:

✔ *The Quality of Mercy,* by Faye Kellerman, features William Shakespeare as a player.

✔ *The Arms of Nemesis,* by Steven Saylor, stars a detective in Ancient Rome.

Historical fantasy and science fiction:

✔ *Taliesin,* by Stephen R. Lawhead (along with its sequels *Merlin* and *Arthur*), is set in Arthurian Britain.

✔ *The Difference Engine,* by William Gibson and Bruce Sterling, tells an alternate history of London in the 1850s, where Charles Babbage has constructed his mechanical computer, the *difference engine.*

Historical general fiction:

✔ *The First Man in Rome,* by Colleen McCullough, along with its sequels, is set in Ancient Rome.

✔ *The Clan of the Cave Bear,* by Jean Auel, along with several sequels, is set in Ice Age Europe.

Historical literary fiction:

✔ *The Red Tent,* by Anita Diamant, features the women in the family of the biblical Jacob.

✔ *The Name of the Rose,* by Umberto Eco, a serial-killer novel, takes place in an anonymous 14th-century Italian abbey. This novel is a historical literary mystery, but it's typically shelved in the thrillers section of bookstores. Go figure.

✔ *Girl with a Pearl Earring,* by Tracy Chevalier, is set in the home of 17th-century artist Jan Vermeer.

You can sell your historical novel, but you must first assign it to one of the well-established categories. A historical novel gives you one competitive advantage: By creating a unique and spellbinding story world, you add zest to your novel's primary category.

Understanding audience-based categories

In some cases, your novel's primary category is defined by your target audience rather than by the kind of story you're writing. (For more on choosing a target audience, see the earlier section "Defining Your Ideal Reader.") Take a look at some of these categories.

Inspirational fiction

Christian publishing houses produce most inspirational fiction, so people often use the terms *inspirational fiction* and *Christian fiction* interchangeably. The category almost always shows one or more characters on a spiritual journey.

The Christian fiction market has been the fastest-growing segment of the publishing world over the last several years. As a high-growth category, it's very open to new writers.

Christian publishers accept fiction in just about any genre (see the earlier section "Genres: Surveying categories based on content"). Be aware that certain subcategories — romance, women's fiction, suspense, and historical romance — dominate this market. Mysteries do fairly well. Fantasy, science fiction, horror, and literary fiction are very tough sells, although there have been some notable successes.

The romance and mystery subcategories tend to be tightly defined in terms of plot requirements, but all other subcategories within inspirational fiction allow you quite a bit of freedom in your story. Foul language and adult situations are almost never allowed to be shown (though they can happen "off-camera").

If you decide to write inspirational fiction, read enough in the category to get a good feel for what's allowed. You must understand and respect your readers' worldview. Study the unwritten rules of the market carefully.

Women's fiction

Women's fiction includes novels specifically geared to women's interests. They may be love stories (requited or not), friendship stories, or stories that otherwise involve women's issues. These novels may have happy endings or unhappy endings. The only real rule with women's fiction is that it should deal with issues specific to women.

This category is very broad and has a lot of overlap with romance and general/literary fiction. As we note in the preceding section, women's fiction is very popular in Christian fiction. Bookstores may choose to shelve women's fiction in any of these categories.

Do you have to be a woman to write women's fiction? No, but we suspect it helps. What you must do is to connect well with your readers, who will be overwhelmingly women. If you write well, you have a good chance of getting published in this category and earning a fair bit of money.

Children's fiction

Children's fiction includes stories for anyone up to about age 12. There are several different age ranges and many different publishers. This is a highly specialized field, with different rules for each age group.

The children's fiction category includes a number of subcategories. Your best bet is to study the Web sites of the publishers who do the particular type of book you want to write. They can tell you what your parameters are.

You must respect your audience. Children know when you're talking down to them. Define your niche carefully and then do your homework. You need to study children's fiction extremely carefully before you try writing it.

For more information on writing for children (and teens), consider picking up a copy of *Writing Children's Books For Dummies,* by Lisa Rojany Buccieri and Peter Economy (Wiley).

Young adult fiction

Young adult (YA) fiction is typically written for the 12-to-18 age bracket. Like children's fiction, this is a very specialized field, and you need to study the existing books carefully.

Young adult fiction offers quite a bit of latitude. The genres are not so precisely defined, and you have freedom to step out and create something entirely new, as J. K. Rowling did with her *Harry Potter* series and Stephenie Meyer did with her *Twilight* series.

You can write YA fiction in most of the genres available for adults — romance, thrillers, mysteries, science fiction, fantasy, or horror. If you choose to write in one of these genres, read a number of similar books and study the guidelines of your target publishers.

Young adults are practically adults, but they don't belong to your generation. You're probably an old fogey to them, so you need to spend enough time with them enough to understand their language and culture.

Picking your category and subcategory

The preceding sections discuss the major categories at some length. Before you begin writing your novel, you need to make two decisions. Get out a piece of paper and answer these questions:

- ✔ What is your book's major category?
- ✔ What is your book's specific subcategory?

Decide this now — rather than after 400 pages of hard work on a novel that may turn out to belong to no discernible category with no particular audience.

After you choose your category, read enough novels in your category so that you're an expert in it. You need to know what's been done a zillion times and what will be considered new and fresh. We can't tell you that — it's up to you to read, read, read until you know your category inside out.

Finding Your Category's Requirements

Different categories have very different requirements. In the earlier sections of this chapter, we talk about identifying your specific category, subcategory, and audience. We also ask you to identify several authors you'd like to emulate in your writing. If you haven't done those tasks yet, do them now, because in this section, you use that information to figure out the special requirements for your book.

Write down the following requirements list for your novel, and as you read this section, fill in the blanks:

✔ Word count: _____

✔ Number of major characters: _____

✔ Story's acceptable levels of the following elements (on a scale of 0 to 10):

- Romantic tension: _____

- Sensuality: _____

- Humor: _____

- Spirituality: _____

- Offensive language: _____

- Action/adventure: _____

- Violence: _____

- Suspense: _____

- Enigma: _____

✔ Emotional driver: _____

Targeting your word count

Novels for adults typically run from 60,000 to 120,000 words or more. An average-length novel is between 80,000 and 100,000 words. These ranges are pretty wide, so you may be thinking that you don't need to worry about your word count. Maybe; maybe not.

Certain publishing houses have tight word-count requirements. This is especially true of specialized lines of romance novels, where the number of pages may be exactly defined and you aren't given much margin of error at all. If you're writing a romance novel, you may already be targeting a particular line. Look up the guidelines on that publisher's Web site and find out right now what the word count of your novel needs to be.

Other categories in which you may have tight word-count requirements are mysteries or science fiction novels that fit into an existing line. If you're targeting one of these, check the publisher's Web site for requirements.

Children's novels are generally much shorter than novels for adults, and books for young adults are often shorter than adult-level novels, but they can be long in exceptional cases. *Harry Potter and the Order of the Phoenix,* by J. K. Rowling, ran to 255,000 words.

For any category, you can always make a rough estimate of your target word count by choosing a book in your category that's about the length of the book you'd like to write. Find a full page of text in the middle of the first chapter and count the words on that page. Multiply this by the number of pages. Round the result to the nearest 5,000 words.

For example, suppose you count 321 words on the second page and you see that the book has 418 pages. Multiplying those two numbers gives you 134,178 words. Rounding that to the nearest 5,000 words gives you an estimate of 135,000 words. Write that down as your target word count. (That's a pretty long book, by the way.)

Accounting for major characters

Your novel will have a certain group of characters who get most of the air-time. If you have too few major characters, you may not have a dense enough storyline. If you have too many, you may dilute your story and confuse your readers. You don't need to pick an exact number of main characters before you write, but you do need to know what a reasonable number is for your category.

How many can you have? The minimum number of characters is obviously one, although most novels have more. The maximum number can be quite large. *The Godfather* had at least ten major characters. *The Lord of the Rings* had dozens.

Again, a lot depends on your category. If you're writing a romance novel, you probably need a hero and heroine and possibly a villain or love interest. That may well be all the major characters you need — it's enough for a classic love triangle — although you'll have plenty of minor characters.

On the other hand, if you're writing a mystery, you need a corpse and a detective. You also need several suspects, some friends for your detective, and some antagonists. That can add up to a dozen important characters.

Think of a few books that are like the one you want to write. How many major characters do they have? Two? Five? Ten? Twenty? Pick a number that seems reasonable and write that down. (***Note:*** You may get a better idea of how many characters you need if you think of which roles you need to fill — heroes, villains, sidekicks, and so on. See Chapter 7 for details.)

Determining levels of action, romance, and all that

Readers of different categories and subcategories have extremely different ideas of what's acceptable in a novel. You need to think about what those expectations are in advance. If you write a novel that isn't acceptable to your audience, then a publisher isn't going to care whether it's acceptable to you; the publisher is in business to sell books.

The purpose of this exercise is to make sure you know — before you write your book — what's appropriate to your reading audience for your category. This can save you years of wasted effort, so it's worth taking some time to do this work now. Here's how to get a sense of reader expectations and set some guidelines for your novel:

1. **Understand the different story aspects, including romantic tension, sensuality, humor, spirituality, offensive language, action/adventure, violence, suspense, and enigma.**

   We discuss these story aspects later in this section.

2. **Consider how much of each aspect appears in other novels in your category.**

Where can you find the official rules on what's acceptable? You can't. That's why you should be reading books in your chosen category — so you can sort out the unspoken rules that everybody knows.

We like to rate books on a scale of 0 to 10 in each story aspect. For example, the amount of violence in *Pride and Prejudice* is very low — we rate it a 0. The amount of romantic tension is high — we give it a 10.

Note: Try to measure quantity, not quality. For example, the amount of violence in the movie *Casablanca* is moderate — we give it a 5. The amount of violence in *Rambo* is much higher — probably a 10. The quantity of violence in each movie is about what its viewers expect, and you could argue that the quality of violence in each case is therefore high. But whenever quality becomes an issue, endless arguments ensue, which we'd rather avoid.

3. **Decide how much of each story aspect is acceptable to your ideal reader.**

Usually, you assign a range of values. For example, if you're writing a romance novel, your audience expects a lot of romantic tension, so you probably want a range of 9–10. For certain categories, your audience won't really care about certain aspects, so you may be able to assign a full range of 0–10.

Can you push the edges of acceptability as you write? Yes, of course. Bend the edges, but don't break them. If you don't know where that fine line is, then read some more books in your category or talk to experienced authors, agents, or editors.

Now look over the following list, which defines the story aspects and gives you a general idea of the categories in which high or low levels of those aspects may be essential:

- **Romantic tension:** *Romantic tension* is the potential for love in a story. Romance novels and women's fiction typically require high levels of romantic tension. Most other genres consider a wide range acceptable — a little, a lot, or anything in between. Children's fiction typically has very little romantic tension.

- **Sensuality:** *Sensuality* is explicit sexual activity in a story. Some romance subcategories accept very little sensuality, and some erotic subcategories require the maximum. Children's fiction and Christian fiction allow essentially none. Most other categories tolerate a fairly wide range of sensuality.

✔ **Humor:** *Humor* is anything that's funny. Most fiction is improved by a bit of humor, but incorporating it is tricky because people's tastes in humor vary widely. All the categories of fiction allow a wide range here. This is the one story aspect you get to decide, and you probably won't violate your reader's expectations, no matter which category you write for.

✔ **Spirituality:** *Spirituality* is a sense of transcendence over the material world. In most categories, less spirituality is considered preferable to more. However, Christian fiction generally prefers more, so long as it keeps within the bounds of historic Christianity. Literary fiction is accepting of a high level of spirituality of just about any flavor, as long as it meets the demanding standards of literary quality. Some fantasy sub-categories also favor high levels of spirituality, often in unconventional directions.

✔ **Offensive language:** *Offensive language* is language that is crude or uses curse words. Most readers in most categories accept a wide range of offensive language these days. Obvious exceptions are children's fiction and Christian fiction, which accept essentially none. Readers of military fiction and certain kinds of thrillers and crime fiction generally expect very high levels of offensive language.

✔ **Action/adventure:** *Action/adventure* includes excitement along the lines of car chases, burning buildings, narrow escapes from death, exploding helicopters, and shooting. It doesn't necessarily include violence, which involves bodily injury. Some categories, such as thrillers and some types of mysteries, expect high levels of action. Other categories, such as women's fiction and romance, generally expect much less. Most other categories accept a wide range.

✔ **Violence:** *Violence* involves bodily injury, blood, broken bones, or death. As with action, violence is not merely accepted but expected in most thrillers and many mysteries. It's far less acceptable in romance, women's fiction, Christian fiction, and children's fiction. All other categories are accepting of a very wide range of violence.

✔ **Suspense:** *Suspense* is the anticipation of something horrible. This is different from both action and violence. The movie *Witness* is an example of a story with quite a lot of suspense but not much action or violence. Thrillers and mysteries generally have very high levels of suspense. Romance, women's fiction, and children's fiction have much less (with the exception of romantic suspense). All other categories allow a very wide range.

✔ **Enigma:** An *enigma* is an unsolved puzzle, secret, or mystery that requires a solution. Mysteries obviously require high levels of this aspect. Thrillers often have quite a lot of enigma (in cases where the reader doesn't know who the villain is), but they can also have none at all (in novels where the reader sees both the hero and villain with equal time). Because any unexplained secret contributes an atmosphere of enigma, this component is very acceptable in any category, even children's fiction or romance, where long-buried family secrets are a staple. However, enigma isn't required in any category except mysteries.

Why don't we simply give you a table of acceptable ranges for all the categories? Because we can't. There are a very large number of subcategories, and nobody could possibly keep track of the tastes of the audiences for all of them for all age ranges. Your job as a writer is to define your target audience and category (as we explain earlier in the chapter), research your tiny little niche of the market, and figure out the boundaries for yourself.

Identifying your story's emotional driver

Fiction is about giving your reader a powerful emotional experience. Therefore, every story must have one or more *emotional drivers* — the particular emotions that you're trying to excite in your reader. It's easy to make a long list of possible emotional drivers: love, lust, fear, horror, jealousy, anger, revenge, greed, sorrow, guilt, and so on.

Decide which emotions your novel will deliver. Choose two or three. They should be appropriate to your category, but choosing very different emotions is quite all right. One of them should be primary; you add the others for extra flavor. Remember that having too many drivers is as bad as having too few, so limit yourself. You can save some for your next novel.

The main requirement here is that if you're writing in a category that demands one particular emotional driver, then that needs to be your primary driver. If you're writing a romance, love has to be your primary driver. If you're writing a thriller, you should use fear or horror instead. Aside from this limitation, you're free to choose almost any combination of emotional drivers that you want, so long as they're all considered acceptable within your category. (For example, the lust driver won't be accepted in children's fiction or Christian fiction; likewise, depression wouldn't fly very well in a James Bond type spy novel.)

Chapter 4

Four Ways to Write a Great Novel

● ●

In This Chapter

▶ Getting it written before getting it right

▶ Investigating four creative paradigms for completing a novel

▶ Understanding why your paradigm matters

▶ Finding and using the right creative paradigm for you

● ●

*P*eople usually write novels in several drafts, and writers agree that the first draft doesn't have to be perfect. Many writers will tell you frankly that their first drafts are a crime against the humanities. But they write a first draft anyway, because you can't write a second draft until you've done a first. So your first task as a writer is to give yourself permission to write a first draft that stinks.

Be aware that there's more than one way to get through that first draft and then edit it to completion. You need to find the creative paradigm that works best for you. By *creative paradigm,* we mean the method you use to write the first draft and then edit it through all successive drafts until it's as perfect as you can make it.

You may be astonished to discover that professional writers have wildly different creative paradigms. Some plan everything meticulously. Others jump right in and just start typing. In this chapter, we explore in detail a number of ways that seasoned writers work, and we give you ideas to help you find your own creative paradigm. In the final analysis, the right creative paradigm is the one that works for you.

Giving Yourself Permission to Write Badly

On the day you sit down to start writing your first novel, you discover something deep about yourself. Some writers pounce on that blank document, eager to slam down the story at warp speed. Others stare at the first empty page, frozen by fear of writing something wrong. Which kind are you?

Staying out of editing mode

If you're having trouble working in creative mode without slipping into editing mode, try one of the following tricks to break the habit:

✔ Write your first draft longhand. Editing handwritten work is a lot harder, so you may be less tempted.

✔ Put a cotton ball on your backspace key so you're reminded not to edit yourself.

✔ Challenge yourself to write 500 words as fast as you can type. Time yourself and see whether you can do it in less than 15 minutes.

Most writers work in two distinct modes:

✔ **Creative mode:** In creative mode, you give yourself the freedom to try different things, with the understanding that they may work and they may not. Writing badly in creative mode is okay. Everyone *expects* that a lot of what you write in creative mode will be bad (and of course, some will be good). Creation is anarchy, so get a little crazy when you're being creative. That's what you're supposed to do.

✔ **Editing mode:** In editing mode, your goal is to clean up the mess that you made in creative mode. You analyze what you wrote, you recognize the good stuff, you throw away the bad stuff, and you straighten it all out so it makes good sense.

Writer's block is what happens when a writer tries to write in both creative mode and editing mode at the same time. Don't do that! It's like driving with your foot on the gas and the brakes at the same time. Creating a little and then editing a little is okay — just don't edit it before you've actually written the words! As the old saying goes, get it written; then get it right.

You always write your first draft in creative mode. When we talk about a *first draft,* we mean the first version you write on the page or type on the screen. Everything after that is *edited copy.* If you're doing your job right, some of your first draft will be excellent, and some will be awful. Your goal is to make sure that all of your final draft is excellent, and the only way to get there is to start with a first draft, no matter how bad.

Give yourself permission to be bad on the first draft. After all, your editor isn't going to see that first draft. Just get it written. Later on, when you go into editing mode, you can worry about making it pretty. After you finish editing, everyone will think that you were brilliant all along. Only you'll know the truth, and you don't have to tell anyone.

On a blank piece of paper, write out this sentence: "I have full permission to write a really bad first draft, because I know that most first drafts by most authors are mostly lame. I'll get it right on the revision." Put today's date at the top and your signature at the bottom and post it over your workspace.

Creative Paradigms: Investigating Various Writing Methods

We've identified and named at least four *creative paradigms,* or writing methods, that novelists use to create the first drafts of their stories:

- **Seat-of-the-pants:** Just write straight through without planning or editing.
- **Edit-as-you-go:** Write without planning but edit thoroughly as you go.
- **Snowflake:** Make a general plan and write, changing the plan along the way.
- **Outline:** Make a detailed plan before you write anything, adhering to it strictly.

When we were planning this book, our editor asked us to identify which of these is the right creative paradigm for writing a novel. But the truth is that such a beast doesn't exist. Good (even *great*) novelists use any of these methods.

In this section, we describe each of these creative paradigms and explain how and why they work. Later, we help you figure out which one's a good fit for you.

Writing without planning or editing

The method of writing without planning or editing is commonly called *seat-of-the-pants* (SOTP) writing. Typically, you start with a few fragments of the story in mind. When you sit down to write, you just start typing, going wherever your fingers take you.

This method is exhilarating, no doubt about it. When you write SOTP fiction, the twists and turns in the plot surprise you as much as they surprise your reader. The story seems to take on a life of its own, and you may well say, "I didn't kill Richard. I walked into the room and found him dead!"

For some SOTP writers, the fun is in the first draft, and editing is a punishment they have to endure. Never knowing what's going to happen, they just enjoy the ride. They write and write — at speeds of up to 2,000 words per hour — happily drilling out story. For these writers, however, the day of reckoning comes on the second draft, when they have to edit it all. Because the entire story was unplanned, they have to rethink some characters. Some plot twists are now obviously mistakes. They have to throw out whole chapters or whole sequences of chapters. And they have to move or revise other chapters heavily.

For other SOTP writers, the first draft is agony, but editing is bliss. Having no plan, every new scene of the first draft is fraught with danger. What if this scene doesn't go anywhere? What if that new character tries to take over the story? What if today's work turns out to be all for nothing? But after the laborious first draft is finished, the fun begins for these writers, because they love revisions. Now they happily cut and paste and delete. They rethink their characters, finding whole new backstories, values, motivations, and goals for them.

If you're going to write by the seat of your pants, you need to be willing to rewrite heavily. When you finish that first draft, it's going to have a lot of characters, plot threads, and ideas — many of which will be inconsistent or incomplete. At that point, you'll understand your story pretty well, but you'll need to be ruthless in your editing and do the following:

- ✔ Rethink your entire novel structure.
- ✔ Fix plot holes and tie up loose ends.
- ✔ Get rid of some characters, combine others, and deepen all of them.

You need to be willing to work hard, to rewrite as many times as you need to get it right. How many revisions? That depends. Some authors report rewriting their novels ten to twenty times — or more. That sounds scary, but authors who do that many rewrites do it because they love to. Many authors also hire freelance editors to help them through the rewriting. Chapter 16 discusses this further.

Stephen King is an SOTP writer. So is Anne Lamott, author of *Bird by Bird*. So is Jerry Jenkins, who co-wrote the *Left Behind* series. If you want to write by the seat of your pants, you're in very good company.

Editing as you go

You may like the wild freedom that seat-of-the-pants writing gives you, but at the same time, you may be terrified of letting the story get away from you. The solution some writers choose is to edit it as they go. Here's how it works:

1. **Write a scene without planning.**

   See chapters 9 and 10 for tips on writing scenes.

2. **Before you go on, stop and edit it.**

3. **Then edit it again and again, as many times as you need, until the scene glows.**

   This is hard work. You may edit it five or ten or twenty times. You may spend an entire day or a whole week working on that one scene.

The benefit of editing as you go is that each time you work over that scene, you understand your story a little better. And your perfectionist heart feels safe when at last you decide to move on to the next scene, secure in the knowledge that the story up to this point works perfectly.

The hazard of editing as you go is that you're still just making up the story as you go along. Because you probably don't know how the story is going to come out and you probably don't know how you're going to get there, you may wrestle with the terrible fear that the book actually isn't going to go anywhere. And your fear may be justified. After all that laborious sanding and buffing and polishing and varnishing of your beautiful scenes, you may have sanded and buffed and polished and varnished your way into a corner that you can't get out of.

Luckily, you're a novelist. You are a remarkably creative novelist, with all sorts of desperate and wicked tricks that your subconscious has been hoarding over a lifetime. If your caffeine level is high enough, and if you're terrified enough, you may just find a new and incredibly cool way out of that corner. That's the joy and the hysteria of writing fiction, and truth be told, there's no greater feeling than brilliantly fixing a busted storyline at 3:00 a.m. on the night before your book is due and e-mailing it in to your editor just as she's getting in to work. There's also no worse feeling than staring at the screen all night in a white panic, knowing that nothing you can do will fix your story and you're going to have to grovel for a deadline extension.

Dean Koontz is an edit-as-you-go writer. If this is your creative paradigm of writing, then know that the method works and works exceptionally well in the right hands.

Planning a little, writing a little

Many writers want a bit of the freedom of the seat-of-the-pants writer, but they also want the security of knowing that the story is going to work out. These writers first do some story planning to get the large-scale structure of the story right. They may create backstories for their characters, map out a three-act structure, write a synopsis, create a list of scenes. But they don't work out every detail in advance. They leave some of that creativity for writing the first draft. Then when they start writing, they've already made most of the big decisions. They still have many small decisions to make, but the main strategy of the story works, and they know before they start writing that it'll work. They're just fuzzy on the details.

Randy prefers this style of writing. Years ago, he wrote a short article on his method and made an analogy to a curious mathematical object known as a *snowflake fractal*. (A *fractal* is an object that you keep drawing and redrawing in ever-finer detail, but it's never actually finished.) Although this analogy was initially a joke, the idea caught fire. To Randy's astonishment, the Snowflake method has become wildly popular around the world, and now hundreds of thousands of people visit the Snowflake page on his Web site (`www.advancedfictionwriting.com`) every year. You can find a detailed description of the ten steps of the Snowflake method in Chapter 18.

The virtue of the Snowflake method (or any other method in which you do an incomplete design before you start writing) is that you have reasonable confidence that your story is going to get from your chosen beginning to your chosen ending. You're free to write rapidly, knowing that you probably won't make any decisions in any given scene that will wreck the main story. You probably won't introduce any characters who'll need reworking later.

The hazard of the Snowflake method is that you may think that your incomplete design is enough to get you home to nirvana. It's not. Sooner or later, your initial design for your storyline is going to show cracks. If you continue on blindly without stopping to do a redesign, then you're setting yourself up for massive revisions later.

If you use the Snowflake method, we recommend that you periodically check your story design to make sure it's still on track. Has your plot drifted? Have you introduced any new characters who need more airtime? Most importantly, are you forcing your story to go in an unnatural direction?

Randy typically does a complete review of his story design after writing about the first quarter of his novel. He repeats this at the halfway mark and the three-quarters mark. Having the story evolve very strongly away from his original plan isn't unusual. That's okay — he finds that the design almost always gets better.

Outlining before you write

Many writers (Peter included) simply can't write anything until they've worked out the whole story. For them, writing a summary of the story first is essential. This summary is typically called a *long synopsis* or an *outline* or a *treatment* or whatever. We call it an *outline* so as not to confuse it with the *synopsis* (two or three pages summarizing the story) that most publishers require before they'll buy a book. A typical outline for a 400-page novel may run 20 to 50 pages or even longer.

Outliners don't want to waste any first-draft material. They want to know every twist and turn in their story in advance. They want to find all the holes in the story logic and plug them before writing one word of the manuscript. Outliners may do as many as five or ten drafts of their outline before they pronounce it done. Then they whiz through the first draft, knowing that the story is already *there* and all they have to do is type the words. If they're good with words, their first draft may be pretty close to their last.

The virtue of the outlining method is that working with a 50-page outline is much easier than working with a 500-page manuscript. You can write it ten times faster, edit it ten times faster, and delete big sections without crying over spilled ink. Holding the big chunks of the story in your mind is also much easier when you're working with an outline than when working with a manuscript. You have less to remember.

The hazard of outlining is that an outline is essentially oriented toward plot, not toward character. So if you're a character-oriented writer, then you'll likely need to augment your outline with some detailed sketches of the characters in your story. If you're a plot-oriented writer, you may get to know your characters only after you've locked them into a story that doesn't fit them very well. You may find yourself adjusting your characters so they fit the storyline. Whenever you do that, you run the risk of having two-dimensional characters, concocted to fit the story.

Robert Ludlum *(The Bourne Identity)* was a famous outliner. Some of his outlines reportedly ran longer than 100 pages. If you're a fan of Ludlum, you know that his plots are enormously complicated, yet he rarely dropped a thread that he didn't ultimately tie off.

Finding a Creative Paradigm that Works for You

There's no one best way to write a novel that works for everyone. Each writer is unique, with particular strengths and weaknesses. You need to find the creative paradigm that plays to your strengths. If you do, you'll find that writing fiction is fun (even when it's hard work). If you choose a paradigm that plays into your weaknesses, you'll find fiction writing to be a horrible, miserable chore, and you may quit writing.

Multiple personalities: Profiling the writer

Everyone knows that all kinds of people are in the world — liberal and conservative, cautious and impetuous, deep and shallow, creative and analytical. If you've ever taken a personality test, such as the Myers-Briggs Type Indicator, then you know how many ways people can be different — at least in the ways people try to label. In the Myers-Briggs scheme of things, four elements go into your personality, and each one has two main options: You're an Extravert or an Introvert, an Intuitive or a Sensor, a Thinker or a Feeler, and a Judger or a Perceiver. Sixteen different combinations of these traits are possible, and your particular combination says a lot about you.

But surely writers are more similar to one another than to the great unwashed masses of nonwriters, aren't they? Writers are creative types, generally pretty intelligent, maybe given to angst more than is good for them, but that's because they're deep thinkers, right? Writers have so much in common that there's probably some typical novelist personality, no?

Well, no. Randy attended a writing retreat once with about 80 other published novelists. One speaker talked about the Myers-Briggs classification scheme and then handed out tests. Randy wondered whether most of the novelists would end up in just a few of the 16 possible groups. To his surprise, nearly every possible combination of traits had at least one writer in it. Randy is an INTP (introvert-intuitive-thinker-perceiver), but one of his good friends is precisely the opposite — an ESFJ (extravert-sensor-feeler-judger). Peter is an ISFJ (introvert-sensor-feeler-judger) — at least this week.

Intrigued, Randy began talking to his fellow novelists to see which methods they use to write their fiction. He found that their creative paradigms vary as widely as their personalities. The point? There's no one writer personality type. Individual writers are very different, and each has his or her own way of approaching the writing process. There's no right or wrong here — just what's right for *you*.

We provide an overview of four creative paradigms in the preceding section. In this section, we explain why you should think about your writing process, and we help you develop a writing strategy that suits you best.

Understanding why method matters

You may wonder why you need to think about creative paradigms at all. Why not just write? The problem is that "just writing" *is* a creative paradigm — it's the seat-of-the-pants method, and it may or may not work for you.

Your creative paradigm gives you a way to manage your novel, which is an enormously complex work of art for three reasons:

✓ **Characters are real people, and real people are complicated.** See Chapters 7 and 12 for the gritty details on building deep characters.

- ✔ **A plot has six different layers of detail, and all six layers need to be working correctly in your story.** See Chapters 8 through 10 and 13 through 15 for a careful discussion of these six layers.

- ✔ **Your novel's theme must pervade every page of your story, without being visible anywhere.** You probably won't understand your novel's theme until after your first draft is written. (If your theme is a great one, literary critics in coming centuries will likely argue fiercely that you never understood your theme at all.)

The human mind isn't well adapted to holding an enormous amount of complexity all at once. Most people can keep no more than about seven different things in their mind at a time. If they need to tackle more than that, they mentally create compartments and shove the extras in those.

The four creative paradigms we discuss in this chapter are four common strategies that novelists use to manage the overwhelming complexity of a novel. When you find the right creative paradigm for you, you'll have a tremendous competitive advantage as a writer. In our experience, the main reason talented writers fail to finish novels is that they're using the wrong creative paradigm.

Developing your creative paradigm

Whether you want to or not, you're going to choose some sort of creative paradigm to write your novel. The question for you is which method will help you manage the layers of the novel and write the best story you can. In most cases, that will be the method that's easiest for you, because it plays to your natural strengths. But whether it's easy or hard, all that matters is that your creative paradigm works better for you than any other method. At the end of the day, nobody is going to know or care how you wrote your novel; all they'll care about is whether it gives them a powerful emotional experience.

Most professional writers find a writing method that works for them early in their careers and stick with it. On the few occasions we've seen experienced novelists try to change their creative paradigms, the results have been disaster. If you're a beginner, now is the time for you to look at all the paradigms, try them out, and choose the one that works for you.

Table 4-1 can help you decide which method may be a good fit (we describe these strategies in detail earlier in "Creative Paradigms: Investigating Various Writing Methods"). Try the creative paradigm that sounds most appealing and see whether your work gives the reader a powerful emotional experience (which is the measure of a novel — see Chapter 2 for details). If it does, then stick with what works. If not, then try combining features from the second-most-appealing creative paradigm or come up with your own method. Don't let anyone tell you that you have to use some particular method of writing your novel.

Table 4-1	Choosing a Creative Paradigm			
Question	*Seat-of-the-Pants*	*Edit-As-You-Go*	*Snowflake*	*Outline*
Do you prefer to plan in advance or plunge right in?	Plunge in	Plunge in	Plan (rarely plunge in)	Plan
Do you prefer each stage of a project to be perfect before you move on, or is leaving loose ends okay?	Loose ends are okay	Perfect it first	Loose ends are okay	Perfect it first (you may write an outline with loose ends but clean them up in another draft of the outline before writing)
Do you hate, tolerate, or enjoy organizing things?	Hate, tolerate, or enjoy	Tolerate or enjoy	Tolerate	Enjoy
Question	Seat-of-the-Pants	Edit-As-You-Go	Snowflake	Outline
Are you a linear thinker, or do you like to think up random story ideas and then pull them all together later?	Usually linear (you write the story in the order it happens)	Linear	Linear or random	Linear or random (you may create scenes at random and then move them around)
Do you prefer to look at the big picture first and then work out the details, or do you prefer to think about the details first and figure out the big picture later?	Details first	Details first	Big picture first	Usually big picture first

Using creative paradigms for s[ ] works and screenplays

What about other kinds of fiction, such as short stories and screenplays? Do you need a creative paradigm for them, too? If so, is it the same one you'd use for a novel?

A novel has many characters and six layers of story structure, and managing them all in your brain is extremely hard; you choose your creative paradigm to help you manage all that complexity in a way that's best for your personality and your brain. So in that light, here's our take on using creative paradigms with other types of fiction:

✔ **Short stories:** We believe that you'll probably do fine with your short story, no matter

which creative paradigm you [ ] simply don't have to manage as much in a short story. A short story has only a few characters and typically has either four or five layers of story structure.

✔ **Screenplays:** A screenplay is generally 100 or more pages, and it's much closer in complexity to a novel, both in the number of characters and in the number of layers of story structure. So we believe that you should use the same creative paradigm for writing a screenplay as you'd use for writing a novel.

Using Your Creative Paradigm to Find Your Story Structure

The story structure of a modern novel has six layers of complexity, and you need to manage each layer so that the direction is clear at every stage (see Chapters 8 through 10 and 13 through 15 for details on these layers). Your reader must always know where your characters think the story is going and why; therefore, you must always know where the story is going and why — and how you'll throw in roadblocks to surprise your characters and your readers. You may not understand this in your first draft, but you need to understand it by the final one.

The problem is that your novel is too complicated for you to figure out all six layers of complexity in one go. You have to take it in stages, first working out one layer of your story structure, then another, and then trying to fit them together bit by bit. This takes a lot of time and effort; fitting them all together on the first try is impossible. This means you need to make several passes through your novel, each time reworking things so the different layers mesh together. You can do this in any order you want, depending on how you work best.

Each of the creative paradigms we cover in the preceding sections is geared toward putting these various layers of story together, fixing up the mismatches, reworking the pieces that don't fit, and then putting them together again, over and over until the story is working on all six layers of story structure. Here's how the process works for each style:

- **Seat-of-the-pants writing:** The seat-of-the-pants method starts with the low-level details. Line by line and paragraph by paragraph, these details work nicely. But at the higher levels of organization — scenes and acts — the story may not work at all. So in the editing stage, you have to rework the whole thing to give those scenes and acts a clear and sensible direction. This is a bottom-up approach.

- **Editing as you go:** The edit-as-you-go method likewise starts with the details. But after you've written a scene, you go back and edit it, thinking now about how this scene works with all the other scenes. If you need to tweak some of those earlier scenes, this is the time to do it. When the scene is finally perfect, the story as a whole works — up to this point in the story. If everything goes well, at the end of the story, everything is still working well.

- **Snowflaking:** The Snowflake method starts with the big picture — usually the main storyline and then the standard three-act structure. Next, you put together a synopsis and then the scenes to fill in the details. If either of these changes the big picture, you edit the storyline and three-act structure. After working back and forth a few times, you're ready to start writing the first draft. While writing, you keep checking to make sure that the big picture is still working and make changes as necessary to keep the story on track. At the end of the first draft, the story should be well-structured and should need only minor editing. This is a top-down approach.

- **Outlining:** As an outliner, you start with the big picture and work out a storyline and three-act structure. As soon as those work, you create a synopsis and the sequence of scenes. Up to this point, you've worked much like the Snowflaker. But now you write a long synopsis instead of a first draft. This long synopsis fills in most of the story ideas, but you tell rather than show each scene. After you finish, if the story works, you go to work on the first draft. At the end of the first draft, you have a well-structured story that needs only minor editing.

Chapter 5

Managing Your Time . . . and Yourself

. . . .

In This Chapter
▶ Creating a writing schedule
▶ Setting up an inspiring writing space
▶ Managing your money
. . . .

You need three major resources to have a successful writing career: time, writing space, and money. If you're going to succeed as a novelist, you must use these resources wisely. Throughout your writing career, you'll want to continuously improve yourself in all three areas, but you have to start somewhere.

In this chapter, we explore all three resources. We start with the resource no one can make any more of: time. Despite rumors to the contrary, there still are only 24 hours in a day, 7 days in a week, and 52 weeks in a year. However, finding the time to write is possible if you carefully and consistently manage your time — and yourself. In this chapter, we also consider the importance of setting up a good place to do your writing, and we wrap up with a brief discussion of managing money.

Finding Time to Write

Writing is a time-intensive occupation. Not only that, but writing is a craft that will improve the more time you spend doing it. We can guarantee that if you dedicate time to learning, practicing, and honing your writing craft, you'll become a better writer. And better writers tend to get published more often — and in higher-quality venues.

If you just want to enjoy writing for writing's sake, then you really don't need to worry about setting up a regular schedule or mapping out your day to make time for your writing. However, if you hope to be published — or if you hope to advance your craft and earn better advances or fees from your publishers — then you need to devote a significant amount of time to writing.

Establishing and sticking to a writing goal — for this week and this year

William Faulkner once said, "I write when the spirit moves me, and the spirit moves me every day." If your ultimate goal is to become a professional novelist, then eventually you'll reach the point where you write every day. But very few writers start out on that kind of schedule. When you're just starting out, you probably *can't* write every day because you have other commitments. But you want to be writing every week — probably at least a couple of times per week. Why? Because you need this time to focus on learning the tools of the craft and improving your writing skills.

Here's our advice for setting aside time to write every week:

1. **Create a specific writing goal.**

   In our experience, your best bet is to start small and steadily work up to longer periods of writing time each week. By starting out small, you'll be able to celebrate smaller and near-term victories on your path to becoming a fiction author. You may start with, say, half an hour or an hour a week. Later, your goal may be to carve out three hours per week of honest writing time or to write five pages of text or 700 words a day. Make sure that whatever goal you choose, it's both measurable and attainable.

2. **Write down your goal.**

   Research indicates that people who write down their goals have a much better chance of reaching them than people who don't write them down. Write your goal on a piece of paper taped to your computer monitor or wall, on a to-do list, or within your scheduling software. Your written goal may look something like this: "This week, I'm going to spend an hour writing. In that hour, I'm going to produce 200 words, and I don't care if they're the crappiest lines I ever write, but I won't quit till they're done."

3. **Find the time to work toward your goal.**

   If you don't know where your writing time will come from, list all the optional things you do each week. Make a quick estimate of how many hours you spend on each of the following:

- Watching TV

- Reading magazines or newspapers

- Browsing the Web

- Socializing with friends

- Doing optional activities related to your job, school, family, or church

- Doing other activities for fun

Some of these activities are likely chewing up anywhere between one and ten hours per week of your time, perhaps more. So here comes the hard part: You need to trade some of these activities for writing time. Start small and allow a few months to wean yourself away from the activities you can do with less — or go entirely without. Maybe for your first week, you commit to watching one hour less TV on Wednesday night.

Avoid robbing your sleep time to write, and don't skimp on exercise. Writing is not just a sedentary activity and a solitary activity — it's a vegetary activity. You can't afford to fall apart physically, so don't consider sleep and exercise to be expendable.

4. Tell anyone who needs to be informed.

That may be your spouse, partner, children, parents, co-workers, or dog-catcher. Tell everyone who needs to know so they won't interrupt you as you work to achieve your goal (and so they don't wonder why you stopped showing up for weekly moose-calling practice).

5. Find someone to hold you accountable for achieving your goal.

Although you may very well be able to commit to a goal and follow through to achieve it, having someone else (a friend, work associate, spouse, or significant other) hold you accountable can keep you motivated. Give this person a copy of your goal and ask your supporter to check in with you periodically to see whether you're meeting your promises. Consider setting up a system in which you promise to pay some sort of fine for failing to achieve your goal. The fine should not be a mere token — it should be stiff enough that you'll do whatever it takes to hit your target.

Randy had a writing buddy once who made this deal: Any week he failed to hit his writing quota, he had to pay 50 dollars. Randy's buddy was just out of graduate school and working at a low-paying job, and 50 bucks hurt. He rarely missed his quota. Guess what? When Randy recently talked with him on the phone, this buddy was raving about the gorgeous cover his publisher had just sent him for his sixth novel.

After you've been writing for a month or so at a steady pace of an hour a week, bump up the pace a little — to two hours a week. We recommend that in their first year of writing, beginning writers ramp up to about five hours of writing per week. More-experienced writers generally devote at least 20 hours a week to their writing, with professional writers often working much more.

Go through the same routine each time: Reset your goal and write it down. Decide what you can cut out of your life to gain the time you need. Inform those who must be informed about your new goal. Finally, make yourself accountable to someone who can exact a penalty if you fail to reach your goal.

Be consistent and keep at your schedule, but don't beat yourself up if you miss a week. Just make an effort to get back to writing the next week. No matter how busy you are, you can squeeze in time to write by examining how you spend your free time and identifying some of that time to repurpose. You're already using up that time — just use it differently.

If you do this, you will improve as a writer. Practice really does make perfect, and this is your primary goal — to become a better writer. The more you write, the better you'll get.

Organizing your time

There's an old saying: if you don't manage your time, your time will manage you. One of the best ways to take control of your schedule is to break your day into blocks of time, with each block devoted to a specific purpose. For example, the first time block in your day (after eating breakfast and taking a shower) may be devoted to reading and responding to e-mail. The second block may be devoted to a library trip to do research or to actual focused writing time. You need to decide how long each block of time will be and which tasks will go within each block.

Schedule your writing block for whatever time of day works best for you — try a variety of times to see when you're most energized, focused, and inspired.

An almost endless variety of activities competes for every writer's attention — anything from taking out the trash to returning phone calls to reading existing books in your genre to attending your friend's soccer game. Making a priority list can ensure that non-writing tasks don't pilfer your writing time. A priority (or to-do) list helps you determine which tasks you'll do each day and in which order you'll do them. Peter has a spiral notebook specifically for such lists.

The idea of a priority list is to keep your most important tasks front and center during the course of your workday — not to have a laundry list of everything you may do within the next year. Make your active list of priorities no more than seven to ten items long. Describe each task in detail in order of importance. As you complete tasks, delete or cross them off.

Looking at time management tools

A number of tools are available to make time management a snap, including the following:

✔ **Personal organizers and day planners:** These paper-based time management systems — which go by names such as Filofax, Day-Timer, and the FranklinCovey Day Planner — are essentially daily calendars on steroids. They're portable, easy to use and update, and they don't need batteries.

✔ **Portable electronic organizers:** Many mobile telephones and personal digital assistants (PDAs) incorporate time management utilities within them. For example, Apple's iPhone offers a variety of time management apps, with such titles as

To-Do's, iProcrastinate Mobile, and Toodledo.

✔ **Computer software:** Microsoft and Apple include simple to-do lists in many of their software offerings (such as Outlook), and you can Google time management software to find all sorts of other options. Remember to keep it simple — few writers need the capabilities in a full-blown project management software package. Ideally, whatever software solution you choose will boot up along with your computer each morning and display your list of to-dos without your having to go out of your way to get it going.

Find a simple system that does what you need it to do and — perhaps most importantly — that you'll use.

Review your list at the beginning of each day to get a feel for what you'll be doing and in what order you'll be doing it. Make any changes you need to bring the list up to date. Are any tasks missing? Or do you see tasks that are no longer relevant and should be removed? Is the order correct? Has one of the tasks become more important than another? Keep your list focused and current, and be sure to use it.

Try to avoid the temptation to skip to easier — but less important — tasks. Why? Because then you'll never get around to your most-important, highest-priority tasks. That said, if you find yourself stuck on a high-priority task and you just can't seem to find the inspiration to get it moving, then move down the list to your next-highest priority. By successfully completing your next task, you may build the momentum you need to carry you through the top of your priority list.

Setting Up Your Ideal Writing Space

Why do you need a creative space for your writing? Can't you just go to a coffee shop and plunk down your laptop? Yes, of course you can. In that case, the coffee shop is part of your writing space. But another part is that laptop. Every writing space has three basic parts:

- ✔ A desk (or table or other flat surface)
- ✔ A chair
- ✔ A computer (or pad of paper and pen or pencil)

If you mooch off the coffee shop for the table and chair, that's perfectly okay, as long as the owners don't mind. (Good luck at mooching a computer off them, though.)

Whoever provides the space, make sure that it's *dedicated* to your writing. All people are creatures of habit. Being creative is easier when you have a special space where you habitually get creative.

Securing the best writing surface

Every writer needs something to write on. Although a pad of paper or laptop computer balanced on your knees may work for short bursts of writing inspiration, you probably need a comfortable and solid surface on which to write for longer periods of time. For most people, this surface is a desk or table. Make sure your desk or table is at an appropriate height — not too high, not too low. (Ergonomics experts usually tell you to keep your wrists in a straight, neutral position while you type, so that determines what "too high" and "too low" mean.)

If space is at a premium in your home, condo, or apartment, then a dining room table can make for an excellent writing surface. If you have room in your home for a proper desk, then be sure that it contains drawers or cubbies for storage and that it's built well enough to last you for more than just a few months.

If space is really at a premium for you — maybe you live in a studio apartment or you share space with several other people — then a wide variety of specialized writing surfaces are available. Consider buying and installing a fold-down desk that you can mount on the wall. These items are designed to be ready at moment's notice when you need them but to stay out of the way when you don't. Alternatively, consider getting a laptop writing table — also known as a lap desk. These writing surfaces are easy to handle, and you can take them anywhere.

Finding the right chair

If you've ever worked an office job, you know just how important your chair is to maintaining your comfort while sitting for long periods of time. And believe us: Writers tend to do a lot of sitting. Here are some things to look for when you buy, beg, or borrow your next chair:

- ✔ Good upper and lower back support
- ✔ An adjustable backrest
- ✔ A comfortable seat cushion
- ✔ Ample room around your hips and thighs
- ✔ Adjustable padded armrests
- ✔ A five-point base with casters

Choosing a computer (if you want to use one)

Many writers today use computers to do all their writing, and for them, computers are where it's at. So why use a computer? Computers allow you to do the following:

- ✔ Easily make changes and corrections to your document
- ✔ Keep track of word count
- ✔ Convert your manuscript into a file that you can quickly and easily send to anyone around the world via e-mail
- ✔ Do online research
- ✔ Easily insert graphics and photographs into your text (this is rare for the actual text of your novel, but common when you're doing research or brainstorming your characters)
- ✔ Store and transport thousands of pages of text on a very small memory stick or thumb drive

Not every writer uses a computer to compose novels, short stories, or other fictional works. More than a few writers find that writing by hand — using a pen or pencil and paper — or even using an old-fashioned typewriter is an essential part of the way they write. If that's the case for you, then that's great — do whatever works best to inspire your creative muse. But no matter how good your handwriting is, you'll need a typed version of your manuscript to submit to your agent or bring to writing conferences. If you don't plan to hire a typist, a computer is most likely in your future.

Fortunately for writers, today's computers are fast, capable, and surprisingly affordable. Here are some features to consider:

- ✔ If you plan to take your computer with you — essential if you plan to do your writing outside of your home — then get a laptop. If you plan to do all your writing at home or in an office, then a desktop computer may be the right choice for you.

✔ If you get a desktop machine, get as large of a monitor as you can reasonably afford. You don't want to have to squint to see your beautiful text on the screen. Most laptop screens are much smaller than desktop monitors, so if you get a laptop you are trading portability for visibility. However, you can often plug in your laptop to a larger monitor on your desk to get the best of both worlds.

✔ Invest in good word processing software. Microsoft Word is the most common choice for professional writers. If you hate all things Microsoft, then make sure that your word processor can read and write files in Microsoft Word format. The free OpenOffice suite of software includes a word processor named Writer that many writers prefer over Word. (See www.openoffice.org to download this free software or browse the web to see if you can find a suitable alternative.)

✔ Get networked. A connection to the Internet — wireless in the case of a laptop computer — is almost mandatory so you can do research and fact checking on the fly (or if you just want to take a break and check your e-mail).

Here are some things you don't need to worry about anymore:

✔ **Speed and storage**. All modern computers are plenty fast enough and have far more than enough memory and storage for your needs.

✔ **Mac versus Windows versus Linux**. Any of these operating systems will do just fine. Use whichever you like. Randy writes on a Mac. Peter writes on a Windows machine. We trade files back and forth with absolutely no compatibility problems, and we don't even know what our editors use. Nobody cares anymore what kind of system you work on.

Putting everything in place

Before you dive into the writing process, get your writing space set up to write. If you're trying to write on a desk that's cluttered with dirty clothes or piles of old newspapers or other debris, you won't be at your best as a writer. Clear off anything that doesn't have something to do with achieving your writing goals.

Put your computer front and center, with the keyboard and monitor in a comfortable place — not hanging off the edge of the desk. Locate your printer nearby (so you don't have to get up every time you print a document), and have a little cup to hold pencils and pens within easy reach. Although many writers now use online dictionaries, encyclopedias, and other references, you may find it useful to have a dictionary and other reference books on your desk.

Our own creative spaces

Randy's creative space has always been a large metal office desk with a good ergonomic chair and a computer. For years, that desk was in a corner of the family room, 3 feet from the door where his kids ran in and out all day. But it was Randy's space. He wrote hundreds of thousands of words in that space. He won a fistful of awards in that space. That space represented writing to Randy.

These days, Randy has an actual office with a door that closes and two large filing cabinets and three enormous bookcases. But the desk and chair and computer are still the same. It's still his sacred space for writing.

Peter used to do a lot of his writing late at night in noisy coffeehouses. In fact, his first few books were all scribbled onto big yellow legal pads that smelled strongly of coffee and cigarette smoke. Something about the swirl of people talking and music playing and the sights and smells of molten caffeine and smoldering smokes flipped his creativity switch.

Today Peter has a home office that's separated from the main living space of his home. He has a large desk and computer and a couple of large windows that let in lots of natural light.

Find your own writing space. Make it yours. Make it special. If possible, reserve it only for writing and only for you. You need this creative space. Take it, guard it, and keep it.

Dealing with Distractions

Wherever you choose to write — whether at home, in a park, or at your local coffeehouse — you soon find that many distractions are available to entice you away from your writing time. Although the occasional distraction can be a good thing (it can get you out of a rut or give you a fresh perspective on your work), ongoing distractions that keep you from writing won't help you get published — or finished. Here are a few tips for dealing with distractions:

- ✔ **Reward yourself for achieving your goals.** Goals may include writing a certain number of pages or words, devoting a certain number of hours to writing each week, or submitting your manuscript to an agent or publisher (see the earlier section "Establishing and sticking to a writing goal — for this week and this year"). When you reward yourself for achieving your goals, you'll be even more motivated to stay on track. The best rewards are ones that you personally find motivating, and they may include things such as treating yourself to lunch at a local restaurant, watching TV for a bit, or taking time to scoop yourself a bowl of ice cream.

✔ **Put up a do-not-disturb sign.** If you have a posse of wild kids or distracting significant others vying for your time, create clear boundaries for your writing space and time. Then announce them to the important people in your life and ask their cooperation and support. Be polite but firm in enforcing the rules — and your boundaries. If, for example, your visiting mother-in-law keeps bothering you to chat, politely explain that you'll be happy to chat after you finish your writing but that she'll need to wait until you're done. It's best if you can schedule time for friends and family, so they don't feel like they're competing with your writing.

Understand that you may have to be flexible. If you're a single parent with kids to entertain and take care of, then you may find that you need to attend to them during the day and work on your writing at night, when they're fast asleep.

✔ **Unplug, turn off, or move the distractions.** Perhaps you can get rid of the distractions that are keeping you from achieving your writing goals. If the television in your writing space keeps calling your name, then move it into another room. If a constant barrage of e-mail messages on your computer keeps you from focusing on writing, close your e-mail program. If a friend calls and wants to talk your ear off, then you may decide that you'll let voice-mail pick up calls when you're working. Writing is a job, so treat it like one.

✔ **Take a short break.** Regular breaks help you clear your mind and then get back to work with a renewed energy and focus. We suggest that you take a break every 60 to 90 minutes and that your breaks last no longer than about five minutes. This will help ensure that you don't lose your precious writing momentum.

Randy likes to walk. Every hour or two, if the weather's good, he takes a five-minute walk around the pond on his property. If the weather's foul, he hits the elliptical machine in his living room for a few minutes. Either way, it boosts his energy levels. Then he drinks a glass of water, looks outside at the ducks on the pond, and has a deep conversation with his cat. For the occasional energy boost, Peter grabs the electric guitar sitting in his home office, plugs it in, and rocks out for a few minutes. And when he really needs a boost, he fires up his espresso machine.

Looking at Money Matters

J. K. Rowling became the richest author in the UK (and perhaps in the world) through her massively popular *Harry Potter* series. Did you know that she was a single mom on welfare when she wrote the first *Harry Potter* book? Tom Clancy quit his day job selling life insurance after his first novel *The Hunt for Red October* became a runaway bestseller. John Grisham quit his job lawyering after *The Firm* made him a superstar.

Although the lives of some very successful novelists make for a great rags-to-riches story, the vast majority of writers don't make a full-time living from it. For many writers, writing fiction is not about making a lot of money. Instead, the satisfaction comes in finding someone who thinks their work is good enough to merit being published in a magazine, e-zine, journal, or book and in having people read their work and enjoy it enough to recommend to their friends and family.

However, many writers do try to make a living — or at least some occasional mad money — from their craft. If that's your hope, then you need a strategy. And even if you consider writing a hobby, you still need to budget money for writing. In this section, we take a close look at why money matters — and what you can do about it.

Budgeting money for writing

Ideas may be free, but writing them down isn't. As a writer, you're going to incur some expenses over the next several years, even though you won't have any income from your writing to offset them. What are those expenses? We can list several possibilities here:

- Computer, printer, and Internet access
- A desk and chair and various office supplies (a few crates of paper for that printer aren't cheap!)
- Books for research, both novels in your genre and nonfiction (the books unavailable at your library or those you prefer to own)
- Field trips, road trips, museum admission, or any other ways you want to do research that don't involve cracking open a book
- Writing classes and workshops
- Writing conferences (including registration and travel expenses)
- Membership dues for any writing associations you join
- Dinner for your star critique buddy, the person who ensures that you stick to your writing schedule, and your best supporters as you write

You may already have bought some of these items. Most people already have a computer and printer before they start writing. If you don't already have a decent desk and chair, however, you need one. You don't want to end up with a back shaped like a pretzel and a chiropractor's bill that costs several times more than that decent desk and chair would've cost in the first place.

You should seriously think about budgeting money for writing conferences now. Quite simply, writing conferences are the quickest and easiest way to make the connections you need to sell your book. This makes them an essential expense — one you can't ignore.

Randy sold his first three books through the contacts he made at writing conferences. After he sold his third book, an agent friend of his called to see whether Randy thought it was about time to start working with an agent. Where did Randy meet this agent? That's right — at a writing conference.

Writing conferences are wonderful, but they do cost money. Even a small, regional one-day conference takes at least $100 out of your pocket. And the larger national multi-day conferences can run you more than $1,000. Start saving money now for writing conferences so that you'll have the money when you're ready. If you take your writing career seriously and follow the recommendations in this book, you may be ready a lot sooner than you think.

Making your living as a writer: Don't expect this to be your day job (yet)

We've heard it said that the top-five-earning writers in the world earn about 60 percent of *all* the dollars earned by writers. This isn't easy to verify, but our experience tells us it's plausible. The pie is split up into a very few huge slices and a lot of tiny slices. Of all the books in print in any given year — about 1.2 million titles — only about 25,000 of them sell more than 5,000 copies during that year. Only a few hundred of those titles sell more than 100,000 copies. According to *Publisher's Weekly* magazine, the average book in America sells about 500 copies.

Long story short, few writers sell enough books to earn a part-time, much less a full-time, living from their craft. However, if your hope is to become a full-time writer earning a full-time paycheck from your work, then you should consider both sides of the equation. On one hand, you need to bring in enough good-paying book deals to keep your financial ship of state afloat. On the other hand, you need to cut your living expenses to allow you to survive on less — giving you the time you need to write.

Can you live on less? If so, how much less? We have two reasons for asking:

- ✔ The less you can live on, the easier you'll find it to earn your entire income from writing.

- ✔ If you start living on less right now, then you can bank the difference and build yourself a buffer so you can quit your day job sooner.

Look at your own finances — and the finances of your family — right now. Got them in front of you? Good. Now ask yourself these questions:

- How much do you earn each month?
- How much do you spend each month?
- How much do you save each month?
- Can you cut your spending and increase your saving? If, for example, you have a mortgage or other large debts, can you pay those down so that your fixed expenses are less?

It's important to remember that you get paid in irregularly-spaced lump sums for your writing. A typical contract will specify that you get a fraction of your advance on signing, another fraction at various milestones, and the rest when the publisher agrees that you've submitted a manuscript of satisfactory quality. Some contracts even delay part of the advance until the publication date. Many books don't earn out their advance, which means that you never get paid another dime on those books, after the initial advance. Novelists simply don't get paid on a nice, weekly schedule. This means you need to manage your cash flow well (unless you're independently wealthy or you have somebody who supports you monetarily in your writing).

Our advice is to make sure you keep your day job until you get your fiction-writing empire fully up and running. If you can't cut expenses significantly, you're going to need the steady income you're already receiving each month to keep afloat and to prosper. Believe us: Worrying about where that next dollar is going to come from (and when it's going to arrive) is an extremely distracting place to be for any writer. You don't need the pressure of money interfering with your writing — there are plenty of distractions already.

Part II

Creating Compelling Fiction

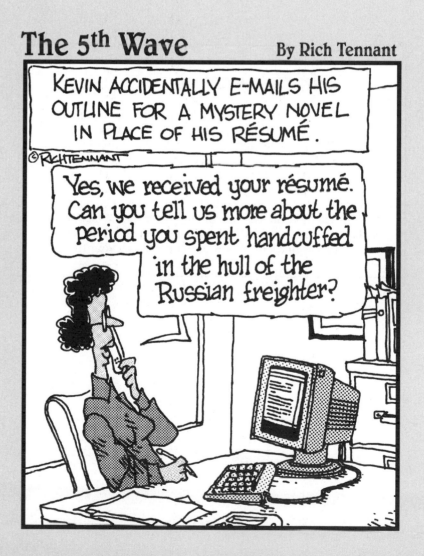

In this part . . .

If you're going to write fiction, then create *compelling* fiction — tell a story that touches a deep emotional chord within your readers. In this part, we explore building your story world — the story's setting — and creating characters who are real and interesting. We then look at the layers of plot, including story structure (the top layers), synopsis and scene (the middle layers), and action, dialogue, interior emotion, interior monologue, description, flashback, and narrative summary (the lowest layer). We put the icing on this part with a look at how to think through your theme.

Chapter 6

Building Your Story World: The Setting for Your Story

. . . .

. . . .

*E*very novel takes place in its own universe, which you create. This universe is not a fragment of some larger universe; it's the whole shebang. Because of that, we prefer the term *story world* rather than smaller-scale terms such as *setting* or *milieu*.

You are the god of the story world you create, and you have complete control over everything that happens there. But this doesn't mean that just anything can happen in your story world. Your story world needs to have an inner logic that drives it.

For starters, the world must have physics, chemistry, geology, meteorology, biology — in other words, you can't ignore scientific laws (even if you've made up some of those laws yourself). To this, you have to add one or more cultural groups, each with rules that define how the characters can interact. And no matter what kind of story world you work with, it must be capable of having a conflict, because without conflict, you have no story. A perfect world is useless to the fiction writer. Your story world requires both good and evil, and you're responsible for creating both in a way that ensures that it's possible for either to win.

Feeling daunted? Shrug it off! You've lived in a story world all your life, and you have a deep intuition for what makes it tick. In this chapter, we help you take apart what you already know and see which pieces are core to telling a story. We also help you research the details of your story world so you can bring it to life.

Note that you have to work much harder on your story world in some categories than others. If you're writing a novel about your hometown, set in the current day, then you don't need to do much work to create your story world. But some kinds of fiction — notably science fiction, fantasy, and historical fiction — require you to imagine a story world that may be very different from yours. Even if your category allows you to pay less attention to story world, remember that looking at your own world in a new way can give you new insights.

Identifying the Parts of a Story World

Every story world has three essential components. Without each of these three components, you simply can't have a story:

- **The natural world:** When you describe the natural world, you create a sense of place. The natural world includes everything there is to know about the physical environment. Normally you don't mess with the laws of physics or chemistry in your novel, but you do have to know the geography, typical weather patterns, and a thousand other details (some of which we cover later in "Researching Your Story World").

- **The cultural groups:** If your novel is set in a small town, you may have only one cultural group. If it's in New York City, you may have characters from five or six ethnic groups interacting (and misunderstanding each other). If you're writing about the planet Zorba, you may have a dozen intelligent species.

- **The backdrop for conflict:** This is the political or cultural or religious or interpersonal climate that makes it possible for your story to have conflict. Without conflict, you have no story.

Table 6-1 shows how these building blocks come into play in three novels.

Table 6-1	Elements of Story World in Three Novels		
Novel	Natural World	Cultural Groups	Backdrop
The Chosen, by Chaim Potok	Brooklyn during the 1940s	A community of Hasidic Jews, the surrounding community of more-liberal Jews, and the broader world of Gentiles	Religious: The Hasidic community intends to raise its children in a tightly cloistered community sheltered from worldly ideas. But in America, you can't prevent children from listening to the radio, reading the newspaper, or visiting the library.
The Clan of the Cave Bear, by Jean Auel	Ice Age Europe in the vicinity of the Black Sea	Humans and Neanderthals	Cultural: Natural tension occurs between two cultures that don't understand or trust each other.
Star Wars: From the Adventures of Luke Skywalker, by George Lucas	"A galaxy far, far away"	Humans, droids, Wookies, and numerous other species	Political: The Rebel Alliance threatens the repressive Galactic Empire.

Creating a Sense of Place

As a fiction writer, your goal is to create a story world that comes fully alive in your reader's mind. This is called *creating a sense of place,* and it's difficult because you have a limited number of words. The average novel is a bit less than 100,000 words, and you need most of those words for telling your story, not for describing your story world.

This means that you can't waste a single word. (If a picture is worth 1,000 words, a 100,000-word novel can show your readers only 100 pictures, which would make a pretty lame story.) You have to do better than that, and this section explains how.

Making description do double duty

In the 19th century, authors routinely took a page or three to describe every little detail of the story world. Look at the opening paragraph from *Ben-Hur: A Tale of the Christ*, by Lew Wallace. Published in 1880, it was the best-selling American novel of the 19th century:

> The Jebel es Zubleh is a mountain fifty miles and more in length, and so narrow that its tracery on the map gives it a likeness to a caterpillar crawling from the south to the north. Standing on its red-and-white cliffs, and looking off under the path of the rising sun, one sees only the Desert of Arabia, where the east winds, so hateful to the vine-growers of Jericho, have kept their playgrounds since the beginning. Its feet are well covered by sands tossed from the Euphrates, there to lie; for the mountain is a wall to the pasture-lands of Moab and Ammon on the west — lands which else had been of the desert a part.

This is *static description,* which is a lot like a still-life painting. Nothing is happening here. You see no characters, no motion, no feeling. It's pure geography.

Nineteenth-century readers loved static descriptions of the setting because descriptions created pictures in their minds, and pictures were rare in the 19th century. Don't write for those readers. Every one of those readers is now dead, and they aren't going to buy your book. You're writing to entertain a reader of the 21st century — one who has seen hundreds or thousands of movies and wants things to happen now. You can't afford to bore your reader with a long, rambling static description of a mountain, a street, a palace, or anything else.

In Chapter 2, we talk about the seven basic tools you have to deliver the goods to your reader. Five of these unfold in your reader's mind like a movie — action, dialogue, interior monologue, interior emotion, and description of sensory inputs (as seen through the eyes of some character in the scene). When you use only these five tools to write a segment of your story, you can say that the segment is written in *immediate scene.* Immediate scene has no narrative summary and no static description. Modern fiction writers tend to use more immediate scene and less static description or narrative summary, because modern readers tend to prefer it.

When you describe any place, any person, any thing in your story, do your best to make that description do double duty. It should do the following:

- ✔ Give the reader a powerful emotional experience.
- ✔ Keep the story moving by integrating smoothly with the action, dialogue, interior monologue, and interior emotion.

Fitting description in the story

If you can, weave your description in as sensory input with the other imme-diate-scene parts of your story — the action, dialogue, interior monologue, and interior emotion. Those are the parts of your story that unroll second by second in your reader's mind. You can't afford to stop the action for a page while you describe some piece of your story world. If you can't describe some-thing naturally within the action of the story, and if you can't describe it from within the mind of one of your characters, then ask yourself why you need to describe it at all.

Do you really need to describe that volcano in pixel-perfect detail? Maybe, if your character is a worried mother who's racing up the trail alongside the red-hot lava field looking for her lost 5-year-old. Maybe, if your character is a young virgin being forced up the stony path to be sacrificed to the gods in the mountain. Maybe, if your character is trudging up the mountain bearing the Ring of Power and searching for the Cracks of Doom. In any of a thousand similar scenes, go ahead and show that volcano. Make your reader's eyes burn with the sulfuric wisps. Make her sweat in the blast-furnace heat. Ripple your reader's stomach with the subsonic rumble of the mountain's innards.

But maybe the volcano plays no immediate role in your scene. The immediate item of interest may instead be the rare and immensely valuable butterfly flit-ting from flower to tree at the base of the volcano. It may be the Lamborghini speeding through the visitor center parking lot, with six police cars in blue-and-red flashing pursuit. It may be a laptop with the secrets of a Fortune 500 com-pany on its hard drive, ready to be stolen while lying on a bench in that parking lot while its owner looks through his binoculars at the view. In these cases, don't show your reader the volcano. Show the butterfly, the Lamborghini, the laptop. Show them in action, from the point of view of a character who cares about them. If your character cares, your reader will, too.

If you have no story reason to describe something, don't. If you have a reason, then describe it, but make the description personal — connect to the senses and emotions of one of the characters. The right description, as seen through the eyes of the right character, can conjure up a place, a time, and a mood in your reader.

Before you write a segment of static description, divorced from any character, ask yourself this first: Are you willing to pay a fine for using static description? (A suitable fine is whatever you earn for one hour of work.) If you're willing to pay that much to achieve the effect you want using static description, then do so. Otherwise, work it in as sensory description as seen by one of the charac-ters, integrated with action, dialogue, interior monologue, and interior emo-tion. Chapter 10 explains this concept in more detail.

Weaving emotive force into your descriptions

Everything in your story world has one of three basic meanings to each character: good, bad, or neutral. Most of the time, most of your story world will be neutral for your character — so skip the description, unless one of the following applies:

- ✔ You absolutely must describe something in order to move the story forward.
- ✔ You need to set up something that will be important later on.

For example, suppose there's a vacant house on the corner of the street where your character Travis lives. Travis walks by that house every day to catch the bus to work, and that house means absolutely nothing to him. The house is neutral to Travis. So give the house a passing mention if it'll become important later — tell readers that it exists — but don't waste a word describing it. If Travis ever needs to go into that house, *then* describe it.

However, maybe Travis's wife Krista kissed her first boyfriend on the porch of that house. For Krista, the rose bush in front of the house carries memories of first love. The house is good to Krista. When she wanders by that house, you may choose to describe it through her eyes, using words that evoke that love. Focus on the fragrance of the red roses, the warm shimmer of sunlight on the windows, the linked hearts rough-carved into the tree beside the porch. When you do that, you're not just describing the house; you're also showing Krista's heart.

Perhaps Jakey, the 10-year-old son of Travis and Krista, believes the house is haunted. Ghosts linger in that house for Jakey, and he's terrified of walking past it after dark. The house is bad for Jakey. When he races past it at midnight, describe it through his eyes using words that evoke terror. Show the dark windows staring out at the street like the eyeholes of a skull. Hear the wind chuffing through the tree, hissing demonic threats. Again, you're not merely describing the house; you're giving your reader emotive hits. That's why your reader reads.

Ruthlessly prune your descriptions so that they create an emotional reaction in your characters, but don't stand still to do so. Show your reader a movie, using the five components of immediate scene. Use concrete details that evoke your character's senses.

Deciding What Drives Your Cultural Groups

Each of your characters is a unique individual with wants and needs. Chapter 7 details how you create compelling characters as *individuals.* However, every individual comes from a larger community — a cultural group — with a shared history, language, science, technology, religion, mythology, purpose, and much more. All these things determine what's likely and what's possible for your characters. We call these things *cultural drivers* because they drive your cultural groups in many ways.

Later, in "Researching Your Story World," we talk about the research you need to do to fully understand your cultural drivers. How much of that research should you show to your reader? The answer depends on the category of fiction you're writing. Historical novels, fantasies, and science fiction novels typically show the reader a more complete picture of cultural drivers. Other categories may show less. You should show your reader as much as she's expecting.

Don't spend time describing the cultural background unless it means something to one of the characters. If any of the cultural drivers is important to one of your characters — enough to affect the storyline — then by all means, tell your reader about that cultural driver. As with description, though, you need to find a way to explain it to your reader so as to

- ✔ Give the reader a powerful emotional experience.
- ✔ Keep the story moving, using action, dialogue, interior monologue, interior emotion, and sensory description.

Revealing cultural drivers with immediate scene

Most cultural drivers aren't easy to show in action, and thoughts or speech that describes them may seem unnatural, which creates a major challenge for a writer. Consider a cultural driver that lies at the core of Tom Clancy's novel *Patriot Games:* the clash between Catholics and Protestants in Northern Ireland. How would you explain this conflict to someone who knows nothing about Ireland or the history of Western Christianity?

You could show part of it using action, as Clancy does, with a violent terrorist attack on the royal family in London. It's easy to show action that's a *result* of a cultural driver. It's much harder to explain the reasons for that cultural driver in the first place. Why so much hate? No gunfire scenes can explain that. To explain something so complex, you need words, which means you need either dialogue or interior monologue.

The problem with using dialogue is that people just don't talk about things that everybody knows. Irish Catholics don't waste time rehearsing for each other the ancient causes of their conflict with Protestants.

If you're going to put in some explanation of a cultural driver in dialogue, you need an outsider character (or a child) who doesn't understand the culture. These characters can believably ask all the questions your reader is asking. If you can't use an outsider or child, then you can feed information to the reader in tiny little slivers of dialogue, leaving it to the reader to fill in the gaps.

You do have another option: interior monologue. But this is even tougher than dialogue, because people rarely spend much time explaining things they already know to themselves. Again, you can show snippets of interior monologue to your reader and trust your reader to be smart enough to put the pieces together.

Exposition: Explaining cultural drivers through narrative summary

Why not use narrative summary to explain cultural drivers to your reader? Narrative summary is efficient, and it may be your only choice for explaining a particularly complex cultural driver, but narrative summary is often boring. You just can't afford to stop the story to deliver a three-page lecture on the history of Scotland under British rule, or the declensions of Russian nouns, or how the tango differs from the polka, or the search by physicists for the Higgs boson, or the intricacies of Zen Buddhism, or what Manifest Destiny meant to an American in 1882.

If you use narrative summary, do your best to keep it short and interesting. Be entertaining. Be brilliant. Be scintillating. For details on narrative summary, flip to Chapter 10.

Combining various elements to show cultural drivers

If giving readers an info dump isn't an option for describing social forces, what's a writer to do? That's what makes writing fiction a battle — and you need to choose your battles carefully. Is there a sound story reason to explain a certain cultural driver? If not, then consider skipping it.

If you do have a good story reason to show a cultural driver, then your best strategy is to mix and match all the tools at your disposal. Use a combination of action, dialogue, and interior monologue to show your reader little snippets of your cultural driver. Then firm it all up with pieces of narrative summary, using as little as necessary. This is a major part of the art of fiction, and nobody ever perfects it.

Chapters 10 and 15 go into detail on how to weave all these components into compelling fiction.

Choosing the Backdrop for Conflict

Your story begins when change begins. That raises a question: Change from *what*, exactly? The answer is change from the status quo. Your responsibility is to know what that status quo is and to communicate it clearly to your reader, along with why the change is happening now. Here's the key question to ask: What weakness in the system makes it possible for change *now*, rather than last month or last year? Read on for information on creating a backdrop.

Defining your backdrop

We use the word *backdrop* to refer to the context for change that marks the beginning of your story. Backdrop has two pieces:

- The status quo — the way things are
- The weak point that makes things ripe for change

You have plenty of options for creating a backdrop. Here are some of the most common scenarios for stories, along with their backdrops. If your story is about change in a city, nation, or world, as in Table 6-2, then the backdrop must include some of the history of that city, nation, or world.

Table 6-2	Common Story Backdrops for Social Change	
Scenario	*Status Quo*	*Weak Point*
War is beginning	Peace	Whatever problem between the nations leads them to decide that the best solution is to fight it out — has some natural resource such as water or oil run dangerously low? Has one nation developed a new weapon? Has one side signed an alliance with a third country?
War is ending	War	One of the sides has become so badly weakened that it now has to sue for peace
War is reaching a turning point	War	Typically some tactical situation that one of the sides can exploit to change the direction of the war; a suddenly vulnerable bridge, mountain pass, supply line, or munitions factory all make prime tactical targets
Cultural change is in the air	Life as it's always been	Almost anything that make the society vulnerable to cultural changes — new technology, immigration of a foreign culture, new ideas, even an explosive new novel
A natural disaster threatens a community or nation	Life as it's always been	Merely that the community or nation is unprepared for this particular type of disaster; whether it's a tidal wave or hurricane or earthquake, it's going to massively interrupt ordinary life

Table 6-3 describes some backdrops for stories that focus on personal change. If your story is about personal change, then the backdrop is mostly the backstory of one or a few characters. But even in these highly personal kinds of stories, the story world is still important. For example, in a story world that tolerates no wife-beating, a battered-wife story couldn't happen; in a story world that assumes wife-beating as normal life, the battered woman's options would be severely limited. Similarly, the larger story world sets the parameters on what sort of personal goals a character can set.

Table 6-3	Common Story Backdrops for Personal Change	
Scenario	**Status Quo**	**Weak Point**
A person decides to change his life for the better	"My ordinary or boring or wretched life"	"I can't live like this any longer" — a wife may decide she's been battered for the last time; an alcoholic may hit the proverbial bottom; a factory worker may realize he can't face the time clock one more day
A person attempts to achieve some personal goal	"My life until now"	"I'm now ready to achieve something new" — a college student who graduates may set a new goal to get a Ph.D.; a runner who's never raced longer than a 10K may set a new goal to finish a marathon
A person decides to get something he wants	"My set of personal possessions"	"I now know that I can't live without having this one great thing" — whether it's a new computer, a new car, or the lost Ark of the Covenant, when a character decides that he won't stop until he gets it, any reader is going to want two questions answered: Why this thing? Why now?
A person is threatened by a change for the worse	"My safe life"	"I'm unprepared for this change that's come into my life" — a layoff, some new and unruly neighbors, or an unexpected divorce can smack into your character from out of the blue

You get to choose the history of your character or cultural group. You get to decide what weak point makes change possible. You get to decide which particular event marks the beginning of change. Then you need to explain it all to your reader, using the tools we talk about earlier for showing cultural drivers: mainly dialogue and narrative summary. In showing the history of a person, you have one extra primary tool you can use: flashback. We describe these tools in Chapter 2, and we show techniques for using them in Chapters 10 and 15.

Defining your story question

As soon as you know what your backdrop is and what change is looming, you have to define a story question. This is almost always a question about a single character in your story. This character is your protagonist, and the *story question* essentially asks whether the character will succeed or fail.

A good story question focuses your story down to a single issue, clearly defining what success looks like and what failure means. Your story question should be

- ✔ **Objective:** The reader should (usually) know how to tell whether the lead character succeeded.
- ✔ **Simple:** The reader should be able to picture what success looks like.
- ✔ **Important:** The reader must believe the story question matters to the character.
- ✔ **Achievable:** The reader should believe that the answer to the story question could be yes.
- ✔ **Difficult:** The reader should believe that the answer to the story question could be no.

Will the Jackal shoot Charles de Gaulle? Will Frodo throw the Ring of Power into the Cracks of Doom? Will Dorothy get home to Kansas? Will Scarlett get Ashley? These story questions drive their stories for hundreds of pages. Every novel needs a story question. The better the story question, the more likely the reader will stay with the book until the end.

Story World Examples from Four Well-Known Novels

In this section, we give examples of the story worlds for a number of novels, including a romance, a historical novel, a thriller, and a science fiction novel. We discuss cultural drivers and show how the backdrop of each story world leads naturally to a story question that defines the essential conflict for the story.

Pride and Prejudice

Pride and Prejudice is a romance novel that Jane Austen wrote in the early 19th century. The story takes place in England in the years 1811 and 1812. The novel centers on the Bennet home at Longbourn, with forays into

London and Derbyshire. The natural world of the novel is therefore a very narrow one. It's one small piece of the world and not a terribly exotic piece.

One cultural driver, however, makes the novel as interesting now as it was when first published. Mr. and Mrs. Bennet have five daughters, but none of them can inherit the Bennet estate of Longbourn because it has been "entailed" away to the nearest male relative, an irritating clergyman named Mr. Collins. The five Bennet girls have good social standing as the daughters of a gentleman, but they have no money, and therefore their prospects are bleak. The girls have no work skills and can't support themselves. Their best hope is to marry men who are so wealthy that they don't care that the girls are penniless. It was no easier to marry into money in 1811 than it is in the 21st century. This cultural driver, entailment, translates directly into gender inequality, giving *Pride and Prejudice* its timeless appeal.

When the story begins, the status quo is that the five Bennet girls are unmarried. The weak point in the status quo is that the two oldest daughters, Jane and Lizzie, are old enough to be married, and they're in danger of becoming old maids if they don't find respectable husbands soon. Their mother determines to marry them off at the first opportunity.

The story starts when change comes to the neighborhood. A wealthy young man, Mr. Bingley, is leasing the nearby Netherfield estate. Bingley has an income of 5,000 pounds per year. If one of the Bennet daughters were to marry him, then the other girls' social standing would rise, and they might marry well also. The heroine, Lizzie Bennet, is the second of the five Bennet daughters. Lizzie makes her own situation more difficult because she dreams of marrying for love, not for money.

So here's the story question: Can Lizzie find a man of good character who will love her despite her poverty?

The Pillars of the Earth

The Pillars of the Earth, by Ken Follet, is a historical novel with strong elements of suspense and romance. Published in 1989, the novel is set in 12th-century England, between the years 1123 and 1174. The story centers on a fictitious town, Kingsbridge, similar to an actual town of that name. The natural world of the story stays entirely within England.

The novel features numerous cultural drivers:

- English barons are doing all they can to weaken King Henry I and his family. The story begins with the sinking of the White Ship and the drowning of Henry's only legitimate heir, William. Civil war wracks England through much of the novel, and by the end, King Henry II — punished for the murder of Archbishop Thomas Becket — no longer stands above the law.

✔ Architecture is changing as Islamic mathematicians and engineers spread their new ideas to Europe through Spain. The new Gothic architecture is displacing the old Romanesque architecture across Europe.

✔ In Kingsbridge, a three-way power struggle continues among the bishop, the prior of the monastery, and the earl. The monks of the monastery want to build a cathedral, but they lack an experienced builder.

When the story begins, the status quo is that King Henry is a powerful king. The weak point is that the aging Henry has only one legitimate heir, William. When Henry's enemies scuttle the White Ship, William's death leaves the succession to the throne in doubt, opening the way for civil turmoil.

Tom Builder, who knows little of royal politics, is the main character in the early part of the book. Tom wants nothing more than to build a cathedral to the glory of God. When he is hired to build the Kingsbridge cathedral, he allies himself with the monastery faction, earning himself the enmity of the other sides. The civil turmoil in England throws huge obstacles in Tom's path.

Here's the story question: Can Tom and his adopted son Jack complete the monastery when it is threatened by civil war, local enemies, and a sea change in architectural design?

Patriot Games

Patriot Games is a thriller by Tom Clancy, published in 1987 and set in the early 1980s. The story takes place partly in London, partly in Ireland, and partly in the U.S.

The main cultural driver is the long-running civil conflict in Northern Ireland between Catholics and Protestants. The status quo is that the Irish Republican Army (IRA) never attacks the royal family. The weak point is that a new faction, the Ulster Liberation Army (ULA), has formed, and it has no scruples about whom it attacks. The ULA is small, secretive, well-financed, highly trained, and heavily armed. Its goals including kidnapping the royal family and subverting the Provisional IRA.

The story begins when the ULA attacks Prince Charles and his wife and infant son in London in broad daylight. Only quick action by Jack Ryan prevents the ULA from succeeding. Ryan is a history professor at the Naval Academy, but he is being romanced by the CIA, which hopes to hire him as an analyst. When Ryan rescues the royal family, he becomes an instant hero in Great Britain — and an instant enemy of the shadowy ULA.

Here's the story question: Can Jack Ryan track down the ULA and bring them to justice before they wreak vengeance on him and his family?

Ender's Game

Ender's Game is a science fiction novel by Orson Scott Card, published in 1985. The story takes place partly on Earth, partly on a planetoid named Eros, and mostly in Battle School — a large spaceship that orbits Earth. The time is at least a century in our future but not much more than that.

Several cultural groups play in *Ender's Game*. Earth has three main political leaders: the Hegemon, the Polemarch, and the Strategos. Most countries speak a language called Standard, but many of them teach their own tongue to their children as a second language. People carry on robust political discussion on the "nets." Behind the façade of international unity lie all the old ugly nationalisms, but these have been temporarily put aside because of the threat of outside invasion.

The backdrop is complex. Some 80 years before the beginning of the story, an alien race of intelligent ant-like creatures ("buggers") tried to invade Earth. Humanity repelled the first invasion with difficulty. When the second invasion came, all seemed lost, but an extraordinary warrior, Mazer Rackham, narrowly defeated the buggers. Earth now anxiously awaits the third invasion, expecting far more terrible weapons.

Human technology has advanced since the second invasion. The key breakthrough came when humans developed "ansible" technology, allowing them to communicate instantly at any distance across the galaxy. Before ansible technology, radio communications allowed the International Fleet to send messages only at the speed of light. That was painfully slow across the vast stretches of the galaxy. The ansible gives Earth a fighting chance, but it won't be enough, because the buggers far outnumber humans.

Humanity's only hope is to find some military genius like Mazer Rackham to repel the buggers. The International Fleet scours the Earth in search of children of exceptional promise and whisks them up to an orbiting Battle School for training. The status quo is that the buggers could arrive at any moment, but humanity is unprepared. The weak point in the status quo is that one 6-year-old boy looks like the first plausible candidate.

Young Andrew Wiggin (nicknamed Ender) is a rare third child on an overpopulated Earth in which few families are allowed more than two children. Ender shows extraordinary military promise. He is smart, tough, and perfectly balanced between his exceptional capacity for empathy and his razor-minded brutality.

Ender's Game is the story of how Ender willingly undergoes a horrific training program to prepare for the buggers' coming invasion. Ender's trainers believe that the next war will end with the annihilation of either humanity or the buggers.

Here's the story question: Can Ender Wiggin rise through the ranks in Battle School and graduate in time to save his people?

Researching Your Story World

Your knowledge of how the world works makes it possible for you to live, eat, hold a job, get a spouse, start a family, have friends, throw a party, celebrate holidays, travel, write a will, file a lawsuit, and get protection from your enemies. If you don't know how these things work in your story world, how will you write about your characters as they try to do each of those things?

Research helps immunize you against that dreaded disease known as *writer's block,* which often comes from just not knowing enough about your story world. It gives you powerful new insights that excite you and that may eventually excite your reader.

What do you need to know about your story world? Everything! But because total knowledge is impossible, your research is always going to be incomplete. For all practical purposes, you need to do enough research to satisfy your reader's expectations. We aren't going to discuss how to do your research here, but here are your obvious sources of information:

- ✔ Personal experience (which you can always expand)
- ✔ Other people
- ✔ Books
- ✔ The Internet
- ✔ The many other sources that you've developed over a long life of learning

Our main concern here is to tell you what sorts of things you actually need to research about your story world — and how much research to do — in order to write your book.

Identifying what you need to know about your story world

You may already have your story world's natural world, cultural groups, and backdrop well in mind (see the earlier sections), or you may still be trying to sort them out. Regardless, asking yourself some questions can help you get the level of detail you need to create a convincing sense of time and place for the reader.

We can never give you a complete list, but here are some of the main topics you need to research (or already know) about your story world:

- ✔ **Geography:** Geography is the physical layout of your world — continents, oceans, rivers, lakes, mountains, and much more. If your story takes place on multiple planets, you need to know the geography of each one. If your story is restricted to one country or city or house, you can restrict your research to the geography of that single location.

- ✔ **Climate:** Climate is defined by the long-term weather patterns of your story world. Is your region sunny all year? Is it perpetually frozen? How much rainfall does it get? What is the average temperature in winter, spring, summer, and fall? (Do you even *have* those four seasons, or are there more or fewer of them? For instance, does your region have a rainy season and a dry season instead? Something else?) How often do you get fog in your story world? Thunderstorms? Hail? Tornadoes? Hurricanes? Earthquakes?

- ✔ **Cultural groups:** What races of people (or other intelligent beings) inhabit your story world? How have they clustered together into family groups, tribes, political units, nations, empires, and federations? Why did they cluster this way? What political conflicts hold these groups in tension with one another?

- ✔ **History:** How long have the cultural groups in your story world been keeping track of their past? Do they keep an oral or written history? What is that history? What wars have they fought? Were there periods of peacetime, and if so, what were they like? What cultural developments have marked progress in your story world?

- ✔ **Languages:** What languages do your various cultural groups speak, and how are these languages related? Are some languages broken out into various dialects? Do some groups speak more than one language, and if so, what is the religious, historical, or political explanation? Do the different groups readily or rarely learn each others' languages?

- ✔ **Culture:** What is the cultural world of your people groups? What do they eat, how do they eat it, and with whom do they eat? How do they choose their life partners, or do they *have* life partners? What do they wear? When do they sleep, or *do* they sleep? What sort of homes do they live in?

  What sort of employment do they seek? Are they entrepreneurs, or do they rely on Big Brother for their security? Are they specialists in their work, or do they do a little of everything?

  What kinds of entertainment help them while away the hours when they aren't working — or do they even *have* any free time? What sports do they play? What art do they create? What literature do they read and write? What legal system protects their rights?

✔ **Science and technology:** What is the level of scientific development of your various cultural groups? What about engineering and technological accomplishments? Do some groups have a technical advantage over others? Do they use this advantage to oppress others militarily or economically, and if so, how? What fractures does this cause in the society of your story world?

✔ **Religion, mythology, and purpose:** How do your various cultural groups explain their origin and the origin of the world? Are these explanations religious, mythological, scientific, or something else? What purpose do your cultural groups believe they have for existing? What future do they see for themselves? Is it a future of peaceful coexistence with other groups or a future of domination over them? Or will the ultimate future mean eliminating other cultural groups completely?

If you're writing science fiction, fantasy, or historical fiction, these questions are just a start, and you'll need to dive deep in your research. On the other hand, if you're following the well-known advice to "write what you know," then you may find that these questions are irrelevant for your story and that you have no research at all on your plate.

Knowing how much research is enough

You do have to quit researching at some point. If you don't, you'll never write your novel. J. R. R. Tolkien constructed Middle Earth over several decades, but he eventually did sit down to write *The Hobbit* and *The Lord of the Rings.*

How much research is enough? You need to know about 100 times as much as you'll actually use in your novel. We can't prove this, but we believe it strongly.

If your story world is the ordinary world in which you live, your research may be mostly done. You've been living in this world long enough to know how to write a novel, so you've likely absorbed far more than this minimum standard.

If you don't know your story world extremely well, then you need to get busy. The amount of research you need to do depends heavily on your category. The following categories require the most research; all the other categories allow you quite a bit of freedom:

✔ **Historical:** Note that historical novels are not an official category; the word *historical* is an adjective that can apply to just about any of the categories we discuss in Chapter 3. But ignoring that technicality, if you're writing a historical novel of any flavor, you need to do great heaping gobs of research.

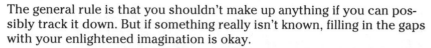

The general rule is that you shouldn't make up anything if you can possibly track it down. But if something really isn't known, filling in the gaps with your enlightened imagination is okay.

✔ **Science fiction and fantasy:** Science fiction and fantasy novels generally require a specialized kind of research called *world-building*. You need to answer the same kinds of questions that you would if you were researching a historical novel, but instead of looking things up in a library, you invent them out of your own rich inner life. The main requirement here is that your story world be internally consistent.

If you're writing science fiction or fantasy, you may find it helpful to study other cultures here on Earth to get an idea of the range of variation that's possible even on a single planet. That may guide you in dreaming up plausible cultures elsewhere.

✔ **Military technothrillers:** Military technothrillers were essentially invented by Tom Clancy, who is famous for his meticulous research. If you're going to write this kind of novel, you need to be accurate when you talk about weapons, equipment, tactics, strategy, and logistics. Your readers will be only too happy to point out any errors, and one blunder can cost you their respect — and their business.

✔ **Legal thrillers:** Legal thrillers typically go fairly deeply into arcane legal details. If you're going this route, you need to do your homework. If you're actually a lawyer, you have the advantage here; if you're not, then hit the books or find a legal eagle who's willing to help you.

If you love research, the painful truth is that you will *never* know enough about your story world to make you happy. You'll always be discovering cool new things. If you take time to write a novel this year, you may find out something next year that proves you wrong in this year's novel. You have to take that risk. Life is short, and research is endless, so come up for air when you've done enough. And "enough" means that you know 100 times as much as you need to write your novel. This means you! We mean it — stop when you know that much.

Whether you're setting a story in your own world or in some foreign one, please, please, *please* remember the flip side of the rule: Don't tell everything you know in one novel. (We've read novels in which the author decided to put in everything he knew. Trust us on this — the epidemiology of bat diseases is not nearly as fascinating to your reader as it is to you.) Tell only 1 percent of what you know. If you take our advice to know 100 times more than what you need, you can write another 99 books without doing one more speck of research.

Being Able to Explain Your Story World to Sell Your Book

Sooner or later, you need to understand your story world well enough to define the backdrop for your story. You need this if you're ever going to explain to an agent or editor what your story's about. Get out a sheet of paper or open a file in your word processor and answer each of the following questions:

- ✔ **What is the natural world for your story?** Describe the limits of geography for events in your story. If your story depends on some natural disaster, describe it. If you're writing fantasy and your story includes magic, describe its limitations. If you're writing science fiction and your story depends on different laws of physics or any other branch of science, explain how it differs from our ordinary world. Limit your answer to one or two paragraphs.

- ✔ **What are the cultural groups in your story?** Describe each cultural group, explaining the main cultural drivers (politics, language, economics, history, laws, sociology, religion, mythology, and so on) that affect your story. Choose no more than three or four of these and explain why they matter.

- ✔ **What makes change possible in your story?** Is it a desire to get something, do something, or become something? Is it a looming disaster to be avoided? What prevented your story from happening earlier? What keeps it from happening later?

Now write a story question for your story. Use our earlier examples as guides, or phrase your story question in a form similar to this one: "Can [lead character] achieve [story goal] in spite of [story obstacle]?"

You may not know your story question yet. You may not understand your story world well enough, or you may not know which pieces of your backdrop are most important yet. But you will eventually. If you don't know this information, don't worry about it now, but keep thinking about it as you write. Someday, possibly when you least expect it, things will fall into place. When that happens, come back to this page and answer the questions here.

The process you follow to find your story doesn't matter. Nor does it matter what order you take to get there. All that matters is that you eventually have a story that you can explain to an agent or editor and that will excite readers. Defining your story backdrop and story question are two pieces of that puzzle.

Chapter 7

Creating Compelling Characters

1 f you want to write truly memorable fiction, your best bet is to start with a wonderful character, one who leaps off the page and into your reader's mind. A great character feels completely real, with a past, a present, and a future. In this chapter, we look at each of the parts of a character and explain how each one works.

Fiction writers spend enormous amounts of time developing and getting to know their main characters, imagining complicated life histories and digging deep to find plausible motivations. This is not wasted time! If you don't know your characters, then your readers won't, either.

In this chapter, we help you figure out a character's past, present, and probable future, and we guide you in revealing that character to the reader. We also help you decide how to filter your story through a character's perceptions, whether that character is telling the story or you're telling the story for her.

Defining Roles: Deciding Who Goes in Your Novel

Of course you'll be original when creating the characters for your novel. And yet you'll probably follow certain well-established patterns in how your characters function in your story. These patterns are known as *archetypes,* and they help your readers make sense of your story. Look at a few of the common archetypes in fiction:

- **Hero (protagonist):** The hero of your story is normally the person your reader is rooting for. Most novels have a strong hero, although usually an imperfect one. Jack Ryan is the hero of numerous Tom Clancy novels. Robert Langdon is the hero of *The Da Vinci Code,* by Dan Brown. In most categories, a hero can be either male or female. Ayla, a young human girl, is the hero of Jean Auel's *Clan of the Cave Bear* series. Kinsey Millhone is the hero of Sue Grafton's mystery series that began with *'A' is for Alibi*.

  In romance novels, the protagonist is the *heroine*. Her love interest normally plays second fiddle, but he's known as the *hero* anyway. Romance novelists commonly refer to this pair of characters as *h/h,* and in this category, all other characters are secondary. In *Gone With the Wind*, Scarlett and Rhett play the h/h roles.

- **Villain (antagonist):** The villain of the story is normally the person who opposes the hero. In a long series, a single hero commonly has many villains, one for each book. The James Bond series, for example, features a new villain in every story. However, you may have a villain who survives to fight again another day, as the Soviet spymaster Karla does in John le Carré's brilliant trilogy: *Tinker, Tailor, Soldier, Spy,* followed by *The Honourable Schoolboy* and ending with *Smiley's People.* The villain may be the lead character, as the Jackal is in *The Day of the Jackal*, by Frederick Forsyth.

- **Antihero:** This is a nontraditional protagonist who lacks certain virtues of the usual hero. An example is Alec Leamas, the seedy spy who turns triple agent in John le Carré's novel *The Spy Who Came in From the Cold.*

- **Sidekick:** This is a close friend of the hero, usually one with qualities that complete the hero. Dr. Watson plays sidekick to Sherlock Holmes, often contributing his brawn and his revolver to the cause of justice. Spock and McCoy are twin sidekicks to Captain Kirk in the *Star Trek* series, bolstering Kirk's logical and emotive sides.

- **Mentor:** This is an older and wiser teacher who guides the hero on his path to maturity. Obi-Wan Kenobi plays mentor to Luke Skywalker in *Star Wars.* Gandalf is Frodo's mentor in *The Lord of the Rings.* The role of mentor is hazardous — often the mentor dies, leaving the hero to fumble along, not yet fully trained.

If you do a little research, you can find long lists of various archetypes, including trickster, shapeshifter, fool, shaman, bully, storyteller, seductress, and many more. These lists may guide your thinking, or you may find them obvious, depending on your own natural talents in creating characters.

It's not uncommon to mix features of two archetypes or to play an archetypal character in an unconventional way. We don't recommend letting your archetypes become stereotypes (see the later section titled "Avoiding stereotypes"), but if archetypal thinking helps you build strong characters, then tap into these powerful ideas and see where they take you.

Backstory: Giving Each Character a Past

Your character was not born yesterday. He has a long and complex family history that goes back into the deep sands of time. He also has an early life with many traumas and triumphs, disasters and decisions. Your character's past is known as *backstory*, and it's critical. In this section, we discuss the importance of backstory, help you start a character sketch, and give you some tips on avoiding stereotypes.

Understanding why backstory matters

A character's past determines what sort of person you have coming into the story. The past is only an imperfect guide to the future, though. Your character has free will and can choose to break loose from his past and pursue a new future. But will he succeed? Your goal as a novelist is to make it plausible that he might, without making it a certainty.

In this section, we explain why backstory matters to you and why it matters less to your readers.

Why backstory should matter to you

You have to understand where your character came from, or you'll never understand what your character wants or why he acts the way he does. If you don't know, then neither will your reader.

Of course, you don't have to figure out your character's backstory all at once. Depending on your creative paradigm, you may not know any backstory before you start writing (see Chapter 4 for a discussion of creative paradigms). But no matter when you develop your backstory, you do have to know it all eventually.

Seat-of-the-pants writers and edit-as-you-go writers rarely work out backstory in advance. Instead, they just start writing the story with what little they know. The more they write, the more they get to know their characters. Bit by bit, the characters reveal themselves — what really happened after the senior prom; that unspeakable incident of the egg in the locker in seventh grade; being forced to eat a spider in kindergarten. By the end of the novel, the writer finally understands her characters and knows their backstories completely. At that point, it's time to rewrite the whole story and work that spider in properly.

Snowflakers and outliners prefer to create all this backstory before they start writing. They do this by thinking about the characters, interviewing them, and writing up detailed character sketches.

Why backstory matters much less to your reader

A hazard is lurking for the unwary writer: As soon as you know all that backstory, you can't help wanting to tell your reader. It's painful for most writers to hear, but the reader is reading your fiction for the story — what's happening right now — not the backstory. The backstory is old news. Yes, it's critical to the right now, but it isn't the right now.

Your job as a fiction writer is to suck the reader into the story so well that eventually she gets curious about why your character behaves the way he does. That's the point where you can slip in a sliver of backstory.

Backstory is like garlic: It livens things up, but a little goes a long, long way. Dole out that backstory in little snippets, leaving the reader curious, wanting to know more. It's far better to have the reader wanting more backstory than wanting less. If you dump too much backstory on the reader early in the book, you may smother the story. We suggest that you know about 10 times more backstory than you tell your reader.

Creating your character's backstory

You can create a backstory for your character any time you want, depending on your favorite creative paradigm (see Chapter 4 for a discussion of these writing methods). Say you've decided that you're ready to develop backstory for a character named Marcus. Normally, you'd do this after you've been reflecting about Marcus for some time and you have some idea what he's like. Take out a sheet of paper or open a document in your word processor and title it "Backstory for Marcus." Then do the following:

1. **Describe your character.**

   Start writing — fast. This is creative work, so don't waste time editing yourself. You can edit the backstory tomorrow. Today, just get it down.

   What does Marcus look like? Write down his birthday and eye color and hair color and anything else that matters to you.

2. Write about his birth, early childhood, and teen years.

Where was Marcus born? Who are his parents (and grandparents if you know about them)? What are his first memories? What's the worst thing that happened to him in kindergarten? What was his favorite subject in grade school, and what was his most hated? Why?

Don't stop, just blaze on. Write about the horrors of junior high. Did Marcus do well in high school, or did he scrape through? Was he a geek, a jock, a heart-throb, a nobody, a goth, or what? Did he date, and if so, what was his girlfriend like? Did he dump her, did she dump him, or did they get married?

3. Take him to adulthood.

Power on through college or trade school or the military or whatever Marcus did as he came to adulthood. Get it all out — the good, the bad, and especially the horrible. What traumatized him? Who were his friends and his family? Who were his enemies? Get it down on paper — it doesn't have to be pretty. Marcus is spilling his guts for you, so keep him talking.

4. Interview your character.

Ask him what he's learned. How does he see his situation now? Most importantly, what would he like to change about his life? What would he like to do that he can't? What would he like to be that he can't? What would he like to have that he can't? You need to know those, because they determine what Marcus's future will look like.

Congratulations! You now have a lot of the details of Marcus's backstory figured out. You'll find this information to be particularly helpful as you continue to develop your story. You aren't done yet, of course. You'll probably keep adding to your backstory of Marcus for quite a while. The important thing for you is to get it on paper so you don't lose it.

Avoiding stereotypes

Part of your backstory includes defining which groups your character belongs to. Your character needs a gender, a nationality, an ethnic group, a political party, a religion, and more. Unless you want to have a really boring story, not all of your characters will have *your* gender, nationality, ethnic group, politics, and religion.

That means you have to do your homework about some other groups. Men and women, for example, tend to dress differently, think differently, act differently, emote differently. The more research you do about gender differences, the more fascinating you'll find them. Likewise, the more you study the nationality, ethnic group, politics, religion, and so on of your character, the more ways you'll find them different from your own. Of course, you want to highlight those differences in your character so it's clear you've done your research.

You may be tempted to build a character who is "typical" of his group in every way. But if you do so, you'll be accused of creating a stereotype — he's the average height, the average weight, the average intelligence. He has the most common eye color, hair color, personality type. He thinks like every other member of his group, has all the usual strengths and all the usual weaknesses. Your character is, in fact, just the average of his group.

How dull is that? Exceptionally dull. How likely is that? Not at all likely. Any mathematician can tell you that a person who is "average" or "typical" in every single way is exceptionally rare. Every group has variation, and every individual varies from the norm in one way or another. But you can't very well make your character different from the norm in every single way, either. Then you'll be accused of not doing your homework or not understanding the other groups. What's the solution?

Make your character "roughly typical" in most ways. Make him "unusual for his group" in a few ways. The more unusual he is, the more awareness he needs to show that he is, in fact, a bit abnormal. A character's feelings about his differences may well play a key role in your novel.

Suppose you're a woman writing a male character. Create him so that he follows the norms, mostly, but perhaps make him a bit more artistic than most guys. Maybe make him a lot more emotionally sensitive than the average Joe. And maybe make him really tall, maybe 6'4". Finally, make sure that he's aware of how he's different, so the reader knows you know. Your guy may be a little embarrassed to be artsy, a lot embarrassed to be so emotive, and reasonably proud of his height. Even if he's not embarrassed, the important thing is that he knows he's different, so your reader isn't misled into thinking you don't know what the norms are.

Motivation: Looking to Your Character's Future

Your character has a past, but more importantly, she has a future. Your character is going somewhere or hopes to go somewhere. But the future is uncertain. Nobody knows what your character will do tomorrow. All you can know is what your character *intends to do* tomorrow. That's roughly what people mean when they talk about your character's *motivation*.

The term *motivation* crops up a lot in books on how to write fiction. It's an ambiguous term, meaning different things to different writers. We think it's a fine word, but we won't be bound by what other people mean by this term. We define it to encompass most of the common meanings. A character's motivation is made up of three essential parts:

- ✔ **Values:** Those things a character holds most strongly to be true.
- ✔ **Ambition:** The one *abstract* thing a character wants in life.
- ✔ **Story goal:** The one *concrete* thing a character thinks will enable her to achieve her ambition.

When you know your character's values, ambition, and story goal, you can always give her credible reasons to act, because you always know her motivation. That's all you need in order to write a powerful, compelling character.

Values: Core truths for your character

Everybody holds certain truths to be self-evident. The great Greek mathematician Euclid derived all of geometry from a very few *postulates,* which he believed to be so obvious that he didn't need to prove them (though one of his postulates was wrong). Thomas Jefferson, when he penned the Declaration of Independence, thought it self-evident that "life, liberty, and the pursuit of happiness" were the common right of all men (even though Jefferson himself owned slaves). If you want to drive your best friend nuts, ask her what makes life worth living. No matter what she answers, keep asking, over and over, "Why does that make life worth living? How do you know?" Eventually, you'll back her into a corner and she'll huff at you, "It just is. It's obvious, and I don't have to explain it." All of these are examples of what we mean by the word *value.*

A *value* is a core truth, something that's "obviously true" to your character. A value needs no explanation, no proof, no reason. A value is true because it's true because it's true.

A value isn't necessarily obvious or true to anyone else. A character may be inconsistent in applying her values, and a value may actually be incorrect.

Making your character's values believable

A special kind of core truth is the answer to the question, "What's the most important thing in the world to you?" Ask a hundred people this question, and you'll probably get at least 20 different answers. Money. Freedom. Security. Friendship. Family. God. Health. Self-esteem. Integrity. Honor. Intellectual honesty. Faith. Fun. Truth. Beauty. The list goes on and on.

It's common to say that people value these things. Please note that our definition of *value* goes beyond what people consider merely important: We define value to be what people believe to be *true*. So if somebody values money, then her core truth value is the statement, "Money is a very important thing in my life."

You can choose any values you want for your character. It's okay if your character can't give a reason for her values. In fact, if she can, then you haven't uncovered her real values yet, and you need to take her deeper.

Make sure *you* can explain your character's reasons, even if she can't. In your character's universe, you are god, and you get to know what she doesn't and can't know. What genetic trait or early experience or cultural influences led her to her values? As soon as you know this, you know all that you need to make those values believable.

You don't have to convince your reader that a character's values are obvious or true or consistent; you only have to convince the reader that the character *believes* her values are obvious and true and consistent. If the character is blinded by cultural drivers or self-interest or genetic predisposition, your reader will understand that (see Chapter 6 for a discussion of cultural drivers).

Aiming for inconsistency: Why values should conflict

Your character should have more than one value. Ideally, each character should have two or three, and they should be *contradictory*. Why? Because that means that at the core of your character is an internal conflict that she can never resolve. Conflict is good in fiction, and internal conflict makes for great fiction. That internal conflict always springs from values that contradict each other.

Suppose, for example, that Darth Vader has a value that says, "Nothing is more important than power." If that's his only value, then Vader is a one-dimensional villain, not particularly deep or interesting. Now suppose Vader adopts a second value that says, "Nothing is more important than my son." Now he has a contradiction. It can't be true that both power and his son are the most important thing in his life. At some point, Vader will have to choose between these values. When that happens, he becomes a far more interesting character, and his story deepens, because he's no longer predictable. When push comes to shove, he might go either way.

Your character is most interesting when his values are most contradictory. When your character is perfectly consistent, he's perfectly predictable. But tie a knot in his soul, and watch him struggle.

Ambitions: Getting abstract, or why Miss America wants "world peace"

Values are good, but they're not enough. Out of a character's values spring a desire for a different story world. Your character wants change, and if you ask her what she wants, she's likely to give you an abstract answer that goes to her deepest yearnings.

Ask a contestant for Miss America what she wants most, and she invariably answers, "World peace." That's a wonderful goal, but it's vague. What does world peace look like, exactly? That's the problem, isn't it? Trying to define *world peace* is pretty darn hard. It takes precision of thought. It takes a serious grasp of the situation. It takes a lot of words. If you try to get specific about world peace, you go way outside the bounds of a sound bite. And that's why Miss America is vague when you ask her this question. She has to speak abstractly in order to speak succinctly. Don't mock her. You'd do no better in her situation.

World peace is abstract — you can neither see nor hear nor feel it. It's an idea. It's vague and squishy. It's an example of what we call an *ambition*. Your character needs an ambition in life. An *ambition* is the one abstract thing that your character wants more than any other.

An ambition must spring from a character's values. The values define the reason for the ambition. If your main character has a value that says, "Money is the most important thing in my life," for example, then her ambition may very reasonably be, "I want to get very rich." That ambition makes perfect sense for that value.

A character can have multiple contradictory values, but she should have only one ambition. Your story needs to be focused, and you achieve that focus by limiting your character to a single ambition.

Note that two characters may have the same ambition but have very different underlying values. For example, you may have a second character who also has the ambition "I want to get very rich," which springs from a value of "Helping the poor is the most important thing in the world." This character wants to get rich and give it all away to the starving millions.

Story goals: Your story's ultimate driver

Knowing your character's ambition is great, but it's not enough to make a story. What does Miss America mean by *world peace?* What does that look like? What would it take to achieve it? Until you have a simple, clear, concrete answer to these questions, all you have is a vague yearning. We call the concrete answer a *story goal,* which is a term we made up because there just isn't a suitable word handy.

A *story goal* is the answer to the question "How exactly do you want to achieve your ambition?" The story goal of your lead character drives your story. As soon as your lead character has a story goal, you have a story. If your lead character has no story goal, then you simply don't have a story.

Consider Frodo Baggins, the lead character in J. R. R. Tolkein's *The Lord of the Rings.* Frodo is a hobbit, living in the Shire, who owns a magic ring. Early in the story, he learns from the wizard Gandalf that this Ring of Power was created by the Dark Lord Sauron in deep antiquity. The Ring contains much of Sauron's evil power, and so it corrupts all who own it. If Sauron regains the Ring, he'll be powerful enough to rule Middle Earth forever. Frodo (like Miss America) wants world peace. That's his ambition. For him, world peace can only come if he throws the Ring into the Cracks of Doom in the land of Mordor. This is the story goal for *The Lord of the Rings,* and it drives the story for many hundreds of pages.

What makes a great story goal

A story goal should have these properties:

- ✔ **Objective:** The reader should know how to tell whether the character achieves the story goal.
- ✔ **Simple:** The reader should be able to picture what success looks like.
- ✔ **Important:** The reader must believe the story goal matters.
- ✔ **Achievable:** The reader should believe that the character has a chance to reach her story goal.
- ✔ **Difficult:** The reader should believe that the character may fail.

In Chapter 6, we talk about the importance of a story question, which has the same properties we list here. That's because the story question amounts to asking, "Will the central character achieve her story goal?"

Why each character needs a story goal

Please note that a story has only one story question, whereas *every* important character in your story should have a story goal. The story question asks whether your lead character will achieve his story goal. But what about those other characters? Aren't their story goals important? Yes, for two reasons:

- ✔ **Those other story goals often oppose the story goal of your lead character.** That's good — it's why your story has conflict.

> ✔ **Each of those story goals defines a separate thread of your story.**
> When you have several major characters, each with his or her own story goal, then you have a rich tapestry of a story.

Each of your characters believes that he or she is the lead character in the story. You may label one the hero, another the villain, another the sidekick, another the mentor, another the fool. But all five think they're the hero. All five have a story goal. All five find the others either helpful or harmful. This is the secret to writing deep characters: No character ever believes he's an extra.

If you'd like to go into more depth in understanding the values, ambitions, and story goals of your characters, we recommend the book *Getting Into Character*, by Brandilyn Collins (Wiley), which asks and answers the question, "What can a fiction writer learn from a method actor?" Collins is a best-selling suspense novelist with a background in drama.

Establishing your character's motivation

Developing your character's motivation is hard, dirty, messy, creative work. You can do it in any order you like. You don't have to define the character's values first, then ambition, and then story goals. You can work out each character's motivation before you write your first draft or afterward or while you're writing. But you must do this work eventually, or your readers will complain that your characters are flat and boring. (A *flat* character is one who lacks depth and is therefore predictable.)

A writing exercise: Motivating Marcus

Say that you've already worked out the backstory for your character Marcus (see the earlier section "Creating your character's backstory") and now you're ready to nail down his motivation. Take a clean sheet of paper or open a new document and title it "Motivation for Marcus." Divide the page into thirds horizontally and add subheads for *values, ambition,* and *story goal.* Work through these steps:

1. **Ask yourself what you already know about the character.**

   Do you know any of Marcus's values — his core truths? Write them down. You don't have to know them all just yet, so write what you know so far. What about his ambition? If you know his abstract goal in life, write it down. Or maybe you know his story goal — the one concrete thing he aims to achieve in this story. Write it down.

2. **Fill in what's missing, starting from where you are and working in both directions.**

   - **If you know one of Marcus's values:** Ask what abstract ambition may spring from that value. Then ask what concrete story goal would best fulfill that ambition.

- **If you know his ambition:** Ask what value it comes from. Then ask what story goal will make his ambition come true.

- **If you know his story goal:** Ask what abstract ambition motivates it. Then ask what value led to that ambition.

3. **Ask yourself what other values your character has.**

   Look for values that conflict with the ones he has already. Try for at least two, maybe three main values in Marcus's life.

4. **Go over your list in both directions, taking care that it all makes sense and that you can explain it to your reader.**

   Does the ambition spring directly from at least one value? Is the story goal the best way for Marcus to achieve his ambition? Does he have conflicting values that will add spice to his story?

Example: Interviewing Frodo Baggins

Nailing down a character's values is often hard. If you have problems, try interviewing your character. Keep asking *why* until he throws up his hands and shouts, "Just because!" When he can't give a rational answer, that's when you've hit a value.

For example, imagine you're J. R. R. Tolkien and you're developing the motivation for Frodo Baggins. You've given Frodo the story goal of throwing the Ring into the Cracks of Doom, but you're a little fuzzy on why Frodo would be willing to take on such a dangerous quest. Here's an imaginary interview that illustrates how you may push Frodo up against the wall and nail down his motivation:

JRRT: Frodo, I understand you plan to leave the Shire and go to Rivendell with the Ring. Ultimately, you're looking for some way or somebody to take the Ring to Mordor and throw it into the Cracks of Doom. You can't be serious. Why would you take on such a ridiculous quest?

FB: Well, Gandalf told me to.

JRRT: Don't be absurd. You're leaving home because Gandalf told you to? Why does he think you should go?

FB: We have to defeat the Dark Lord Sauron.

JRRT: That's quite a leap, isn't it? Aren't there other ways to defeat Sauron? Why not smash the Ring right here? Grab a hammer and give it a whack?

FB: No can do. Gandalf said that the Ring contains Sauron's power. No hobbit could destroy it. No fire in Middle Earth is hot enough, other than the Cracks of Doom, where it was forged in the depths of time.

JRRT (grinning): Nice one, there — the "depths of time." I'll have to remember that. But why you? No offense, Frodo, but you're not a very impressive guy. If this is so important to Gandalf, why doesn't he do it?

FB: The Ring corrupts anyone who has it. Gandalf is a great wizard, and the Ring would pull him into evil through his desire to do good.

JRRT: And why won't the Ring corrupt you then?

FB (stammering): Gandalf . . . didn't really explain that. I guess I'm not important enough to corrupt. I just don't want Sauron to take over the Shire.

JRRT (leaning forward): Oh? Why?

FB: Because he'll destroy it. If Sauron gets the Ring, he'll crush it under his boot. I'm scared to death of him, but . . . I have to help defeat him somehow.

JRRT: Aha! That's your ambition, isn't it? You want to defeat Sauron?

FB: I suppose so. It's not enough to push him back or contain him. He has to be beaten, now and forever.

JRRT (writing): Frodo's ambition is to defeat the Dark Lord Sauron. That's great. A very fine ambition. But now let me ask again. Why?

FB: I told you. Sauron will destroy the Shire.

JRRT: So? Why is that so bad?

FB: It's my home.

JRRT: Why not go elsewhere?

FB: I don't want to go elsewhere. The Shire is my home, and I want to live here.

JRRT: Why here?

FB (getting angry): I already told you. I want to live in the Shire. It's my home, and I love it.

JRRT: Why do you love it?

FB: Just because I love it. That's all the reason I need.

JRRT (rubbing hands together): Frodo, I think we've found your value. You love the Shire more than anything else, don't you?

FB (scratching his chin): Yes, I suppose that's true. Yes, absolutely. I never thought of that before. I guess I thought it was obvious.

JRRT: That's fine. I love England, so I can empathize. But there's something I don't understand. You love the Shire. You'd do anything to save the Shire. So now you're going to *leave* the Shire? Why would you do that if you love it so much? Are you sure you really love it?

FB (thinking for a long time): I don't think you understand. I love the Shire, and I don't want to leave. But I have to, for a while, because part of what I love is the other hobbits. The Shire isn't just the land — it's the hobbits who live there.

JRRT: Hobbits are foolish, stupid, bumbling, irritating, and idiotic. Why would you care about them? Aren't elves much more entertaining?

FB: Hobbits are all that. I'm all that, too. Whether I like it or not, those hobbits are my people, and I care about them, no matter how stupid and bumbling they are.

JRRT: Why?

FB: I can't explain it. I just do.

JRRT (scribbling feverishly): Excellent! We've got your second value. You love your fellow hobbits more than anything. You love the Shire more than anything. But you can't save your fellow hobbits unless you leave the Shire — possibly forever.

FB (shaking): Stop it! When you say it like that, I don't want to go. And yet, I have to go. I hate this. I wish somebody else had this cursed Ring.

JRRT: Thanks for your time, Frodo. I think I understand you better now.

Going deep: Researching your character's psychology

Building great characters is a bottomless well — you can always go deeper. Throughout this chapter, we look at things from a pragmatic novelist's point of view. You may well decide, however, that you want to know more about psychology. If you do, bravo! It's a task you'll never finish, but getting started is still worthwhile.

You have many options in studying psychology, none of which require you to go back to school. Start by looking inside yourself. What makes you tick? Why do you do the things you do? What are your own values, ambitions, and goals in life? What might explain your values? You may even want to explore some of your own personality issues with a counselor, psychologist, or psychiatrist. (If people ask where you got the psychological insight, tell them you merely did your homework.)

If you prefer a less hands-on approach, you can find any number of books on psychology, both academic and popular approaches. Although psychology is a science, plenty of pseudoscience out there is masquerading as psychology. But even the wackiest pseudopsychology theory may still give you some insights into your characters. At the very least, a little book study can help you avoid blunders like calling a character schizophrenic when you actually meant that he has multiple personality disorder.

You may be one of those intuitive types who prefers to learn everything you know about people by watching them. If so, you're in good company. That's all the research that many novelists ever do. But if you choose to dive deep into human psychology, you'll enrich yourself and your story. Just remember to come up for air long enough to actually write some fiction.

Point of View (POV): Getting Some Perspective on Character

Most of your story isn't about your character's past or future; fiction is about what's happening right now. To show a character acting right now, you use a *point of view,* or POV — a lens through which you show your character's world (and the story) to the reader.

Your choice of POV is closely related to your choice of *narrator* — the person who's telling the story. For most POVs, the narrator is essentially the unnamed author, but it can be a character in the story (if you're writing in first person).

Most POVs require you to choose a focal character for each scene — one character that you want your reader to identify with during that scene. This focal character is sometimes called the *viewpoint character,* sometimes the *point-of-view character,* but most often the *POV character.*

Over the years, fiction writers have chosen a number of strategies for POV, which we describe in Table 7-1. The two most common strategies, which we list first, have writers choose only one POV character per scene and stick with that character for the entire scene. However, some choices of POV let you have more than one POV character per scene, and one option doesn't let you have *any* POV characters at all — you can't get inside any character's head.

Table 7-1	Options for Point of View		
POV	*Description*	*POV Characters per Scene*	*Narrator*
First person	Write from inside the head of the POV charac-ter, using the pronoun *I.*	One	A character in the story
Third person	Write from inside the head of the POV charac-ter, using the pronoun *he* or *she.*	One	The author
Third person objective	Write from outside the head of a focal charac-ter, using the pronoun *he* or *she.*	None — you never get inside the head of any character	The author

(continued)

Table 7-1 *(continued)*

POV	Description	POV Characters per Scene	Narrator
Head-hopping	Write from inside the heads of multiple characters in the same scene, using the pronouns *he* or *she*.	Multiple	The author
Omniscient	Write from inside or outside the heads of multiple characters or from the perspective of a god-like persona who knows things that none of the characters can know.	Multiple	The author
Second person	Write from inside the head of the POV character, using the pronoun *you*.	One	The author

Unless you have a compelling reason to do otherwise, we recommend that you choose only one POV character per scene and stick with that character for the entire scene. Your goal as a fiction writer is to give your reader a powerful emotional experience, and humans find it easiest to identify strongly with only one person at a time. In each scene, you make the reader see what your POV character sees, hear what he hears, smell what he smells, taste what he tastes, do what he does, and feel what he feels.

In this section, you look at each of these strategies in turn and see what advantages and disadvantages they give.

First-person POV

When you write a scene in first-person POV, you make the POV character the narrator of the story. This has the advantage of being simple and natural and intimate. Getting deeply inside the character is easy. If the character is having a powerful emotional experience, the reader is also very likely to have one.

A question of trust: Unreliable narrators

A first-person narrator is allowed to be *unreliable.* This can mean that the narrator is self-deceived, unintelligent, uninformed, misinformed, irrational, a liar, or even insane. A fine example of a first-person novel with a somewhat unreliable narrator is Mark Twain's *The Adventures of Huckleberry Finn,* in which young Huck accurately tells his story but often misinterprets what happened or is blinded by the racist culture he's immersed in. Huck Finn clearly has different values than Twain.

Using an unreliable narrator can add depth to the character telling the story, but it does take

some finesse. If you use an unreliable narrator, include some hints early in the story so the reader knows to treat the character's version of events with some skepticism or at least senses that something is off. And throughout the book, add some clues in dialogue and action that help confirm or deny what the narrator says. That way, you give the reader some sense of what really happened and ensure that inconsistencies in the story look like character traits rather than mistakes.

Novels written in first-person POV often have only a single POV character for the entire book. That can be a disadvantage if the action is happening on several fronts at once, because one person can be in only one place at a time. A way around the problem of using a limited point of view is to have several POV characters, each narrating their scenes in first person. Switching narrators can be a little confusing, however, so if you do this, always make it clear who *I* is at the very beginning of every scene.

Look at an example taken from a Sherlock Holmes novel, *A Study in Scarlet,* by Sir Arthur Conan Doyle. In the story, Holmes and his friend Dr. Watson have been asked to help two moderately competent Scotland Yard inspectors, Gregson and Lestrade, investigate a murder. Here is a snippet of the scene, written in first person with Watson as the POV character:

> Still I had had such extraordinary evidence of the quickness of his perceptive faculties, that I had no doubt that he could see a great deal which was hidden from me.

> At the door of the house we were met by a tall, white-faced, flaxen-haired man, with a notebook in his hand, who rushed forward and wrung my companion's hand with effusion. "It is indeed kind of you to come," he said, "I have had everything left untouched."

> "Except that!" my friend answered, pointing at the pathway. "If a herd of buffaloes had passed along, there could not be a greater mess. No doubt, however, you had drawn your own conclusions, Gregson, before you permitted this."

"I have had so much to do inside the house," the detective said evasively. "My colleague, Mr. Lestrade, is here. I had relied upon him to look after this."

Holmes glanced at me and raised his eyebrows sardonically. "With two such men as yourself and Lestrade upon the ground, there will not be much for a third party to find out," he said.

Outlander, by Diana Gabaldon, is written in first-person POV with a reliable narrator. *The Time Traveler's Wife,* by Audrey Niffenegger, uses two first-person narrators, with each scene starting out stating the POV character's name explicitly. *River God*, by Wilbur Smith, features a vain and mostly reliable narrator writing in first-person. *The Curious Incident of the Dog in the Night-time*, by Mark Haddon, uses an autistic boy who is somewhat unreliable as a narrator because of his inability to understand social cues.

Third-person POV

When you write a scene in third-person POV, you refer to the POV character by name and use third-person pronouns such as *he* or *she*. This is the most common POV in modern fiction, and it has the advantage of being simple and natural. With a little work, it's not difficult to get as deeply inside the head of the POV character as you can in first-person POV, because you have access to all the thoughts and feelings of the POV character.

Here we've rewritten Sir Arthur Conan Doyle's original scene in third person:

Still Watson had had such extraordinary evidence of the quickness of Holmes's perceptive faculties, that he had no doubt that Holmes could see a great deal which was hidden from him.

At the door of the house they were met by a tall, white-faced, flaxen-haired man, with a notebook in his hand, who rushed forward and wrung Holmes's hand with effusion. "It is indeed kind of you to come," he said, "I have had everything left untouched."

"Except that!" Holmes answered, pointing at the pathway. "If a herd of buffaloes had passed along, there could not be a greater mess. No doubt, however, you had drawn your own conclusions, Gregson, before you permitted this."

"I have had so much to do inside the house," the detective said evasively. "My colleague, Mr. Lestrade, is here. I had relied upon him to look after this."

Holmes glanced at Watson and raised his eyebrows sardonically. "With two such men as yourself and Lestrade upon the ground, there will not be much for a third party to find out," he said.

Compare the first paragraph of this version to the first paragraph as written in first person in the preceding section. Notice how tricky it is to distinguish between the two men. We were forced to use *Holmes* twice, rather than using the pronoun *he* the second time. Otherwise, this example isn't much different from the first-person POV case.

Third-person POV is very widely used. We particularly like the third-person POV in *The Pillars of the Earth*, by Ken Follett; *Ender's Game*, by Orson Scott Card; *The Little Drummer Girl*, by John le Carré; and *Dies The Fire*, by S. M. Stirling.

Objective third-person POV

When you write a scene in objective third-person POV, you never get inside the character's head, so you can't use interior monologue or interior emotion. It's as if you're showing the story with a movie camera pointed at the focal character. This has the advantage of making your story intensely visual, but it has the disadvantage that thoughts and emotions simply can't be easily deduced from body language and facial expressions.

In objective third person, you don't have a POV character at all (because we define a POV character as a character whose head you can get inside). Instead, you have a *focal character* on whom you focus your camera. If you want to give your novel a cinematic feel, this is one way to do it, but be warned that it's hard work and it's probably not for beginners.

Here is our Sherlock passage rewritten into objective third-person POV:

> At the door of the house they were met by a tall, white-faced, flaxen-haired man, with a notebook in his hand, who rushed forward and wrung Holmes's hand with effusion. "It is indeed kind of you to come," he said, "I have had everything left untouched."
>
> "Except that!" Holmes answered, pointing at the pathway. "If a herd of buffaloes had passed along, there could not be a greater mess. No doubt, however, you had drawn your own conclusions, Gregson, before you permitted this."
>
> "I have had so much to do inside the house," the detective said. "My colleague, Mr. Lestrade, is here. I had relied upon him to look after this."
>
> Holmes glanced at Watson and raised his eyebrows. "With two such men as yourself and Lestrade upon the ground, there will not be much for a third party to find out," he said.

We've had to strike out the first paragraph of the original. When using this POV, you can't show the reader the verbatim thoughts or internal feelings of the characters — that's the definition of this POV. Of course, you can *suggest* to the reader the thoughts and feelings of the characters while staying outside their heads, using body language, facial expressions, voice tones, and all the other cues that actors use to portray thoughts and feelings on-screen, but it requires quite a bit of skill.

When working in objective third-person POV, you may be tempted to cheat by having the characters verbalize their thoughts and emotions in ways that sound phony. Don't cheat. Writing well in this POV takes a sure touch, and if you don't have that touch, then you're probably better off using regular third-person.

Dashiell Hammett uses the objective third-person POV effectively in *The Maltese Falcon*.

Head-hopping POV

Some writers use a form of third-person POV in which they get inside the heads of multiple characters in the same scene. This has the advantage that the reader now knows what everyone is thinking. However, the reader no longer identifies as strongly with any single character, so most fiction teachers discourage writers from using this strategy.

The easiest way to give the reader a powerful emotional experience is to persuade her that she *is* one of the characters, and that means choosing just one.

Take a look at the Holmes snippet with some sloppy head-hopping thrown in:

> Still Watson had had such extraordinary evidence of the quickness of Holmes's perceptive faculties, that he had no doubt that Holmes could see a great deal which was hidden from him.
>
> At the door of the house they were met by a tall, white-faced, flaxen-haired man, with a notebook in his hand, who rushed forward and wrung Holmes's hand with effusion. "It is indeed kind of you to come," he said, "I have had everything left untouched."
>
> "Except that!" Holmes answered, pointing at the pathway. "If a herd of buffaloes had passed along, there could not be a greater mess. No doubt, however, you had drawn your own conclusions, Gregson, before you permitted this."
>
> "I have had so much to do inside the house," Gregson said, embarrassed at having failed Holmes again. He realized that he could blame Lestrade for the blunder. "My colleague, Mr. Lestrade, is here. I had relied upon him to look after this."

> Holmes glanced at Watson and raised his eyebrows sardonically, wondering what sort of idiot Gregson took him for. "With two such men as yourself and Lestrade upon the ground, there will not be much for a third party to find out," he said.

We've inserted bits of interior monologue in the fourth and fifth paragraphs, allowing the reader to hear the thoughts of Gregson and Holmes. Notice that doing this jerks the reader out of Watson's head and really adds nothing to the story. If you're tempted to hop between heads, ask yourself why. Are you really willing to weaken your reader's powerful emotional experience in order to explain a bit more of what the characters are thinking?

As we note earlier, many writing teachers strongly discourage the head-hopping POV. However, plenty of best-selling novels hop heads with abandon. *Gone With the Wind*, by Margaret Mitchell, hasn't done too badly in the market, despite plenty of head-hopping.

Omniscient POV

The writer who uses omniscient POV knows all and wants to tell all to the reader. The advantage is that the author can ensure that the reader doesn't miss the point. The disadvantage is that part of the fun of reading fiction is figuring things out. Although a number of 19th-century novelists used omniscient POV extensively, most fiction teachers today consider omniscient POV a felony offense.

The truth is that although doing a good job using omniscient is difficult, it's possible, and this POV allows you to paint your story on a very broad canvas. If you're going to use this POV, make sure you know your craft, because it's much easier to do it poorly than to do it well.

Here is our segment of *A Study in Scarlet* written with some rather badly done omniscient pieces thrown in:

> Still Watson had had such extraordinary evidence of the quickness of Holmes's perceptive faculties, that he had no doubt that Holmes could see a great deal which was hidden from him. Had he known how much Holmes had already deduced from the tracks of carriage wheels in the road, he would have been even more amazed.
>
> At the door of the house they were met by a tall, white-faced, flaxen-haired man, with a notebook in his hand, one Tobias Gregson, who rushed forward and wrung Holmes's hand with effusion. "It is indeed kind of you to come," he said, "I have had everything left untouched." This was not strictly true, but Watson would discover this soon enough.

"Except that!" Holmes answered, pointing at the pathway. "If a herd of buffaloes had passed along, there could not be a greater mess. No doubt, however, you had drawn your own conclusions, Gregson, before you permitted this." Holmes often liked to tweak Gregson, though he considered him the least incompetent of any man in Scotland Yard.

"I have had so much to do inside the house," Gregson said, exaggerating as he often did. If Gregson had a weakness, it was his ego, which he'd inherited from his grandfather. "My colleague, Mr. Lestrade, is here. I had relied upon him to look after this."

Holmes glanced at Watson and raised his eyebrows sardonically, wondering what sort of idiot Gregson took him for. "With two such men as yourself and Lestrade upon the ground, there will not be much for a third party to find out," he said. Holmes thought that this bit of humor would fly above both Gregson and Lestrade's heads, but he didn't realize that they actually took his point rather well.

Of course, we were trying to do a bad job, but we didn't have to try very hard. When you write in omniscient POV, you may find it irresistible to add in extra little bits, as we've done in each of the paragraphs here. Look at how we've intruded on the story and cut the tension. If you're tempted to write in omniscient POV, rewrite your passage in normal third person and ask whether it's better than the original.

Few modern authors write with an omniscient POV, but one book that uses it effectively in many scenes is *The Godfather* by Mario Puzo.

Second-person POV

Only a rare writer successfully writes a story in second-person POV. When you choose this viewpoint, you're telling the story using the pronoun *you* instead of the character's name. This has the advantage of being intensely personal. A major disadvantage is that the reader may well balk at some actions of the POV character. If the reader *ever* says, "I wouldn't do that," then you've lost your reader for that scene.

There's a very rare variation on this that uses the imperative voice. In this voice, you're telling the reader what to do. An example of this is the short story "How to Become a Writer," by Lorrie Moore.

Here's the Sherlock scene with you in Watson's shoes:

Still you had had such extraordinary evidence of the quickness of his perceptive faculties, that you had no doubt that he could see a great deal which was hidden from you.

At the door of the house you and Holmes were met by a tall, white-faced, flaxen-haired man, with a notebook in his hand, who rushed forward and wrung your companion's hand with effusion. "It is indeed kind of you to come," he said, "I have had everything left untouched."

"Except that!" your friend answered, pointing at the pathway. "If a herd of buffaloes had passed along, there could not be a greater mess. No doubt, however, you had drawn your own conclusions, Gregson, before you permitted this."

"I have had so much to do inside the house," the detective said evasively. "My colleague, Mr. Lestrade, is here. I had relied upon him to look after this."

Holmes glanced at you and raised his eyebrows sardonically. "With two such men as yourself and Lestrade upon the ground, there will not be much for a third party to find out," he said.

Second-person POV can work, but you'd better be exceptionally good at it. You need to be able to persuade the reader at every point that the POV character's actions really are exactly what the reader would do. This POV can easily become tiresome and irritating to the reader, and the constant repetition of *you* can get very old.

Bright Lights, Big City, by Jay McInerney, is one of the very few novels written in the second person.

Choosing between Past and Present Tense

Closely linked to the idea of POV is the tense of a scene. Almost all fiction writers use either past tense or present tense, and they typically talk about their choice of POV and verb tenses in the same breath — "I'm writing in first-person, present," or "Joe always writes in third-person, past."

Past tense is far more common than present tense, and it's a little easier to write. You may like present tense because you believe it's different and cool. Writing in present tense certainly gives your fiction a strong sense of *immediacy* — of happening right now. If you're using first-person POV, then the narration in present tense implies to the reader that the character is a right-now kind of person. But be aware that many readers feel uncomfortable reading present tense, and although they may agree that it's different, these readers disagree with you about its being cool.

Tense matters: Delivering backstory when you're using past or present

If you're writing your main story in present tense, then to tell a sliver of backstory, you switch your verbs temporarily to past tense. Here's an example, in which the backstory starts in the second sentence:

> As I leaf through my diary from seventh grade, I spot an entry about Mr. McDaniel, my science teacher. Mr. McDaniel was the only good thing that happened to me in all three years of junior high. He wore a beard, and in 1970, that was a novelty on a teacher. And he saw some sort of promise in me that nobody else saw.

Using the right verb tense for backstory is a little more complicated if you're writing your main story in past tense. Many writers want to switch to past-perfect tense for the entire back-story, constantly using the word *had.* But that quickly ties you in knots. The solution is to use *had* once, the first time you use a verb in the backstory. After that, switch back to ordinary past tense. Your reader will follow this nicely. Here's the example in past tense:

> As Rupert leafed through his diary from seventh grade, he spotted an entry about Mr. McDaniel, his science teacher. Mr. McDaniel was the only good thing that had happened to Rupert in all three years of junior high. Mr. M. wore a beard, and in 1970, that was a novelty on a teacher. And he saw some sort of promise in Rupert that nobody else saw.

To write in present tense, change all simple past-tense verbs to simple present-tense verbs. For example, *ran* becomes *runs* and *punched* becomes *punches.* You may find that certain verbs cause problems when you do this. For example, the sentence "I guessed that he was Little John" can't just become "I guess that he is Little John" because "I guess" is a *colloquialism* — a casual, conversational expression — meaning "I suppose." So you may have to change the verb to get the awkward sentence "I make a guess that he is Little John" or "I'm guessing that he is Little John." Most verbs don't cause problems, but be aware that a few do.

Writing in present tense requires only a little more skill than writing in past tense, and we certainly don't want to discourage you from using it if you think it's right for your story. Even if you're a beginning writer, you should be able to write just about as well in present tense as in past tense. Just bear in mind that some readers dislike present tense for no other reason than they dislike it.

The Time Traveler's Wife, by Audrey Niffenegger, is a terrific example of a present tense novel, as is *The Speed of Dark*, by Elizabeth Moon.

Revealing Your Characters to the Reader

Creating characters using the methods we've outlined so far in this chapter is the easy part. The hard part is revealing your characters to your reader while keeping the story moving. You generally don't want to stop the story cold while you spend a few pages explaining a character's motivation or back-story. Yes, you can use narrative summary to explain these, but often you'll choose to show the reader who your character is instead of telling your reader about your character.

So how do you show your character to your reader? You have several valuable tools: action, dialogue, interior monologue, interior emotion, description, and flashback. We discuss these at length in Chapter 10, but it's appropriate to mention here some ways in which each of these reveal character. With each method, we include a small example snippet in a scene featuring a used-car salesman greeting a pair of potential buyers.

- **Dialogue:** You can find out plenty about a character by what he says. Most people are only too happy to talk about themselves, and your characters are no exception. Of course, a character can lie, but even lies tell you how he wants to be perceived, which tells you something about him. You can also figure out a ton just from the way he speaks — his tone of voice, his speed in speaking, his word choices, his grammatical errors, his use or misuse of logic, his judgments of other characters. All of these give the reader hints about whether they like or dislike the character, trust him or distrust him, respect him, fear him, or scorn him. Look at the following example and see what you can pick up from the dialogue. What do you think of the narrator and his boss after reading this dialogue?

  > "Go get 'em." Shriver pointed at the couple walking through the lot inspecting stickers.

  > "I'm on it." I pounced out of my chair and winked at my boss. "Take no prisoners, eh?"

  > Shriver grunted and pointed. "Go, go, go!"

  > I looked in the mirror and adjusted my tie. "They'll think I'm Jesus feeding the multitudes before I'm through."

- **Action:** A character who behaves heroically is different from one who behaves like a coward. Yes, a character can behave deceptively, but even so, his actions and body language hint at whether he's happy, sad, angry, excited, discouraged, afraid, bored, or amused. They also tell a lot about what he thinks and feels about the other characters.

The old aphorism "actions speak louder than words" is doubly true in revealing character. When a character's actions say one thing and his words say another, readers always believe the actions.

Read the next example and see what the actions show you. Do you think the customers are likely to buy anything?

> I stepped outside into the brilliant July sunshine and strode toward the pair, sizing them up. The man was kicking tires on our loss-leader model. I kid you not — actually kicking the tires. The woman was holding her purse tight to her side, her fingers clenched around the clasp as she squinted at the sticker. Her mouth was a line so thin, you'd need a razorpoint pen to put her lipstick on.

✔ **Description:** The way a character looks is a window into how he perceives himself. If he's an elitist, his immaculate style of dress tells you instantly that he's from the upper crust. If he's an absent-minded intellectual, you see it by the other-universe look in his eyes, even if his hair isn't quite the mop of an Einstein. If he's a geeky loner, you know it, even if he left his pocket protector home. In this example, what do the descriptions of the characters tell you about the family dynamics of this couple?

> "Hey there!" I said, stepping into their personal zone. "Great day, isn't it? What can I do for you folks today?"

> The man looked at me, and yet he didn't look at me, his eyes shifting up almost to contact with mine, then flickering away. I couldn't quite tell if he'd shaved today. His hand was hard and callused and greasy when we shook. His wife slunk back behind him. Her eyes had that hollow, hungry look of a beaten dog, and her lank, shoulder-length hair hung down onto a dress that fit her like a potato sack.

✔ **Interior monologue:** If you know what a character's thinking, then you have direct access to his inner being. As with dialogue, you find out even more by the way he expresses his thoughts internally — his word choices, grammar, logic, and value judgments on other characters all tell you who he really is, even if he himself isn't aware of it. Based on the interior monologue, do you think the narrator is as enthusiastic as he sounds?

> "Can we test drive this one?" The man jerked his head at the cadaverous Fiat that Shriver calls the Frantic Italian Attempt at Transportation.

> "Absolutely, sir, I'll just need your driver's license and we can take this rocket out on the road." If I made this sale, the commission would be all of about eighteen bucks. *Shriver is going to laugh his socks off at me.*

✔ **Interior emotion:** Different characters have different ranges of emotion. Some people constantly overreact to everything, as if their emotional response circuitry only has one setting — full volume. Other people take everything in stride, barely flinching even when the sky really is falling. The way your characters react emotively can tell your reader volumes. In this example, what new thing do you guess about the narrator from his interior emotion?

> "Molly, give me my wallet." The man turned to look at her.
>
> She fumbled in her purse, first slowly, then frantically. "Frankie, it ain't—"
>
> He backhanded her hard across the right cheek. "Stupid little bitch!"
>
> A burst of molten lead exploded in my gut. All of a sudden, I couldn't hear anything except the ten thousand hornets buzzing in my brain.

✔ **Flashback:** We recommend that you be wary of overusing flashback; however, it can be a valuable tool in exposing part of a character's back-story, throwing a floodlight on his real essence.

Don't waste a flashback on trivial incidents. If you're going to use this tool, take your reader to the worst times of your character's life. Your reader will empathize with your character in a whole new way if you take them both into the character's private hell.

In the following example, how do you think our narrator's flashback is going to play out, given only the first two paragraphs? When the flash-back ends, what new direction do you think this scene will go?

> I'm 8 years old and the old man is hitting Mama again. Another sharp, tight slap rips through the bedroom wall, then her con-trolled little gasp, then the one word hissed out. "Bitch!"
>
> My fists knot up into hammers of rage, such as only a 63-pound superhero can bring to bear on the forces of evil.

We've laid things on extra thick in the examples here to get our point across in minimal space. Our examples are designed to highlight our teaching points, not for literary merit. In your novel, you have vastly more space to work, and you can afford to be a lot more subtle.

Chapter 8

Storyline and Three-Act Structure: The Top Layers of Your Plot

*S*tory structure — a succinct sketch of your story that captures its essence — is the key to selling your story to a publisher, and it's critical to your success as a writer. The reason it's such a great selling tool is that when you can explain your story in just a few words, people instantly know whether this story is for them or not. It's important to you because it helps you keep focused as you write and edit your novel.

The modern novel is an extremely complex art form. The plot of a novel has six layers of complexity. In this chapter, we discuss the two highest-level layers: the storyline and the three-act structure. We cover the other layers (synopsis, scene list, scene, and clips) in Chapters 9 and 10.

Giving the Big Picture of Story Structure: Your Storyline

If you want to write a commercially successful novel, then you need to sell your book seven times. We call this sequence the *selling chain*. Here's what the selling chain looks like:

1. You or preferably your agent sells the concept to an acquisitions editor, who decides to take it to her publishing committee for review.

2. The editor sells the idea to the publishing committee, which is responsible for making the decision to publish the book. The publisher then offers you a contract that specifies your royalties and advance payments.

3. When the book goes into production, the editor sells the concept to the sales team, which has to get orders from the bookstores and chains.

4. The sales team sells the book to professional buyers, who place orders for bookstores and chains of bookstores.

5. The catalog copy and back-cover copy sell the idea to the sales staff in bookstores, who interact with readers every day.

6. The back-cover copy or the bookstore's sales staff sells the book to readers, who come into bookstores looking for something to read.

7. The first wave of readers sells the idea to their friends because they enjoyed the book so much they can't stop talking about it.

The selling chain is essential. If you break any link in the chain, your book will almost certainly fail to do well.

Please note one important fact: The people in the selling chain don't know your story as well as you do, but each of them needs to find some way to communicate his or her excitement about your novel to the next link in the chain. If you want them to do their job, then giving them the tool they need is your responsibility. That tool is a short, one-sentence summary of your novel. We call this sentence the *storyline*. The storyline of your novel captures the essence of the story.

You need to put on your minimalist hat when thinking about your storyline. The question is not how much you can add to the story; it's how much you can take away. In this section, we show you how to write one.

Understanding the value of a storyline

You won't die if you don't write a storyline, and you'll still be able to write a novel. So why spend the time writing one? Consider a scenario where a storyline comes in useful:

> You're at a writing conference in a large hotel, waiting for the elevator. When it arrives, you walk in and a high-powered agent steps in beside you. You give her a friendly smile. She squints at your name tag and says, "Hi, what sort of fiction are you writing?"
>
> The door chings shut and you feel your heart thudding just beneath your vocal cords. "I . . . well, see, there's this guy," you say, "and he's working in the bus factory. No wait, I changed that. He's driving a bus for the city. And there's this girl, too. Not really his girlfriend, see, but he'd like that, only she doesn't know he exists. I mean she kind of knows who he is, but not really. And he keeps having dreams about —"
>
> The door opens at the next floor and the agent steps out. "Wow, sounds great. Got to run."

You stand there rubbing your sweaty palms on your shirt, kicking yourself, because you hardly got started. Matter of fact, you never even got to the cool part of your story, which is that the guy who drives the bus is having dreams of an impending terrorist attack on Disneyland, just like the dreams he was having in early September 2001. No matter. That agent is gone, and you've blown whatever chance you had.

Rewind that movie halfway and play the last bit of it again:

The door chings shut and you feel your heart thudding just beneath your vocal cords. "I'm writing a paranormal suspense novel about a bus driver who has dreams about a terrorist attack on Disneyland, just like the dreams he was having in September 2001."

The door opens at the next floor and the agent steps out. She turns around and studies your name tag again and she's got a funny look on her face. "Listen, I'm on my way to an appointment, but that's exactly the kind of book I love to read. Can we talk? Here's my card with my cellphone. Call me in an hour."

See the difference? In both cases, you have the same great story. In the first case, you don't know how to present it in one sentence. In the second case, you do.

If you don't write a great storyline, then everyone in your selling chain will make up a storyline of his or her own. None of these people know your story as well as you do, nor do they love it as much as you do. They'll do their best, but the storylines they come up with may fail to capture the heart of your story. If your agent or editor knows your storyline right from the start, she'll make sure that everybody else in the selling chain knows it, too. The simpler your storyline is, the easier it'll be to pass it down the chain.

The storyline isn't merely a selling tool; it can serve to focus your own creative efforts during the arduous months when you're planning and writing your novel. Knowing what your story is "really about" can keep you on track when the inevitable rabbit trails pop up. Even if you don't figure out your storyline until after you write your first draft, it can be a powerful tool in helping you cut out the nonessentials when you get into revisions. Although the storyline isn't essential, it can be as valuable to you, the writer, as it is to all those links in the selling chain.

Writing a great storyline

The purpose of the storyline is to get one of two possible reactions from the hearer:

- ✔ Wow! I like that. Tell me more.
- ✔ Sorry, I'm really not interested.

Your storyline needs to tell people immediately whether they belong to your target audience (see Chapter 3 for a detailed explanation of how you decide on your ideal reader). Remember that you'll never write a book that appeals to everyone. If someone doesn't fit in your target audience, that's okay. You fail quickly, which allows you to move on to the next person. But if someone does belong to your target audience, then you succeed quickly.

Here are the essential features of a good storyline:

- ✔ **It's short.** You want it to be short so you can memorize it easily and say it quickly — and so can everyone else in your selling chain.

- ✔ **It's emotive.** Fiction is about creating a powerful emotional experience, so your storyline needs to tell what emotive experience your story will deliver.

- ✔ **It arouses curiosity.** Your storyline shouldn't give away the story. It should raise a story question that demands an answer.

If you want to know how to write a good storyline, look at the bestseller lists. They often provide a one-sentence summary of each book. Study how those sentences arouse curiosity and punch emotive buttons in just a few words.

Here are some common features of successful storylines. They aren't essential, but they're good guidelines:

- ✔ Shoot for 25 words or less. If you can do it in less than 15 words, you get extra credit.

- ✔ Limit your storyline to just a few characters. One or two is ideal. Three is the maximum.

- ✔ Tell only one thread of the story, either the most essential one or the most interesting one.

- ✔ Most of the time, don't name the characters. Instead, describe each, aiming for internal inconsistency that promises conflict. A "one-armed trapeze artist" is infinitely more interesting than "Joe." (However, whenever a famous character — such as Houdini or physics pioneer Marie Curie — plays a role in your novel, consider bending this rule and naming him or her in your storyline.)

- ✔ When writing the storyline for a historical novel, tell the time period and geographical setting if they add potency to the brew.

- ✔ Use adjectives that evoke empathy or cast a character as an outsider. The word *young* frequently shows up in storylines because it implies vulnerability and appeals to modern youth-oriented culture. References to gender may set up romantic tension or show characters who cross stereotypes. You can tolerate some redundancy if it heightens the wallop.

✔ Don't be afraid to use a small amount of hype with a verb such as *battles* or *struggles*.

✔ Backload the storyline by putting a surprise or some emotively punchy words at the end of the sentence.

You can write your storyline at any time. A lot depends on which creative paradigm you follow (see Chapter 4 for a discussion of creative paradigms). If you're a seat-of-the-pants writer or an edit-as-you-go writer, you'll probably do best to write your storyline after your first draft, when you understand your story well. If you're a Snowflaker or an outliner, you may want to take a first cut at your storyline before you start writing. We recommend that you revisit your storyline frequently, constantly honing it to make it sharper, brighter, and more potent.

The following steps can help you compose a storyline. You may want to experiment first by writing storylines for some published novels — we provide some example storylines in the next section. When you're ready, you can take a shot at writing a storyline for your own novel.

1. **Pick the character to focus your storyline on.**

   Normally, this is your lead character, but it can also be your villain or someone else. Here are some questions to jiggle your neurons to help you find your best storyline:

   • Which of your characters has the biggest contradiction in his values? (See Chapter 7 for a discussion of character values.)

   • Which of your characters plays the strongest role in the story?

   • Which of your characters has the toughest obstacle or the biggest paradox?

   • What is the story goal for each of your primary characters? (See Chapter 7 for an explanation of story goals.)

2. **Write a sentence about that character that suggests a possible story question.**

   The *story question* asks whether your character will succeed or fail to meet his story goal (see Chapters 6 and 7 for more on story questions).

3. **Edit the sentence.**

   Writing a strong storyline takes a lot of practice, and you may not get yours right on the first try. (If you do, you're probably a marketing genius.) Getting it wrong the first ten or twenty tries is perfectly okay, so long as you get it right the *last* time. So ask yourself some questions — is the character interesting? Is the plot simple? Are the words emotive?

Do you need to establish a setting? Can you backload the sentence with either surprise or emotional zing?

Remember: A storyline must strip out everything that isn't essential. It must even throw away many elements that *are* essential at lower levels in your story structure. Be ruthless in simplifying your storyline. The question isn't how much you can pack in; the question is how much you can take out and still make a lasting impression.

4. **Save it for later.**

Your storyline almost certainly isn't perfect. Look at it again next week or next month and try to improve on it. For some tips on reworking your storyline, flip to Chapter 13.

Examples: Looking at storylines for 20 best-selling novels

Please remember that writing a storyline is an art, not a science. There's really no one best way to write a storyline. The purpose of a storyline is to arouse interest — to make your target reader say, "Ooh! Tell me more."

The best way to figure out how to write a storyline is to look at some examples. Try your hand at writing storylines for the following novels, and then compare your efforts to ours. Practice won't make perfect, but it will make you better. In the publishing game, *better* may be good enough.

Bending the rules with *Transgression*

At book signings, Randy sold many copies of his first novel, *Transgression,* using an 11-word storyline: "A physicist travels back in time to kill the apostle Paul." That always got either a yawn or a wow response. Randy followed up the wowsers with the sentence, "By the way, I'm a physicist myself, and I know all about time travel."

Notice that Randy bent one of his guidelines (he gave the name of the apostle Paul, a famous character) because that added a high emotive punch, which was all the stronger because it was backloaded to the end of the sentence.

If you've read *Transgression,* then you know that neither of the two primary characters in the story are even mentioned in the storyline. That's okay. The point of this storyline was to raise the story question: Will the physicist kill that pesky Paul, or won't he?

Here are storylines for 20 novels, in alphabetical order by title. Our examples range from 14 to 27 words, with an average of about 19 words. Study these examples. If you work at it, you can probably do better.

- *Blink,* **by Ted Dekker (Christian thriller):** "A young Saudi woman on the run from her family links up with a Berkeley physics prodigy who is just discovering that he can see the future."

  What makes this storyline work is its unconventional mix: The devout Muslim woman and the agnostic physics student create an irresistible lure to Dekker's core audience, conservative Christians who love a taut thriller. We've backloaded the one paranormal element — seeing the future — that makes this story special.

- *The Clan of the Cave Bear,* **by Jean Auel (historical):** "A young human girl in Ice Age Europe struggles to survive persecution by her adoptive clan of Neanderthals."

  Here we mention only one character, the young human girl Ayla, who is 4 at the beginning of the story. Why don't we mention the other characters in the story? Because less is more. By not mentioning them specifically, we leave room for the zinger at the end — she lives among Neanderthals. This is another example of backloading the emotive punch.

- *Contact,* **by Carl Sagan (science fiction):** "A young female astronomer discovers radio signals from alien beings in a nearby star system."

  This storyline highlights the gender of the central character, cutting against the grain of the stereotypical male scientist. This automatically arouses empathy, because the protagonist is an outsider. The word *alien* is always good for emotive appeal, especially in science fiction.

- *The Da Vinci Code,* **by Dan Brown (thriller):** "A Harvard symbologist and a female French cryptographer solve the puzzle of the Holy Grail in a race against death across Europe."

  Highlighting male and female characters promises a bit of romantic tension, which is always good, even if it's not central to the story. In this case, the storyline is already high-octane, with three separate phrases that generate emotive responses: "Holy Grail" connotes religion, "race against death" is a stock phrase for thrillers, and "Europe" adds an exotic flavor that appeals to Americans.

- *The Firm,* **by John Grisham (legal thriller):** "A brilliant young lawyer gets a fabulous job at a firm that is a cover for a Mafia money-laundering operation."

  This storyline focuses on a single character, shifting him rapidly from a high positive ("fabulous job") to a high negative ("Mafia money-laundering operation.") A little hype at the beginning ("brilliant young lawyer") is standard practice, whereas a kicker is backloaded at the end.

✔ *Girl with a Pearl Earring,* **by Tracy Chevalier (literary historical):** "A young servant girl in 17th-century Holland lies at the center of a marital dispute in the home of renowned painter Johannes Vermeer."

This storyline, like the story itself, is painted in muted colors. We backload the sentence by naming the famous artist who plays a central role in the story.

✔ *Gorky Park,* **by Martin Cruz Smith (mystery):** "A Moscow homicide detective investigates a bizarre triple murder and runs afoul of the KGB and FBI."

Homicide detectives are commonplace characters, so we focus first on what makes this one special: he works in Moscow. We follow up with the word *bizarre,* a hype word acceptable for storylines in this genre. The reader isn't surprised that a Moscow cop might ruffle KGB feathers, but we drastically raise the stakes by backloading the sentence with the word *FBI.* The reader of this genre will demand to know why the FBI may be in cahoots with the KGB.

✔ *The Hunt for Red October,* **by Tom Clancy (military technothriller):** "A Russian sub captain leads the Soviet navy on a merry chase while he tries to hand over the latest Soviet submarine to the Americans."

This storyline focuses on a lesser character, the Russian sub captain. We don't mention the protagonist of the story at all — Clancy's meal-ticket character Jack Ryan. Why not? Because if you have a powerful enough story question, then a powerful hero is implied. Ryan is a strong character, but we don't need him to pique interest. Our storyline is loaded with emotive hit points that were particularly potent in the early 1980s, as the Cold War came to its peak.

✔ *The Kite Runner,* **by Khaled Hosseini (literary):** "A boy raised in Afghanistan grows up with the shame of having failed to fight the gang of boys who raped his closest friend."

We start with a word designed to intrigue the reader: *Afghanistan.* Given the author's name, the reader will immediately guess that the novel is an insider look at that mysterious country. We follow up on this with a series of emotive hits — *shame, failed, fight, gang, raped, friend.* The storyline promises something different, and the book delivers.

✔ *The Lord of the Rings,* **by J. R. R. Tolkien (fantasy):** "A hobbit learns that destroying his magic ring is the key to saving Middle Earth from the Dark Lord."

Notice how very many characters we've left out of this storyline: The wizards, the elves, the orcs, the Ents, Gollum, Shelob, Tom Bombadil. We've also left out all the important places: The Shire, Rivendell, Lothlorien, Rohan, Minas Tirith, even Mordor. We've stripped it down to our hero Frodo and the Dark Lord. In a battle between good and evil, just showing the symbol of good and the symbol of evil is okay.

✔ ***The Lovely Bones,*** **by Alice Sebold (literary):** "A young girl watches the turmoil in her family from heaven after being raped and murdered by a neighbor."

This storyline highlights the unusual story premise — watching from heaven. Note how we backload several traumatic words ("raped and murdered by a neighbor"). The story is too harrowing for some readers, and this storyline tells them immediately that they won't be able to handle it.

✔ ***The Man From St. Petersburg,*** **by Ken Follett (historical thriller):** "In 1914, a Russian anarchist tries to assassinate the aristocrat who is negotiating his country's entrance into World War I."

This storyline starts with a date, 1914, which is necessary info for any historical novel. Now count the emotive hit points: "Russian anarchist," "assassinate," "aristocrat," "World War I." If you've read this novel, you know that the story has four major characters, each with an important story thread, and that a young Winston Churchill also plays a significant role. We've chosen to mention only one major character (the assassin), along with one minor character (the Russian nobleman). Why skip over three major characters? Because less is more. Focus your storyline down to the sharpest point you can. Why skip over Churchill? Because we couldn't figure out a way to do so without overinflating the storyline. See whether you can improve this storyline by adding Churchill and subtracting something else.

✔ ***My Name is Asher Lev,*** **by Chaim Potok (literary):** "An orthodox Jewish artist struggles to reconcile his art, his religion, and his family."

Here we highlight an intrinsic personal conflict — orthodox Judaism historically ignored the visual arts because the Second Commandment prohibits making images. To excel in his work, the artist Asher Lev must cut against the grain of centuries of tradition. We backload this storyline with the words "his family," which highlight the fact that religious rebels always pay a heavy personal cost.

✔ ***Outlander,*** **by Diana Gabaldon (time-travel romance):** "A young English nurse searches for the way back home after time-traveling from 1945 to 1743 Scotland."

Don't underestimate the power of a simple word like *home.* Going home again carries enormous emotive overtones for many readers. Because this is a time-travel novel that doesn't begin in the present day, the storyline shows both endpoints in time. We've backloaded this sentence with a date and place (1743 Scotland) that will carry some freight for any reader who knows about Bonnie Prince Charlie and the failed Jacobite Rising in 1745.

✔ *The Pillars of the Earth,* **by Ken Follett (historical thriller):** "A stone-mason in 12th-century England battles to build his life's dream, a cathedral."

This book is widely agreed to be Follett's finest work, yet the storyline is stark. We have a lowly stonemason trying to build a cathedral. The storyline only needs to spark interest. Either the reader cares whether a lone stonemason can build a cathedral, or she doesn't. The storyline should arouse curiosity in those who care, and it should warn off those who don't.

✔ *Pride and Prejudice,* **by Jane Austen (romance):** "A young English woman from a peculiar family is pursued by an arrogant and wealthy young man."

This storyline puts on display the weaknesses of both the young woman ("from a peculiar family") and her suitor ("arrogant"). It raises the questions of whether the man will succeed and whether the reader should want him to.

✔ *River God,* **by Wilbur Smith (historical action-adventure):** "A genius eunuch slave in 18th-century B.C.E. Egypt must survive palace intrigues between his mistress and her evil father."

In this example, we show three characters: the slave, his female owner, and her father. The conflict pits two against one, but even so, it's clearly an unfair battle. Neither a slave nor a woman carries the political clout of a man of high birth. We highlight two features of high interest in one character here — the slave is both a genius and a eunuch. Both features make him unusual.

✔ *The Speed of Dark,* **by Elizabeth Moon (literary):** "An autistic savant must choose whether to accept a new treatment that would make him normal and change his identity forever."

This storyline mentions only one character, one who's intrinsically interesting: an "autistic savant." Again, we've backloaded the sentence with a kicker that appeals to a broad audience ("change his identity forever"). Most people would resist very strongly any attempt to change their identities. Why do we use the word *forever?* Isn't that already implied? Perhaps, but it carries emotive freight, so we can justify using the extra word.

✔ *The Spy Who Came In from the Cold,* **by John le Carré (spy thriller):** "A British spy 'retires in disgrace' as cover for a deeply laid plan to entrap the head of counterespionage in East Berlin."

This storyline defines the hook for one of the finest spy novels ever written. Everybody loves a sting operation, especially in a spy novel. Count the emotive hit points: "British spy," "disgrace," "entrap," "counterespionage," and "East Berlin." This novel is essential reading for anyone who writes thrillers.

> ✔ ***The Time Traveler's Wife,*** **by Audrey Niffenegger (literary):** "A young girl grows up in the company of a strange time-traveling visitor who appears and disappears at random."
>
> We highlight the chaotic relationship at the center of this novel by using the words *strange* and *random.*

Three-Act Structure: Setting Up Three Disasters

A novel needs to be simple enough to explain in a single sentence, but it also needs to be complex enough to fill up a few hundred pages and engage your reader for hours. We now discuss the next level of complexity after the storyline — the well-known *three-act structure,* which is widely used to analyze stories. This structure does the following:

> ✔ It lets you hold the main points of the story in your head in one coherent flow.
>
> ✔ It lets you communicate those main points to industry professionals in a way they're expecting (as we discuss later in "Summarizing Your Three-Act Structure for Interested Parties").

In this section, we show you why three-act structure is important, break down the acts, explain how to escalate a story's excitement, and give you some hints on timing.

 You may be wondering whether using three acts is required for a novel. No, of course not. There are no unbreakable rules in fiction; you can use any structure for your novel that works. However, we strongly recommend mastering the three-act structure because it fits the structure of so many novels. Everyone in the industry understands this structure, so it gives you a tool for communicating your story to other people. It also works. Even if you decide that the three-act structure isn't right for your novel, you'll find it valuable to ponder *why* it doesn't work for your novel. That should give you some deep insights into your story.

Looking at the value of a three-act structure

When you have an agent interested in your storyline, you need to give her the bones of the story next: the setup, a sequence of major disasters (each worse than the one before), and then the ending. That's the three-act structure.

Imagine a scenario where you met an agent at a writing conference earlier and gave her a one-sentence storyline that got you to first base: She asked you for an appointment (we give you this scenario earlier in "Understanding the value of a storyline"). We now take that scenario a little further to show why three-act structure is important. Suppose you sit down with the agent to discuss your novel, and all she knows so far is that your story is about a bus driver who's having dreams about a terrorist attack on Disneyland, just like the dreams he was having in September 2001:

> Naturally, you're a bit nervous as you begin the session. You've never done one of these 15-minute appointments before, but the agent evidently has. "I really like your storyline," she says. "Tell me more about your story."
>
> You fold both hands in your lap to keep them from shaking. "Well, so he calls Homeland Security, and they believe him, and together they stop the terrorist attack."
>
> The agent's mouth drops open, and she stares at you for a few seconds. "That's not a novel," she says. "That's a newspaper report. Is that all there is to your story?"
>
> Great drops of sweat slither down your sides. "That's all I've got so far, but it's a start, isn't it?"

No, it isn't a start. It's the end of this interview, because you really have no story. A story needs conflict. Obstacles. Disasters. What kind of disasters? Disasters that escalate. Here we rewind a bit to show you what happens if you have a three-act structure with a series of increasingly bad disasters. We begin with your response when the agent asks for more information about your story:

> You fold both hands in your lap to keep them from shaking. "Well, so he calls Homeland Security every day for a week, and they finally commit him to a psychiatric institution for observation for 72 hours."
>
> The agent leans forward in her chair. "I like that. That's a pretty good disaster. So what does he do then?"
>
> You take a deep breath and feel your pulse start to slow down a little. "After two days, he calls this girl he knows on his cellphone and she helps him escape, but now the cops launch a manhunt."
>
> The agent is nodding encouragement. "Good, good. Then what?"
>
> A faint smile tugs at the edges of your mouth. "He has another dream that reveals the terrorists' timeline, but then there's a shootout with the cops and the girl gets wounded and captured."
>
> The agent returns your smile. "Then what?"

You're feeling much calmer now. "He goes to the hospital where she's under heavy guard, lures the cops into a high-speed chase through most of L.A., and leads them to the terrorists' weapons cache."

The agent leans back in her chair and studies you for a long moment. "Have you got a sample chapter I could look at?"

If the agent asks for a sample, it all comes down to whether you can write. Maybe you can; maybe you can't. But presenting your three-act structure can earn you the right to be read.

Timing the acts and disasters

Aristotle famously said that a story has a beginning, a middle, and an end. The three parts of the three-act structure correspond exactly to Aristotle's beginning, middle, and end. Act 1 is the beginning; Act 2, the middle; and Act 3, the end.

We believe that a powerful technique for punctuating the three-act structure is what we call the *three-disaster structure*. The three-disaster structure is just a piece of the three-act structure, but it's an important piece. The acts are the large pieces of the story; the disasters are the points that connect them. We like to think of the timing of the three-act structure like a football game, as follows:

1. **Act 1 takes up roughly the first quarter and ends with a major disaster.**

   The first disaster comes at the end of Act 1 and links it to Act 2.

2. **Act 2 takes up the second and third quarters, and each quarter ends with an even worse disaster.**

   The second disaster comes at the midpoint of Act 2 (ending the second quarter) and serves as an antidote to what people often call the *sagging middle*. The third disaster strikes at the end of Act 2 (ending the third quarter) and links it to Act 3.

3. **Act 3 takes up the last quarter and includes a *climax* (also called a *resolution*), which answers the *story question* — the question of whether your lead character will succeed.**

   The climax typically falls late in the fourth quarter, and everything after it serves to wind down the story.

Here's how the three-act structure works: Tension rises in Act 1, which ends in a disaster that fully commits the lead character to the story. Tension rises further until the middle of Act 2, when a second disaster strikes, even worse than the first. After a brief recovery, the tension ramps up even harder, right up to the end of Act 2, when the third and worst disaster breaks. This forces the lead character to find a way to resolve the story somewhere in Act 3.

Introducing a great beginning

The *beginning* of your story (Act 1) takes the reader into your story world and introduces the main characters. They may not yet have a story goal. They may simply be living life and trying to get by. Or they may each have rather dull and boring goals they're trying to reach. Or they may know from the very first paragraph what important story goals they want.

Consider the beginning of a classic movie, *Star Wars Episode 4: A New Hope*. This first *Star Wars* movie caused an enormous sensation when it released in 1977. (**Note:** The story actually appeared first as a novel — George Lucas's *Star Wars: From the Adventures of Luke Skywalker* — published a few months before the movie hit screens.)

In the beginning of the story, young Luke Skywalker takes possession of two droids bearing a mysterious message from a beautiful princess. The princess is begging for help. Luke would help her if he could, but he has no idea who she is, what she needs, or what he can do for her.

The droid R2-D2 escapes, and Luke pursues him. After being attacked by vicious sand-people, Luke meets Obi-Wan Kenobi, the intended recipient of the message. Kenobi tells him that the droid has plans for the Death Star, which must be taken to the planet Alderaan to help the rebel alliance defeat the Emperor. He asks Luke to join him. Luke refuses reluctantly. He's already given his word to stay at his dull farming job with Uncle Owen and Aunt Beru through the season. He can't just pick up and leave the planet, can he?

Luke would like to join this story, but he can't commit. He needs something to force him to make a break with the past. What might cause him to commit? What causes the lead character in most novels to commit irrevocably to the story? It takes a disaster — something to reset the character's priorities.

The end of the beginning: Getting commitment with the first disaster

By the end of Act 1, each character must know his or her story goal and must be firmly committed to it. Why committed? Because if the characters won't commit, then the reader won't, either.

The purpose of the beginning of your novel is to bring your lead character to a point of no return. Before this point, he can refuse his role as lead character of the story. After this point, he's all in and he isn't going back. Your lead character commits (and your reader commits) when you give him a disaster that brings his role in the story into sharp focus. Generally, no small disaster will do; it needs to be something big, something life-changing. At that point, your reader emotionally commits to your story for the long haul, because she wants to see the story question answered: Will the lead character achieve his story goal, or won't he?

In *Star Wars*, Luke and General Kenobi discover a ruined transport — the one owned by the jawas from whom Luke's uncle bought the droids. In a flash, Luke realizes that his uncle and aunt are in horrible danger. He leaps in his transport and flies back home. He arrives at the farm and finds Uncle Owen and Aunt Beru murdered, slaughtered by Storm Troopers.

That's the first major disaster. Luke makes his decision instantly. He no longer owes his aunt and uncle labor. Instead, he owes them vengeance. He decides to leave the planet and join the Rebellion. He'll go to Alderaan with Kenobi and help destroy the Death Star.

Until now, Luke has had small and unimportant goals. Now he has a big one. He has a story goal, and it drives the rest of the story: Join the Rebellion and destroy the Death Star. The disaster has turned Luke from a dithering farm boy into a man with a mission. That's the purpose of the first disaster. The beginning is over, and the long middle of the story has begun.

Supporting the middle with a second major disaster

The middle of your novel (Act 2) takes up at least half of your book, just as the second and third quarters of a football game take up half the game. Many things happen in the middle act; the problem is that no matter how interesting they are, they all start looking alike after a while.

What's the solution? Another disaster. Something bigger than the one before. Something that snaps your lead character's head back hard enough to give him a concussion. This disaster should come at roughly the midpoint of your story.

Your lead character will have numerous smaller setbacks throughout the second act. However, the second disaster will be major — the worst thing that's happened in the story so far.

In *Star Wars*, the intrepid Luke and General Kenobi join forces with Han Solo and Chewbacca. After some adventures in the cantina, they escape Luke's home planet on the *Millennium Falcon* and pop into hyperspace for a trip to Alderaan. When they arrive, they find the planet gone, which is bad, but it carries no serious emotive punch for Luke. He didn't personally know any of the billions of dead. This isn't the disaster you're looking for.

The Death Star pulls in Luke's ship with a tractor beam. He and the others hide out, sneak aboard the Death Star, and then discover and rescue Princess Leia. Obi-Wan Kenobi disables the tractor beam. As they all head back to the ship to escape, Darth Vader intercepts Kenobi and the two warriors battle with light sabers. The viewer expects an exciting battle and an even more exciting escape. Instead, Vader kills Kenobi.

That's a disaster, and it's huge. Kenobi was Luke's mentor, and he was the effective leader of the group. Psychologically, they've been decapitated. They escape the Death Star, fight off the pursuit, and set course for the rebel planet. Luke continues training in the Force. Luke and Leia are intent on fighting in the rebellion. Han Solo intends to collect his reward and pay off Jabba the Hutt. The problem now is that this story could go on forever, or the heroic team could splinter. What's going to force this story to end — and end well?

Leading to the end: Tackling the third disaster

Your story needs some reason to focus itself on an ending. That reason normally comes from a new major disaster, the third and worst. Like the first disaster, this one forces a decision. But this time, the decision is mutual between hero and villain. It's a decision on both sides to pursue a final confrontation, and it comes at the end of Act 2.

Please note that the third disaster/decision is *not* the final confrontation itself. The decision leads up to the final confrontation, which you show in Act 3. Everything that comes after this third disaster/decision forms the ending of your story.

In *Star Wars*, the third disaster comes when the rebels discover that they've been tracked by the Death Star. It's approaching their base quickly. When it arrives, it'll annihilate the rebel planet, which has been the secret base of operations. The rebel alliance now faces a decision. Should they run for it, scattering in a thousand directions? Or should they stand and fight the Death Star, using the information in R2-D2's memory?

They choose to stand and fight. That's the decision that launches the ending. Note that this decision is irrevocable. If they win, they'll never have to face the Death Star again. If they lose, there won't be enough of them left to scrape off the Emperor's shoe. They have to win — and so does the Death Star.

Your third disaster need not be the actual occurrence of a catastrophe. It can be the *threat* of a catastrophe. The important feature is that it forces the final showdown. That's its purpose in the story structure. You may argue that the approach of the Death Star doesn't seem like a disaster, because nothing horrible has happened yet. You'd probably feel differently if you were on the rebel planet watching the approach of the Death Star, knowing that within a few hours, it may kill you, shatter the rebellion, and leave the galaxy helpless in the hands of the evil emperor.

Wrapping up: Why endings work — or don't

The ending (Act 3) now follows from the decision to pursue a final confrontation (see the preceding section). There's preparation, of course. Both sides get ready. Both know that the difference between victory and defeat is a razor-blade's width. The battle could go either way, but neither side will back down.

An ending must answer the story question of whether the main character will achieve his story goal. (See Chapters 6 and 7 for details on story questions.) A story question must be objective, simple, important, achievable, and difficult. You have three options as a storyteller:

- ✔ **Happy ending:** Answer the story question with a "yes, hooray!"

- ✔ **Unhappy ending:** Answer the story question with a "no, boohoo."

- ✔ **Bittersweet ending:** Answer the story question with a "yes, but" or with a "no, but."

Any of these endings work, as long as the answer follows from the characters' values and is plausible within the story world you've created.

Your ending will not work if you do any of the following:

- ✔ You fail to answer the story question at all.

- ✔ You answer the story question in a way that rings false to the values of the characters.

✔ You answer the story question in a way that violates the basic rules of your story world. This is often called a *deus ex machina* ("god from the machine") ending, named after the annoying habit of Greek tragedians to resolve their stories by lowering a god from a crane onto the stage to wrap up the story. Aristotle criticized Euripedes for rescuing Medea in just this way.

In *Star Wars*, the story question is "Will Luke and his friends defeat the Empire by destroying the Death Star?" This question comes into clear focus at the end of Act I.

The rebels have a tiny hope of victory — they must fire a precisely aimed proton torpedo into a small hatch in the exterior of the Death Star. But the approach to the hatch will take them through a heavily armed trench. Before they can reach the trench, they must fight through a swarm of TIE fighters. Han Solo's piloting skills make him ideal for the mission, but he leaves to pay his debt to Jabba the Hutt. The deck is stacked against the alliance, but they do have Luke, and Luke has the Force.

The battle rages, and many rebels are blasted apart. At last, Luke is alone in the trench with a single remaining proton torpedo. If he can fire it, he might destroy the Death Star. But Darth Vader is on his tail in a TIE fighter and gaining on him. It's clear that Vader will fire first. This race between Luke and Vader is the final confrontation.

Then there's an explosion. Darth Vader has been winged by Han Solo, who is joining in the battle after all. Vader spirals away, out of the game. Luke fires his proton torpedo. It zooms down the hatch into the guts of the Death Star. A brilliant explosion lights up the galaxy. That explosion is the climax of the story.

But why does Han Solo return? Is this a *deus ex machina?* Not at all. Han Solo left in the first place because it was logical for him to leave, given his values. He came back because it was logical for him to return, given his values. (See Chapter 7 for a discussion of values and the importance of giving your characters conflicting values.)

Han Solo values two things: His life and his reputation. Repeatedly through the movie, you see Solo doing things to rescue himself and others, and he makes it clear that he likes being alive. But you also see him flinch when Princess Leia or Luke insults him. Han Solo sees himself as a bold, adventurous cowboy, afraid of nothing, able to shoot a bounty hunter in a cantina while wearing a cool, nonchalant grin.

Han decides to skip out of the final battle because he wants to pay off Jabba the Hutt, who's put a price on his head. That's reasonable, because Solo values his life. But Luke accuses him of being a coward before he leaves. That nettles Han more than he's willing to admit. He leaves the planet, but he can't get that accusation out of his head. Is he a coward? No. He's afraid of nothing. Han finally decides that he'd rather risk his life than be thought a coward. So he returns, rescues Luke from Vader, and enables the defeat of the Death Star. Ultimately, it's the victory of one of Han Solo's values over another that makes the ending of *Star Wars* work.

Summarizing Your Three-Act Structure for Interested Parties

When selling your story to an agent or editor, we recommend that you present your three-act structure as a five-sentence paragraph with this format:

1. The first sentence sets up the story by introducing the lead characters and the story world.

2. The second sentence summarizes the beginning and presents the first disaster to force a decision that frames the story question.

3. The third sentence summarizes the first part of the middle, leading up to the second disaster.

4. The fourth sentence summarizes the second part of the middle, leading up to the third disaster, which forces a decision to pursue the final confrontation.

5. The fifth sentence explains how the story ends, including the final confrontation and any wrap-up that you feel you need to explain.

In this section, we provide some example paragraphs that summarize three-act structures, and we help you write your own.

Examples: Summarizing The Matarese Circle and Pride and Prejudice

Before you try writing a three-act structure for your novel, check out some examples. We can summarize the three-act structure of Robert Ludlum's classic spy novel *The Matarese Circle* in a paragraph — the three disasters are in italics:

Brandon Scofield is an aging U.S. covert agent who's been inexplicably pushed out of the service on an idiotic pretext. After evading an assassination attempt, he discovers that *his own government is trying to kill him and that his only hope is to join forces with Vasili Taleniekov, the ex-KGB agent who murdered Scofield's wife.* Forging an uneasy alliance, Scofield and Taleniekov uncover a shadowy international conspiracy led by corporate billionaires, but the stakes rise when *one of the billionaires is murdered by his controller.* After pursuing leads in Russia, Germany, and England, Scofield must make a hard decision when *his girlfriend Toni and his ally Taleniekov are kidnapped by the conspirators,* who invite Scofield to surrender to them in Boston. Scofield flies to Boston, discovers one final shattering secret, and then walks unarmed into the lair of the conspirators to "surrender."

The Matarese Circle is arguably Robert Ludlum's finest single-book work. (Ludlum also authored a three-book series involving Jason Bourne, which is his best-known work.) *The Matarese Circle* is a complex plot-driven book, so the paragraph about three-act structure is necessarily complex. We've hinted at the ending without giving it away. Now we analyze the three disasters:

- ✔ **Scofield discovers that his own government tried to kill him and that he must team up with his archenemy Taleniekov to survive.** This disaster forces Scofield into the wrenching decision to join up with Taleniekov.

- ✔ **One of the billionaire conspirators is murdered by his controller.** This escalates the tension. When you discover that the powerful enemy you feared is a weak pawn in the hands of someone even more powerful, your stakes go up dramatically.

- ✔ **Scofield's girlfriend Toni and his ally Taleniekov are kidnapped.** This third disaster forces Scofield's terrifying decision to agree to a final confrontation with the shadowy circle of conspirators.

Now we consider a complex character-driven novel, Jane Austen's *Pride and Prejudice,* which has many strong characters and several story threads. Here is our one-paragraph summary of its three-act structure, taking care to focus on the main story thread — the romance between Lizzie Bennet and Mr. Darcy:

When Lizzie Bennet and her sisters meet some wealthy young men at a ball, Lizzie takes a keen dislike to one of them, Mr. Darcy. Lizzie's sister Jane falls in love with Darcy's friend Mr. Bingley, and Lizzie takes an interest in Mr. Wickham — whom she then learns *has been financially ruined by Darcy.* When Lizzie visits her married friend in Hunsford some months later, Mr. Darcy seeks her out and proposes marriage to her, but *she rejects him flat out.* Lizzie soon finds out that Darcy is a better man than she had thought, and she is beginning to regret her rejection when her sister *Lydia runs away to live in sin with Mr. Wickham.* When Lizzie learns that Mr. Darcy rescued her sister's reputation and when he learns that she no longer hates him, the two realize that they were made for each other.

Note that this analysis presents the story with Lizzie as the lead character, but all three disasters are disasters from Darcy's point of view. Here are the disasters:

- **Wickham tells Lizzie that Darcy financially ruined him.** This lie causes Lizzie to treat Darcy even more coldly. However, Darcy is a man who decides on a thing and then stays resolute to it. He continues to pursue Lizzie, however hopeless it seems.

- **Darcy bungles his marriage proposal, offending Lizzie badly and causing her to burn her bridges in rejecting him.** Darcy now knows that he has no chance, and yet he remains hopelessly in love with her.

- **Wickham runs off with Lizzie's sister Lydia, ruining the marriage prospects of all five sisters.** Darcy is tormented by this, knowing that Wickham could not have seduced Lydia if he, Darcy, had not kept silent about Wickham's evil character. He decides to rescue Lydia, and this decision leads to the happy ending with Lizzie.

Describing your own three-act structure

We want to reiterate that you can develop your three-act structure at any time, depending on which creative paradigm works best for you (see Chapter 4 for details on these writing methods). If now is a good time to write your three-act structure, then here are some steps that should help you develop a one-paragraph summary that you can use to explain your story to an interested agent or editor:

1. **Write a first sentence that introduces one or more characters and sets up the conflict.**

   Name your principal characters and tell any essential information. You may even include key backstory details.

2. **Write three sentences, each describing a major disaster in your story.**

   The three disasters should be from a single character's point of view, usually the lead character's.

3. **Write a final sentence that explains how you resolve the story.**

   If you don't reveal the details of the resolution, you should at least give some clear hints about how the story question will be answered.

4. Rework the sentence containing your first disaster, adding in the decision that sets the story goal.

5. Rework the sentence containing your third disaster, explaining why it forces the final confrontation.

6. Polish the entire paragraph until it flows naturally.

7. Save your one-paragraph summary in a safe place and come back to it periodically and make sure that it actually describes the story you're writing.

You can change this paragraph if you need to. It's okay for your story to evolve as you get to understand your characters better and as you discover what really drives your story.

Additional reading for high-level story structure

Here are some of our favorite books that deal with high-level story structure:

✔ *Plot & Structure,* **by James Scott Bell (Writer's Digest):** This book is ideal for beginning writers, although writers at all levels find it useful.

✔ *Techniques of the Selling Writer,* **by Dwight Swain (University of Oklahoma Press):** We especially recommend to you the chapters titled "Fiction Strategy" and "Beginning,

Middle, End" for plenty of detailed info on story structure.

✔ *The Writer's Journey,* **by Christopher Vogler (Michael Wiese Productions):** This book expands the usual three-act structure into a 12-step "Hero's Journey." Vogler calls the first disaster *crossing the threshold.* Depending on the story, he calls either the second or third disaster the *ordeal.*

Chapter 9

Synopsis, Scene List, and Scene: Your Middle Layers of Plot

- -

In This Chapter

▶ Deciding which layer to write first

▶ Writing a two-page synopsis

▶ Writing your scene list

▶ Structuring scenes

- -

The modern novel's plot typically has six layers of complexity. In Chapter 8, we discuss the two highest layers of plot, the storyline and the three-act structure. In this chapter, we look at the middle three layers: synopsis, scene list, and scene. We cover the lowest layer of plot — action, dialogue, and all that — in Chapter 10.

Before looking at the middle layers in detail, consider the order in which you'd like to work on your story structure. The next section gives you a run-down on the approach you should use regarding your writing order.

Deciding Which Order to Work In

Sometimes success depends on doing things in the right order. If you put on your socks first and then your shoes, your day will go a lot smoother than if you put on your shoes first and then your socks. But sometimes, the order doesn't matter. Your day will go just as well, whether you put on your left or your right sock first. Yet you probably put them on in the same order every day because putting one of them on first feels right.

Developing your story structure is one of those things where the order doesn't matter, though you probably do have a preference. In Chapter 4, we talk about the importance of having a creative paradigm, which sets the order in which you create your novel. All that really matters is that you choose the creative paradigm that works best for you. In Chapter 4, we list four very common ones (Seat-of-the-Pants, Edit-As-You-Go, Snowflake, Outline), but you're free to develop your own paradigm that works best for you.

Your creative paradigm will likely be either bottom-up or top-down:

- **Top-down:** A top-down paradigm starts with the highest layer of complexity and works down to the details. The Snowflake paradigm is a top-down approach, because you start with a high-level concept — a storyline — and expand it to a three-act structure and go on to lower and more detailed layers of complexity. The Outline paradigm is also a top-down approach.

 If you prefer a top-down approach, read this chapter in order: You first see how to write a synopsis, then a scene list, and then a scene.

 When you're ready to create your story structure, write your storyline first and then define the three-act structure of your novel, using the ideas in Chapter 8. After you have those, write a synopsis and then a scene list using the ideas in this chapter.

- **Bottom-up:** A bottom-up paradigm starts with the lowest layer of complexity — the actual words of the story — and organizes it in higher and higher levels. The Seat-of-the-Pants paradigm is a bottom-up approach, because you write your story first and then you analyze it later and eventually you figure out what it all means. Likewise, the Edit-As-You-Go paradigm is bottom-up.

 If you prefer a bottom-up approach, read the main sections of this chapter in reverse order. You see first how to structure your scenes, then how to make a scene list, and then how to write a synopsis.

 When you're ready to create your story, write your first draft first and then analyze each scene's structure to make sure it's pulling its weight as a scene. When you know that all your scenes are well-structured, make a scene list and rearrange your scenes to be in the best possible order. Then write your synopsis from your scene list. If it's a good synopsis, you should be able to summarize it into a single paragraph that represents the three-act structure that we discuss in Chapter 8. When you have a solid one-paragraph summary, boil it down to a one-sentence summary, and you'll have the storyline that we talk about in Chapter 8.

Writing the Synopsis

Almost always, you must have a synopsis to sell your novel. A *synopsis* is a document roughly two pages long that describes your plot, and it's an essential part of your book's sales process. To get an agent, or to sell your book to a publisher, you need to write a query or a proposal (see Chapter 16 for all the details on writing these). Either an agent or a publisher will want to see a synopsis. Therefore, knowing how to write a good synopsis is mandatory for every novelist.

Writing a two-page synopsis seems to be the most traumatic writing experience many novelists ever face. We've seen excellent writers paralyzed because they didn't know what's expected. Not only that, many editors agree that the synopsis is boring. Most writers hate writing the synopsis and tend to write either too much or too little. In this section, we show you the simple principles you need to get it right and do it quickly.

There really isn't any mystery. Here are the basics:

- Write in third person.
- Write in present tense.
- Summarize your entire story in about two single-spaced pages. That gives you about 1,000 words.

A typical novel has around 100 scenes. If you include every single one in a synopsis of 1,000 words, then you'd have to shrink every scene down to 10 words, which is just not enough. What's a writer to do?

Each paragraph in your synopsis should summarize a *sequence* of related scenes, not a single scene. A sequence may be anywhere from three to seven scenes. The paragraph strips that sequence down to the essentials, focusing on those scenes that are most important and skipping completely over scenes that are peripheral.

You have two easy ways to build your synopsis, depending on whether you're working top-down or bottom-up: Either you start with your three-act structure and flesh it out, or you start with your scene list and slim it down.

Taking it from the top: Fleshing out your three-act structure

If you're a top-down thinker, then start with your three-act structure. (See Chapter 8 for a thorough explanation of the three-act structure.) You should have a one-paragraph summary that defines your three-act structure. That paragraph has five sentences. Expand them as follows:

1. **Expand the first sentence (the story setup) into a paragraph or two, describing the story backdrop.**

2. **Expand the second sentence (leading up to the first disaster) into about half a page.**

   Use two or three paragraphs to tell how you'll get to your crucial first disaster and the decision that defines your story question.

3. **Expand the third sentence (leading up to the second disaster) into another half page.**

   Again, use no more than three or four paragraphs to summarize the high points of the story. Don't worry about glossing over details or ignoring some story threads. Cut to the bone.

4. **Expand the fourth sentence (leading up to the third disaster) into yet another half page.**

   Once again, use no more than three or four paragraphs. Be brutal in leaving out details. The publisher does not care about those cool subplots you cooked up; the publisher cares whether the main story works.

5. **Expand the fifth sentence (the ending) into three paragraphs that tell how the ending works out.**

You really don't need any more than that for your synopsis. Don't allow a mere two pages of typing to traumatize you. You may find that your synopsis is boring. Guess what — editors expect it to be boring. Your synopsis is like a table of contents; its purpose is to show that you have enough meat in your story to fill up a book. Nobody reads a table of contents for entertainment, and nobody reads a synopsis for entertainment, either.

Bottoms up! Building around sequences of scenes

If you're a bottom-up thinker, then you can use your scene list to create a synopsis. Your scene list (which we discuss later in "Developing Your Scene List") will be much too long, so you have to trim it down harshly. Here's how:

1. **Cut and paste your list of scenes into a fresh document in your word processor.**

   This probably means that you'll have about 100 very short paragraphs in your document to start with. Your goal is to combine these into 15 to 20 longer paragraphs, taking up no more than two pages.

2. **Start at the top, scan down through the first few scenes, and decide which ones seem to be related.**

   Pick three to seven scenes. These scenes form a *scene sequence*.

3. **Add in some blank lines above the scene sequence and write a new, fresh paragraph that summarizes the gist of that scene sequence.**

   Shoot for a paragraph of five to eight lines. Delete the original scene sequence, because you now have a single paragraph that summarizes those scenes.

4. **Repeat Steps 2 and 3 until you've summarized and deleted all the original scenes.**

5. **Read through the whole synopsis and edit it down to two pages.**

   Be disciplined. Be brutal if you must. Your agent or publisher will not love you if you turn in a 50-page synopsis.

Knowing how much detail you need

Each paragraph in your synopsis summarizes a whole sequence of scenes in your novel. Your synopsis is high-level summary, and it can't tell all the details of your story. It can't tell all your amazing plot twists. It likely can't even mention all your characters.

Your synopsis should focus on the three or four most important characters. Mentioning some of the minor characters in passing is okay, but stick to the story thread for your lead character. Explaining the theme of your story isn't necessary. (See Chapter 11 for a discussion of your theme and how to find it.) You may not even know your theme yet when you write your synopsis. That's okay.

The bottom line is this: If your synopsis has more than two single-spaced pages, then it has too much detail. Cut some out, and keep cutting until you're down to two pages. This discipline will force you to think about which parts of your story are critical and which are just nice extras.

The synopsis must stand alone. Assume that anyone reading the synopsis knows *nothing* about your book. When you introduce each new character, add a phrase or even a sentence to tell just a little about him. You don't need much — just enough to make your synopsis comprehensible.

Example: A synopsis of Ender's Game

Ender's Game is a science fiction novel by Orson Scott Card. The novel won both the Hugo Award and the Nebula Award. (If you read only one science fiction novel in your life, make it *Ender's Game*. You won't be disappointed.)

We've chosen this novel as an example because it's relatively simple to analyze. The novel's lead character is Andrew "Ender" Wiggin, and he's the POV character for the vast majority of scenes. The story unfolds linearly. The novel itself is very strong in four of the pillars of fiction that we identify in Chapter 2: story world, character, plot, and theme.

Ender Wiggin is a boy chosen for rigorous military training in Battle School. Earth is expecting a fresh attack soon by an alien race of ant-like "buggers" who nearly destroyed humanity 80 years earlier. The buggers have superior technology and will certainly overwhelm Earth — unless a leader as talented as Alexander the Great can be found. Is Ender that leader? If so, can he be trained in time to save his people from annihilation? That's the story question that *Ender's Game* raises.

Because we want to avoid spoilers, we analyze only the first quarter of the book — Act 1 of the novel. Here is our synopsis of that first quarter, which summarizes 31 scenes:

An impending alien invasion is threatening earth in the near future, and military leaders around the planet are looking for a young leader with the brains and guts to save human civilization. After three years of being electronically monitored by the military authorities, 6-year-old Ender Wiggin finally has his electronic monitor removed. Everyone thinks that he's been rejected as a candidate for military training, but the top brass have a real-life test lined up for him.

When several bullies surround Ender after school to beat him up, he first tries to talk his way out of trouble, but then he launches a savage attack on the leader. To ensure that the bullies never bother him again, Ender brutalizes the downed boy and gives the others a terrifying warning.

Hopeful that Ender might be "the one," the military takes him from his family and sends him with a number of other boys on the next launch to the orbiting Battle School. The officer in charge, Colonel Graff, praises Ender so lavishly that the other boys make him a pariah. Ender feels lonely and afraid, but he soon befriends one of the insiders, Alai, and helps him take over leadership of the launch group. Soon enough, Ender and Alai have welded a dysfunctional unit into a team.

Before Ender can relax, the trainers promote him into a mock army with much older boys. Ender's new commander, Bonzo Madrid, rejects Ender as a useless paperweight and orders him to do nothing during the mock battles that his army fights. In his first few battles, Ender obeys Bonzo's orders. In his fourth, Ender disobeys orders, fires on the enemy, and turns certain defeat into a draw. Humiliated, Bonzo retaliates by trading Ender away to another army and then beating him up. Resolving never to be a victim again, Ender registers for personal combat training.

Developing Your Scene List

A scene list helps you keep track of your scenes. To develop a scene list, you write a short summary of each scene. Managing all those summaries is challenging, but in this section, we show you two common techniques to make it easier.

Unlike with the synopsis (see the preceding section), you don't have to develop a scene list to sell your book. If you don't write a scene list, nobody will ever know or care. So why write one?

Scenes are the fundamental unit of fiction. Therefore, making a list of your scenes gives you a powerful organizing tool for designing your story before you write it and for editing your novel after you write it. Which would you rather shuffle around: 100 lines summarizing your scenes or 400 pages of text?

Back before computers were common, writers made scene lists by writing a sentence for each scene on a 3-x-5 index card. Then they could easily spread out their story on the living room floor and move things around until they got the scenes in the perfect order — which worked great until Rover chased Lassie through the pile, or until the writer wanted to try out an alternative arrangement without losing the original order. In either case, a stack of 3-x-5 cards was a hassle.

We recommend replacing those 3-x-5 cards with a computer. You can organize all your scenes using a word processor or a text editor, but a spreadsheet works even better. Try programs such as Microsoft Excel; Numbers (part of the Apple iWork suite); the free OpenOffice suite (www.openoffice.org), which runs on all computer systems; or Google Spreadsheet (docs.google.com), which you can access via the Internet anywhere, anytime. If you've never used a spreadsheet, ask a spreadsheet-savvy friend to teach you how to do simple lists. You can pick up the essentials in a few minutes, and you'll find it an extraordinary tool for managing your list of scenes.

You have two easy ways to fill in the details in your scene list, depending on whether you're working top-down or bottom-up. Either you can start from your synopsis and flesh it out, or you can start with your manuscript and summarize it.

Top-down: Fleshing out your synopsis

If you're a top-down thinker, then start with your synopsis, which is roughly a two-page summary of your story (see the earlier section "Writing the Synopsis"). Look at each paragraph in the synopsis and ask how you can break that down into scenes. Each scene will take place at a single location and at a single point in time. It will have a few characters, and it will move the plot forward.

For each scene that you imagine, add one line to your spreadsheet (or to a 3-x-5 card) describing the basics of what will happen in that scene. You don't have to spell out all the details. Leave that fun for later. Right now, just get the big chunks right.

Try to break each paragraph of your synopsis into several distinct scenes. (Three to seven scenes is about right.) When you get to the end of the synopsis, your scene list is done. If you're using a spreadsheet program, save it as a file.

Feel free to try out different orders of scenes in your list. Editing your scene list in a spreadsheet is extremely easy. You can delete lines, add new lines, edit them, and move them around. Every time you make significant changes to your scene list, save it as a new file. (This is much easier than trying to make copies of 3-x-5 cards.)

Bottom-up: Summarizing your manuscript

If you're a bottom-up thinker, making a scene list from your manuscript is simple. Read through the manuscript and summarize each scene in a single line of your spreadsheet (or on a 3-x-5 card). Remember that you don't have to capture all the details. Your manuscript already has all those details anyway, so you won't lose them.

Skimming through your manuscript and adding a line in your spreadsheet (or a card in your stack of 3-x-5 cards) for every scene in your manuscript takes only an hour or two. This may be the most valuable hour you ever spend on your entire novel. When you finish, you have a concise summary of your story that you can see all in one place.

If you're truly a bottom-up thinker, you probably have a large amount of work to do to reorganize your story (especially if you're a Seat-of-the-Pants writer). Your scene list is your power tool for helping you do that organization. Every line in your scene list represents hundreds of sentences in your first draft. Editing your scene list is far, far easier than shuffling scenes around in that big bad bulky manuscript. (See Chapter 13 for more comments on editing the high-level structure of your story.)

Example: A scene list of Ender's Game

We continue using *Ender's Game* as an example story. In the earlier section "Writing the Synopsis," we show an example synopsis of the first quarter of the novel. Here is the corresponding scene list, which we created by reading each scene in the first several chapters of the novel and writing a sentence or three about each one. Note that our scene list has considerably more detail than our synopsis.

- ✔ Two military officers discuss Ender Wiggin. He looks like a good candidate for Battle School, but is he too malleable? They decide to surround him with enemies and see how he does before making a final decision.

- ✔ The doctor removes Ender's monitor, a traumatic procedure that nearly kills him.

- ✔ Ender returns to his normal classroom, where the other children see that he's had his monitor removed. A pack of bullies attacks Ender after school. He defends himself by brutally attacking the leader of the gang.

- ✔ The officers wonder if Ender defended himself so savagely for the "right reasons." They agree to watch how Ender handles his cruel brother Peter.

- ✔ Peter bullies Ender and threatens to kill him, but his sister Valentine talks Peter out of it.

- ✔ The officers discuss how to get Ender to leave home and decide that dishonesty is the best policy, although they will tell him the truth if necessary.

- ✔ Colonel Graff visits Ender, questions him about his motives in the attack on the bullies, and then offers him a chance to go to Battle School.

- ✔ Ender is reluctant to accept the offer but finally realizes that he really has little choice and agrees to go to Battle School with the next launch group.

- ✔ The officers worry that Ender will fit in too well with the other boys, harming his military creativity, so they decide to isolate him psychologically from his peers.

- ✔ Lavishly praised by Colonel Graff during the launch, Ender is bullied by one of the other boys, Bernard. Ender defends himself and accidentally breaks Bernard's arm.

- ✔ Ender confronts Colonel Graff for inciting Bernard to bully him. Graff responds brusquely, and Ender realizes that he can't count on Graff ever to help him.

✔ The officers worry that they'll ruin Ender and decide that he will be allowed to have friends but he must never have a parent figure.

✔ Ender settles into his room and gets oriented to Battle School, but he is already a pariah within his peer group of fellow "launchies."

✔ Ender feels lonely and afraid, but he resolves to be strong and show no fear.

✔ Ender goes to the game room, plays an older boy in a difficult war game, and wins two out of three. The older boys sneer at him because he's so young.

✔ Ender uses his computer system to undermine Bernard, the bully of his launch group. He succeeds and gains a few friends, but Bernard is now his confirmed enemy.

✔ The officers are worried that Ender is poisoning his launch group by causing division. They decide to do nothing, forcing Ender to weld his peers together through his own efforts.

✔ Ender befriends Alai, Bernard's best friend. Soon, Alai is the leader of the entire launch group, and there are no longer any outsiders.

✔ Ender plays a video game and finds a way to beat the unbeatable Giant — by doing the unthinkable.

✔ The officers are shocked at the way Ender has found to beat the Giant and decide to let him rest for a short time before his next ordeal.

✔ Ender agrees to help Alai build a new security system but then discovers he has been promoted to one of the "armies" — at a far earlier age than anyone has ever been promoted before.

✔ Ender goes to the game room and plays until the game shuts down and the computer orders him to report to his new "Salamander Army."

✔ Ender reports to Salamander Army for duty and is completely rejected by his commander, Bonzo Madrid. He is befriended by outcast Petra, the only girl in the unit.

✔ Ender goes to the bathroom and is recognized by boys in another army, who remember his exploits in the game room. He realizes that at least a few of the older boys know who he is, and he resolves that soon everybody will know him.

✔ Ender gets some training from Petra, but Bonzo refuses to let him practice with the rest of the army.

✔ Lacking training partners in his own army, Ender begins training the young boys from his launch group. His commander Bonzo orders him to stop doing so.

✔ Ender persuades Bonzo to let him train the launchies in order to make himself valuable enough that Bonzo can trade him away to another army.

✔ Ender participates in his first mock battle under Bonzo's strict orders to do nothing. His army loses and at the end, he is the only soldier not totally "disabled." After the battle, everyone realizes that Ender could have forced a draw if he had disobeyed orders and fired his weapon.

✔ Ender takes part in another mock battle. His side is losing, and so Ender violates his orders by shooting several of the enemy soldiers. This turns certain defeat into a draw, but his commander Bonzo is furious with him.

✔ Bonzo trades Ender to Rat army, then beats him up for disobeying orders.

✔ Unwilling to be beaten up ever again, Ender registers for a course in personal combat.

Extending your scene list

If you use a spreadsheet to manage your scene list, you'll find that you can extend it in many ways. You can add a column to track the POV character for each scene. (See Chapter 7 for an explanation of POV characters.) You can add a column to track the date and time of each scene, which is great if you have a complex timeline for your story. You can add a column to estimate the number of pages for each scene. Since spreadsheets make it easy to add a column of numbers, you can even make a projection of how long your novel will be. Spreadsheets also make it easy to color-code rows or columns, so if you want to assign a different color to each POV character, you can do that easily.

If you rearrange the scenes in your spreadsheet, those extra columns won't get scrambled, because spreadsheet software makes it easy for you to move rows as single units. (Again, ask a tech-savvy friend if you need help on this.)

Setting Up the Structure of Individual Scenes

The scene is the fundamental unit of fiction. Therefore, you must master the art of writing scenes. Each scene is a mini-story, with a beginning, middle, and end of its own. At the end of each scene, at least one of the characters must have gone through some sort of change. Otherwise, the scene isn't pulling its weight. Modern fiction has two different kinds of scenes, each with a simple structure. In this section, we show you both structures and explain how they work together to give your reader a powerful emotional experience.

A *scene* takes place in a single location at a single point in time. It has a beginning, a middle, and an end, and its purpose is to give the reader a powerful emotional experience by showing the scene while focusing on one special character — the focal character. You want your reader to identify emotionally with that focal character.

In most cases, the focal character is identical to the POV character. If you use an omniscient or multiple point of view, the scene has more than one POV character, but the dominant one is your focal character. If you use a third-person objective point of view, then you don't have any POV character, but your scene still has a focal character. (See Chapter 7 for a discussion of point-of-view, focal characters, and POV characters.)

Fiction is infinitely diverse. Anything can happen. And yet the structure of scenes in most modern fiction is exceptionally simple. That's because scenes are quite short. You can classify each scene based on what happens in its beginning, middle, and end.

A modern novel normally has several dozen scenes. Many novels have more than a hundred. Each scene can range in length from a few paragraphs to a dozen pages or more.

As we note at the beginning of this section, modern fiction has only two basic kinds of scenes:

- ✔ **Proactive scene:** This type of scene includes a goal, a conflict, and a setback.
- ✔ **Reactive scene:** This type of scene includes a reaction, a dilemma, and a decision.

In the following sections, we look at each of these scene types in detail.

Setting the proactive scene

The most common type of scene follows a precise sequence. We call it a *proactive* scene because it's easier than calling it a *goal-conflict-setback* scene. In your novel, probably the majority of your scenes will be proactive scenes. A typical proactive scene looks like this:

1. **Goal: At the beginning of the scene, the POV character has some goal that he hopes to achieve by the end of the scene.**

2. **Conflict: During the middle of the scene, the POV character tries repeatedly to achieve his goal, but he runs into obstacle after obstacle as the scene unfolds.**

3. **Setback: At the end of the scene, the POV character hits a nasty setback.**

   Normally, he fails to reach his goal and is now worse off than he was before. Occasionally, he achieves what he wanted, but something bad happens to nullify this minor victory.

Here's a summary of an example proactive scene:

> So far, the writing conference has cost you $400, a six-hour flight, and a lot of apologizing for missing your son's rugby tournament, but it's worth it. You have a meeting with an agent, and you're sure she's the one who'll take you over that last hurdle to publication.
>
> You sit down at the table, ready to start the nice-weather-we're-having routine. Right off the bat, she begins grilling you on your story — plot, characters, and the ontological implications of time travel. You stumble through your answers. As her eyes get colder, you begin stuttering. When you reach a frazzled state of incoherent mumbling, she asks to read your chapter. As her finger moves down the page, her face tightens into a hard scowl. "Sorry," she says. "This scene has no structure at all. I wouldn't touch this project with a sixty-foot pole."

Here, the goal is to interest the editor in your novel, the conflict arises when she asks you a long series of tough questions, and the setback occurs when she rejects your work and humiliates you.

What is your scene's goal?

You should try to establish two things very early in each proactive scene:

- ✔ Who is the primary POV character?
- ✔ What is his or her goal for this scene?

The goal for each proactive scene should be

- ✔ **Simple:** You want the goal to be simple to understand because a scene is simple — it's one small piece of your story.
- ✔ **Objective:** A goal should be objective so your reader can easily visualize what success looks like.

✔ **Worthwhile:** Otherwise, why would you be wasting ink on it?

✔ **Achievable:** A goal that can't be achieved within the scene kills the tension for that scene.

✔ **Difficult:** A trivially easy goal won't keep your reader up late flipping the pages.

Conflict is key

Most of your scene should be conflict. We recommend that a proactive scene be about 80 to 90 percent conflict. That's a lot. If you establish your goal early, then you can spend almost the entire scene throwing one obstacle after another at your POV character. Your character will dodge those obstacles and will keep trying to reach his goal. Don't let him give up early. Make him sweat. The harder you work him, the more your reader will invest in him emotionally. You can and must be cruel to your POV character; your readers will love you for it. In Chapter 10, we discuss techniques for showing this conflict in exquisite detail.

Hitting the setback

We recommend that you hit your POV character with a setback as late in the proactive scene as possible. It's quite possible to let the hammer fall in the closing paragraph, the last sentence, even the final word. Here are some ideas to keep in mind with your setback:

✔ It should be an objective failure to reach the goal of the scene. (When the editor says no, that's pretty objective. You can hear it.)

✔ It should be a result of the POV character's persistence in trying to achieve his goal.

✔ It should leave the POV character worse off than he was at the start of the scene.

✔ It should be unexpected, if possible, but it should also follow logically from the way the scene plays out.

Following up with the reactive scene

The reactive scene usually follows immediately after a proactive scene and looks like this:

1. **Reaction: At the beginning of the reactive scene, the POV character is reeling from the setback in the previous scene.**

   She spends some time reacting emotionally and finally gets control of her feelings.

2. **Dilemma: During the middle of the reactive scene, the POV character has to figure out what to do next.**

   If her setback was significant enough, then she has no good options. She has a dilemma, and she must think hard to choose from the least-bad option.

3. **Decision: Eventually, the POV character makes a decision.**

   That provides her with a goal for her next scene, which is normally a proactive scene.

Here's a summary of an example reactive scene:

> For a second, you can't breathe. In your worst nightmare, this isn't what you expected. You stumble away in a fog, hoping desperately that you don't break down before you can find a place to be alone. You stagger outside into the blinding sun and find a safe, quiet spot under an ancient oak tree. After a few minutes, the mental haze starts to lift. You wipe your eyes and take a few deep breaths. You release your manuscript from your clammy death-grip. Okay, fine. You struck out. What now? You could go back and argue with her, but that's probably going to make things worse. You could quit writing, but . . . writing is your life. You could try to figure out what she meant by "scene structure" but honestly, you thought you knew that already. What the heck are you going to do? A friend walks by, sees your teary face, and asks if you're okay. You explain what's happened. Your friend suggests that you take your manuscript over to the walk-in critique table and have a professional writer give you some constructive suggestions. "You're crazy," you say. "How much more is that going to cost me?" Your friend pulls you to your feet and picks up your manuscript. "Didn't you pay attention in orientation? It's free. They said it's the most overlooked part of the conference. But you'd better hurry, because they close in ten minutes." You feel a grin sliding onto your face. "I'm on my way."

In the example, the reaction to the rejection is visceral — you can't breathe. You stagger away. Your mind is in a fog. In your dilemma, you consider several options: arguing with the editor, quitting writing, and trying to figure things out on your own — all bad options. Your friend suggests a fourth option — getting some help at the walk-in critique table. That's an easy decision to make, once you learn that it's an option.

Going for the reaction

The *reaction* part of a reactive scene can be either long or short, depending on how big of a setback your character is responding to and on how emotional the character is. The reaction is mainly emotion. If your novel is an introspective one, then you can deliver many of your powerful emotional experiences right here in the reaction. If your novel is more geared to action, then you probably want to keep the reaction short and swift.

The reaction part of your reactive scene is raw emotion. It will last only as long as your POV character has emotions to spend on it. Eventually, your character will calm down and begin to think more rationally. That's when your reaction ends and you need to move on.

What is the dilemma?

The dilemma is not emotional; it's intellectual. Your POV character has a problem. How is she going to solve it? She has options, but all those options are bad options. If she has any good options, then you haven't given her a strong enough setback in the previous scene.

Your character will mull the options at some length. How long? That depends on how terrible the situation is and how good your character is at analyzing facts and making decisions. The dilemma may take a long time to sort through, or your character may zip through it quickly.

Deciding on the decision

At some point, your POV character has to decide. She can't dither forever. When she makes a decision, she needs to commit to it. A decision should have all these features:

- ✔ **Simple:** Your character needs clarity of vision with her decision.
- ✔ **Objective:** Your reader needs to be able to visualize exactly what your character wants next.
- ✔ **Worthwhile:** Your reader must believe the character would actually make this decision, based on her values.
- ✔ **Achievable:** Your reader must believe that success really may be just a chapter away.
- ✔ **Difficult:** Your reader must have some doubts that this decision will work.

At 3:00 a.m., your reader needs a reason to turn over the page instead of turning out the lights. A decision that's simple, objective, worthwhile, achievable, and difficult gives your reader that reason.

Notice that this decision sounds an awful lot like the goal of a proactive scene. That's exactly what a decision is — a choice to pursue a new goal.

Coming full circle with your scenes

A proactive scene starts a character out with a goal, hits him with loads of conflict, and then rocks him back with a setback. A reactive scene picks up immediately afterward, taking that character through an emotional reaction, then working him through an intellectual dilemma, and finally taking him to a decision — to pursue a new goal.

In theory, therefore, you can write a proactive scene and follow it up with a reactive scene and follow *that* with a new proactive scene, alternating forever. That's a fine theory, and it works often in practice but not always. Here are a couple of reasons you may not follow this strict alternation of proactive and reactive scenes in your fiction:

✔ **To pick up the pace of your story:** Modern commercial fiction often blazes through the story at a gallop. In fast-action fiction, the proactive scenes run long, and the author may fly through the reactive scene in a paragraph of narrative summary. The author may even skip the reactive scene, leaving it to the reader to figure out what reaction, dilemma, and decision the POV character worked through.

✔ **To switch POV characters after a scene:** If you do that, you probably can't show your POV character's emotive reaction from the setback in the previous scene. So when do you show it? Maybe later, when you switch back to that POV character for a new scene. Or maybe never, if the POV character can explain her reaction, dilemma, and decision to some other character.

Whether you show your reactive scene to the reader or not, you need to know what happens in it. That tells you what goal your character will have further down the road. Also, a lot depends on your genre, reader expectations, and your skill as an author. The modern trend is to cut reactive scenes to the bone.

Scene structure in Gone With the Wind

Consider this example early in the novel *Gone With the Wind*, by Margaret Mitchell. Scarlett O'Hara is infatuated with Ashley Wilkes and expects to induce him to marry her someday. When she discovers that Ashley has gotten engaged to Melanie Hamilton, Scarlett can hardly believe it and vows to speak to him at the next day's barbecue and ball at the Wilkes plantation. During the afternoon lull, when the other young women are napping, Scarlett steals away to confront Ashley in the infamous library scene. Here's an analysis of this proactive scene:

✔ **Goal:** Scarlett plans to meet Ashley, confess her love to him, and per-suade him to marry her instead of Melanie.

✔ **Conflict:** Ashley explains repeatedly that what Scarlett wants is impos-sible. They're too different. Yes, he cares for her, but he needs to marry a woman with a personality like his. Scarlett is furious as she sees her dream vanishing and tells him she hates him and slaps him hard. He leaves her, and she's so furious, she throws a fine china bowl across the room.

✔ **Setback:** Rhett Butler — a dishonorable scoundrel, has been napping on the couch and has heard every word. Rhett laughs at her, and Scarlett is humiliated.

A reactive scene follows directly after the proactive scene:

✔ **Reaction:** Scarlett is lightheaded with fury. She can hardly catch her breath and fears she may faint. She's terrified that word of her meeting with Ashley might get out. Nobody can know.

✔ **Dilemma:** Should Scarlett join the napping girls? Impossible — she over-hears them talking about her. Honey Wilkes is accusing Scarlett of being "fast." Should she leave? Impossible — Melanie is defending Scarlett, which is too hideous for words. Worse, Honey has somehow caught on that Scarlett loves Ashley. Should Scarlett go home? Impossible — that would leave the field open to Honey's poison gossip, and people might believe it. Scarlett can't continue listening, so she hurries downstairs and runs into Charles, who is Melanie's brother and Honey's beau. Charles sees that Scarlett is disturbed and takes her aside. Earlier in the day, Charles had become infatuated with her and even worked up the courage to ask her to marry him. Now, with news of war freshly arrived, Charles is planning to fight the Yankees. He asks if Scarlett will wait for him.

✔ **Decision:** Scarlett sees that if she marries Charles, it will solve all her problems. It will show Ashley that she was only flirting with him and wasn't serious. It will kill Melanie to have Scarlett as a sister-in-law. It will destroy Honey's plans to marry Charles. Scarlett decides to accept Charles's proposal on the spot.

Scene structure in *Patriot Games*

Now look at a much faster-paced example from a thriller, *Patriot Games,* writ-ten by Tom Clancy. The lead character is Jack Ryan, a history professor at the Naval Academy in Annapolis.

Recommended reading

Here are some books we recommend for further reading on these middle layers of story structure:

✔ *Story*, **by Robert McKee:** McKee is a famous teacher of screenwriting, and his book *Story* is a classic. (He and his book play a role in the movie *Adaptation*, starring Nicolas Cage.) This is an advanced book, which we recommend here mainly because of McKee's discussion of sequences of scenes. Although McKee doesn't say explicitly that each paragraph of your synopsis should summarize a sequence of scenes, we got this idea after reading his work. We believe he has highlighted this particular level of story structure better than anyone else has.

✔ *Techniques of the Selling Writer,* **by Dwight Swain:** Swain was a published fiction writer and a long-time teacher of fiction at the University of Oklahoma. He is best known for his analysis of *scenes* and *sequels.* Because both of these are actually scenes in the usual sense, we've taken the liberty of relabeling these. Swain's *scene* is identical to our *proactive scene,* and his *sequel* is identical to our *reactive scene.*

✔ *Plot & Structure,* **by James Scott Bell:** Bell is a best-selling novelist and former fiction columnist for *Writer's Digest.* His book is the best and simplest work we know on story structure.

Chapter one begins with Ryan on a research trip in London. After a day in the library, he has just met up with his wife and daughter in Hyde Park, when they hear an explosion only 50 feet away. Ryan turns and sees two gunman shooting up both sides of a disabled Rolls Royce with automatic weapons. Here's an analysis of the proactive scene and the reactive scene that follows:

✔ **Goal:** Ryan instantly decides to stop this attack — with his own body.

✔ **Conflict:** Ryan charges the gunman on the near side of the car and blindsides him with a flying tackle that snaps bones. Ryan snatches the gunman's pistol, knowing that he still needs to take out the man on the other side, who has an AK-47. But what about the man he's just tackled? Is he conscious? There's no time to find out, so Ryan pumps a bullet into the man's hip to disable him. He locates the other gunman, who has now discarded his AK-47 for a pistol. The gunman sees Jack. Both men fire. Jack feels a fiery impact in his left shoulder, but his own bullet hits the terrorist in the chest. Jack squeezes off another shot that hits the killer in the face, killing him instantly.

✔ **Setback:** Ryan himself is shot — quite badly.

✔ **Reaction:** Ryan feels dizzy, breathless, gasping for air.

✔ **Dilemma:** One of the palace guards is racing toward Ryan with a gun. The man can't possibly know that Ryan is a good guy. Jack is holding a gun at the scene of a terrorist attack. What should he do?

✔ **Decision:** Ryan spends no time agonizing over this dilemma. He takes the clip out of his pistol, drops it on the ground, sets the gun down, too, and steps away from them. He'll just have to trust that the guardsman won't shoot him.

Chapter 10

Action, Dialogue, and More: The Lowest Layer of Your Plot

. . . .

In This Chapter

▶ Writing action

▶ Portraying dialogue, thoughts, and emotion

▶ Using description

▶ Reliving the past with flashbacks

▶ Fast-forwarding with narrative summary

▶ Putting it all together

. . . .

The modern novel has six layers of complexity in its plot. Chapter 8 explains the first two layers, storyline and three-act structure. Chapter 9 covers the middle three layers, synopsis, scene list, and scene. In this chapter, we discuss the lowest layer of plot, in which your story unfolds paragraph by paragraph.

Your goal as a novelist is to give your reader a powerful emotional experience. Most of the techniques for doing that require you to plug your reader directly into the senses of your point-of-view (POV) character. When an editor asks you to "show, don't tell" your story, this is what she's asking you to do.

You have five primary tools for showing your story: action, dialogue, interior emotion, interior monologue, and description. You can use action and dialogue for any character in any scene. You can use interior emotion and interior monologue only for your POV characters. Normally, you can use description only for your non-POV characters, with a few important exceptions. You also have two other tools for your story — flashback and narrative summary. Each of these has a place if you handle them right.

To become a successful fiction writer, you need to understand the art of combining all these tools together to give your reader the illusion of actually being one of the characters in your story. In this chapter, we describe the tools and explain how they work together.

Using Seven Core Tools for Showing and Telling

Have you ever had an agent or editor scrawl, "show, don't tell," on your manuscript and return it to you without further explanation? Isn't that infuriating? Of course it is, for the simple reason that the editor has *told* you to "show, don't tell," but she has not *shown* you how to "show, don't tell." Editors never explain what "show, don't tell" means because they assume you already know it.

Showing means presenting the story to the reader using sensory information. The reader wants to see the story, hear it, smell it, feel it, and taste it, all the while experiencing the thoughts and feelings of a living, breathing character. *Telling* means summarizing the story for the reader in a way that skips past the sensory information and goes straight to the facts.

You have five main tools that you can use for showing your story. In order of their importance to you, these are

- ✔ Action
- ✔ Dialogue
- ✔ Interior emotion
- ✔ Interior monologue
- ✔ Description

You can mix these as you like within a paragraph, so long as it makes sense to do so. You can even mix them within a sentence. But you don't have to mix them. If you like, you can have an entire paragraph or more that uses just one of these tools.

Please note that the previously-mentioned tools can also be used in narrative summary to *tell* your story. Since we are most interested in how to use these to *show* your story, we need to sharpen our definitions of action, dialogue, interior emotion, interior monologue, and description so that they refer specifically to *showing*, not *telling*. See the following sections for exact definitions of what we mean by all of these terms, along with examples of how to use them.

You also have two other tools at your disposal:

- ✔ **Flashback:** In a flashback, you transition back in time to an earlier scene where you show part of the story using all the usual suspects — action, dialogue, interior emotion, interior monologue, and description — and then you transition back to the current time. You must provide the reader with some sort of cue to signal both the beginning and end of the flashback.

> ✔ **Narrative summary:** Narrative summary is what editors call *telling*. Narrative summary is a concise and efficient way to pass lots of information to the reader. It bypasses your reader's sensory organs and goes straight to the cognitive center of his mind.

In this section, we analyze these seven tools and show you how to put them together effectively at the lowest layer of plot complexity — to show and tell your story like a professional fiction writer.

Action

Action is stuff happening right now, instant by instant. Action never summarizes; action shows. Beginning writers often imagine that action is about big stuff happening fast — car chases, gun battles, and exploding helicopters. Although those can occasionally be important parts of the action in a scene, they're rarely the most important thing to your reader. Action is normally the ordinary, everyday movements and gestures that your characters make. A man kissing his wife, a girl petting her dog, a leaf falling from a tree — all of these are actions, and any of them may carry emotive freight with your character (and therefore with your reader).

Action matters only if it involves characters the reader cares about. An exploding helicopter with nobody in it means nothing. An exploding helicopter with your 3-year-old daughter in it means *everything*. Never show an action that doesn't mean anything to one of your characters.

Look at the following two action paragraphs. The scene doesn't involve much movement, but each action expresses something:

> Your editor smiles at you when she sees you approaching her appointment table. She's talking on her cellphone, but she gestures to the seat across the table, points to her watch, and holds up her index finger. *One minute.*

> You collapse in the chair, glad to have a little extra time to prepare while she wraps up her call. You reach into your leather portfolio and pull out your latest synopsis and sample chapters, the sequel to the novel that this editor bought from you last year.

Notice that the two paragraphs are fundamentally different. The first focuses on the editor, whom readers view from the outside, because she's not a POV character. Readers can't read her mind, yet they can know a great deal about her thoughts and emotions by her actions and facial expressions — her non-verbal communication. The second paragraph focuses on the POV character, and there we see not only actions but also some thoughts and feelings.

Look at all you can figure out about your editor from a few sentences about her gestures:

- ✔ She smiles, telling you she's happy to see you.

- ✔ She's talking on her cellphone, telling you she's a busy woman.

- ✔ She gestures to the seat across the table, welcoming you and reinforcing the message that she's glad to see you.

- ✔ She points to her watch, indicating she's aware of the time and she's conscious she's encroaching on your appointment time.

- ✔ She holds up one finger. In context, this can only mean that she wants you to wait one minute. The text makes this explicit by adding the sentence *One minute* in italics.

All of these combine to give you a simple message. The editor is happy to see you but she's busy. You'd better deliver a good writing sample, or she may not be so happy 15 minutes from now.

The actions of the POV character also tell a nonverbal story — the way you collapse into the chair says that you're tired, but the fact that you reach into your portfolio shows that you're prepared. When showing the actions of the POV character, it's common to add in thoughts or feelings to get the reader more fully inside the skin of the character. The example passage notes your thought that you appreciate having extra time to prepare. For tips on mixing in this kind of information, see the later sections titled "Interior emotion" and "Interior monologue."

In fiction, as in real life, actions speak louder than words. If a character's actions send a different message than her dialogue does, the reader will always believe the actions.

See Dr. Margie Lawson's online course, *Empowering Characters' Emotions* (www.margielawson.com), for more information on using actions for nonverbal communication.

Many novels do an excellent job of showing actions. Some examples are: *The Maltese Falcon,* by Dashiell Hammett; *The Spy Who Came in From the Cold,* by John le Carré; *Dies the Fire,* by S. M. Stirling; and *River God,* by Wilbur Smith.

Dialogue

Dialogue refers to words spoken aloud by your characters. Even if only one character is present, if he speaks aloud, that qualifies as dialogue. Writers distinguish between *direct dialogue* (quoting the exact words of the character), *indirect dialogue* (giving the gist of the words of the character), and *summary dialogue* (giving a summary of an entire conversation in narrative summary). When we use the term "dialogue," we mean either direct dialogue or indirect dialogue, the two forms of dialogue that qualify as *showing*. Summary dialogue is *telling*.

Here are some rules on showing dialogue:

- ✔ **Show direct dialogue word-for-word in quotation marks.** Don't summarize what the speaker says. Show it, word-for-word:

  "Tell me truly, and don't lie to me, Ashley Wilkes!" Scarlett said. "Do you think I'm beautiful?"

- ✔ **Show indirect dialogue nearly word-for-word, without quotation marks.** Here, you can summarize a little, but you still need to attribute the dialogue to a character:

  Scarlett asked if Ashley thought she was beautiful.

- ✔ **Use a *tag* to tell who's speaking.** You can use a simple "he said," as a tag or you can use an *action tag* that names a character and shows him doing something. If it's obvious who the speaker is, you can eliminate the tag altogether, but never leave the reader in doubt about who's speaking (and try not to have characters say each other's names too much).

  Avoid using fancy tags, such as "he explained," or "she expostulated." A simple one like "he said" or "she asked" is nearly invisible and therefore best. Also avoid adverbs in your tags, such as, "he said patronizingly," or, "she said sarcastically." If he's really patronizing or she's really sarcastic, the words themselves will show it.

- ✔ **Put the dialogue for each character in a separate paragraph.** Show the tag in the same paragraph as the dialogue, even if it's an action tag.

Look at another three paragraphs in our continuing scene, each showing dialogue spoken by a different character:

  Your editor closes her phone. "So! What have you got for me today?" She leans forward, reaching for your manuscript.

  You push the stack across the table. "It's another paranormal suspense novel. Our hero, the bus driver, is kidnapped by North Korean agents who try to force him to reveal the date of the coming attack by the American imperialists."

  "Plagiarist!" screams a voice behind you. "You ripped off my idea!"

Opposing sides: Remember that dialogue is war!

Dialogue is war! Every dialogue should be a controlled conflict between at least two characters with opposing agendas. The main purpose of dialogue is to advance the conflict of the story.

You can't have a war unless the opposing sides actually oppose each other. In the first two paragraphs of our example dialogue, the editor and you have identical goals — to discuss your manuscript. The reader is looking for conflict here, finding none, and wondering when it will kick in. Only when the third character shows up do we have conflict. That character has a completely different agenda than you or your editor does. The new character wants to bash heads — yours, in fact. Now we have conflict.

In our example, we've made the conflict overt. But conflict can be hidden under a surface politeness, as long as the different characters have different goals. (See Chapter 9 for a discussion of the importance of a goal in a proactive scene.) For example, in a famous scene near the end of *Pride and Prejudice*, Lady Catherine de Bourgh arrives at the home of Lizzie Bennet. Lady Catherine's goal is to make Lizzie deny that she intends to wed the Lady's nephew, Mr. Darcy. Lizzie has little hope of ever marrying Darcy, but she hates the old woman and refuses to make any such promise. Her goal is to preserve her own dignity. The dialogue between the two is fierce — and yet icily polite, with Lizzie consistently turning de Bourgh's logic back against her. The conflict comes from the sharply differing goals.

Keeping your dialogue off balance

When the reader knows what the characters are going to say next, there can be little conflict. But when the characters surprise each other (and the reader), then the plot begins sparking.

In our example, the dialogue looks nicely balanced, even tame, until the third character enters from nowhere. You have several ways to throw a dialogue off balance. You can introduce

- New characters
- New facts
- New events

One of your characters may have a conflict between his own values, forcing him to make a hard, unpredictable choice. (See Chapter 7 on the importance of conflicting values in a character.) Any of these will throw the dialogue off balance and keep your reader guessing.

Giving each character a voice

Voice is the particular way that a character puts together words to express rational speech and rational thought. Huck Finn has a strong and distinctive voice; so does Scarlett O'Hara; so does Albus Dumbledore. Nobody could possibly confuse Huck with Scarlett or Dumbledore. In fiction, a character's voice is important in establishing reader identification and revealing character. Your main tools for showing voice are dialogue and interior monologue, which we discuss later in this chapter. (For more on voice, flip to Chapter 12.)

Numerous novels have wonderful dialogue. A few examples are *Pride and Prejudice*, by Jane Austen; *The Chosen*, by Chaim Potok; and *Ender's Game*, by Orson Scott Card.

See *Self-Editing for Fiction Writers,* by Renni Browne and Dave King (Harper), for more information on dialogue. See *Stein on Writing*, by Sol Stein (St. Martin's Griffin), for some insights into creating overt conflict in dialogue by giving characters different scripts. See *Getting Into Character* by Brandilyn Collins (Wiley), for a clear presentation of writing subtle conflict into dialogue using subtexting.

Interior emotion

Interior emotion refers to the internal physiological sensations you feel in the grip of strong emotions. It's common in fiction to tell a character's emotions. For example, you can tell the reader that Frodo is afraid. That is not interior emotion, it's narrative summary. If you want to *show* his fear, then you need to make the reader feel Frodo's pulse ramping up, his hands turning clammy and cold, and the back of his neck prickling with a thousand tiny needles. That is interior emotion — when the physical sensations show the fear.

You use interior emotion only for a POV character. That's what a POV character is — a character whose skin you can get inside. Your reader reads in order to have a powerful emotional experience. By showing interior emotion, you have a terrific opportunity to deliver the very drug your reader craves — emotion.

The next paragraph shows an example of interior emotion, followed by interior monologue (which we cover in the next section), followed by action, all focusing on the POV character in the scene. The interior emotion is in the first sentence of the paragraph.

> A hot ball of adrenaline wells up in your belly. That voice. You know that voice. But from where? You spin around to look.

Showing your reader an emotion is far stronger than telling your reader that emotion. You tell the emotion by naming it. You show the emotion by showing the character's physiological reactions at moments of high tension.

Keep asking yourself, "How does my character feel? *What* does my character feel?" If you can answer those questions with a physiological response, then you have a potent way to give your reader a powerful emotional experience.

We strongly commend Dr. Margie Lawson's online course, *Empowering Character Emotions* (www.margielawson.com), for an encyclopedic study of how to show character emotions through physiological responses. Here's a short list of guidelines to get you started:

- ✔ Show interior emotion only for the POV character. If you're writing in objective third person, then you have no POV character and therefore you have chosen not to use interior emotion. If you're writing in omniscient or head-hopping POV, then you can show interior emotion for more than one character in a given scene. Weigh the advantages of this against the disadvantage of your reader losing identification with the lead character in the scene.

- ✔ Focus on involuntary physiological responses. What happens in your character's hands, feet, belly, neck, face? What metaphor can you use to recreate this sensation?

- ✔ Don't name the emotion, which tells the reader the emotion. Instead, show it.

- ✔ Less is more. Don't overuse the method. Use it when you need a moment of sharp and vivid emotion.

You may think that our term *interior emotion* is redundant. Isn't emotion always interior? Yes, of course it is, but you don't always get inside your character to show emotion. Quite often you merely tell about your character's emotions, using narrative summary. We use the term *interior emotion* to refer only to those occasions when you get directly inside your character to show the internal physical responses to those emotions.

Emotion often leaves visible exterior traces, in body language and facial expressions. Therefore, you have ways to show the emotions of the other characters in your scene — through the character's actions and through a description of the character, especially her facial expression.

Virtually all novels use interior emotion to show the feelings of the characters. Some of our favorites include: The entire *Harry Potter* series, by J. K. Rowling; *No Second Chance*, by Harlan Coben; and *The Pillars of the Earth*, by Ken Follett.

Interior monologue

Interior monologue means the actual thoughts your character is thinking. Just as with dialogue, writers distinguish between *direct interior monologue* (telling the exact words of the thought), *indirect interior monologue* (giving the gist of the thought), and *summary interior monologue*. When we use the term "interior monologue," we mean either direct or indirect interior monologue, both of which are *showing*. Summary interior monologue is *telling*.

Not only do thoughts convey information, but they also give readers insight into character. They're one of two tools you have to show your character's *voice,* which is how that character puts words together. The other tool is dialogue. (For information on character voice, see Chapter 12 and the earlier "Dialogue" section.)

As with interior emotion, you use interior monologue only for a POV character, never for a non-POV character. Look at the middle three sentences in this example paragraph, all of which are interior monologue.

> A hot ball of adrenaline wells up in your belly. That voice. You know that voice. But from where? You spin around to look.

We highly recommend the chapter titled "Interior Monologue" in *Self-Editing for Fiction Writers,* by Renni Browne and Dave King (Harper).

Here are some guidelines for writing interior monologue:

- ✔ Show interior monologue only for the POV character. If you're writing in objective third-person POV, then you have no POV character. If you're writing in omniscient or head-hopping POV, then you have several.

- ✔ For direct interior monologue, use present tense if the thoughts are about the present, even if you're telling your story in past tense. Example: "Jack studied the tiger through his binoculars. *I hate that beast.*"

- ✔ Use italics only for direct interior monologue, not for indirect. Many writers these days don't use italics at all, not even for direct interior monologue. You have some freedom to choose your style, but be consistent.

- ✔ You never need to add the words "he thought" in interior monologue. The reader is smart enough to know that the POV character is thinking your interior monologue.

- ✔ For indirect interior monologue, use past tense if you're telling your story in past tense. Example: "Jack studied the tiger through his binoculars. He hated the beast that had killed his daughter."

- ✔ Use indirect interior monologue when you want to insert a small amount of explanatory material. In the preceding example, we add an explanation of why Jack hates the tiger — because it killed his daughter. Real people don't explain their reasons to themselves, so this kind of explanation wouldn't be appropriate as direct interior monologue.

- ✔ Don't lie to your reader using interior monologue. Your characters must tell themselves the truth — so far as they know it. Your reader will be furious if you deceive her using interior monologue. However, your reader won't mind if it's obvious that the character is fooling herself.

Some novels that use interior monologue very effectively are: *The Speed of Dark*, by Elizabeth Moon; *The Time Traveler's Wife*, by Audrey Niffenegger; and *Rich Man, Poor Man*, by Irwin Shaw.

Description

Description creates a word picture in the reader's mind, much like an image in a movie. Look at the following paragraph, a description of a new character who's about to attack the POV character:

> Long, greasy black hair. A scar down his left cheek disappearing into a scruffy sideburn, speckled gray. He's wearing black leather and stainless steel chains. Dangling from his right hand is a pair of those wooden-stick martial-arts things — nunchakus? His pupils are dilated to the size of quarters, and a stream of tobacco juice dribbles through the stubble on his chin.

Here are some guidelines on writing description:

- ✔ Show only what the POV character can see, hear, smell, taste, or touch. Normally, this means that you aren't able to show a description of the POV character unless he's looking in the mirror. However, if you're using third-person objective, omniscient, or head-hopping POVs, then you have the freedom to show a description of any character.

- ✔ Use strong nouns and verbs. If you're tempted to use adjectives, ask whether a stronger noun will serve you better. If you feel the need for an adverb, ask whether a sharper verb is called for.

- ✔ Pinpoint concrete details that imply the many details you aren't showing.

- ✔ Filter the description through the mind and emotions of the POV character (if you have one) so his voice comes through.

- ✔ Use description of non-POV characters to show what they're thinking and feeling via nonverbal communication. Their body language, facial expressions, and tone of voice all can give your reader insights into these characters' thoughts and feelings.

Looking out: Using a POV character's senses

As a novelist, think like a screenwriter when you write descriptions. If you have only one POV character in your scene, imagine that he has a camera mounted on his forehead. What would that camera see? Describe that and only that. You're not allowed to describe anything your POV character can't see, hear, smell, taste, or touch.

Why this limitation? Why not show everything there is to see? The answer is that by limiting yourself to what the POV character can sense, you're reinforcing the powerful illusion that your reader actually is the POV character. Because your POV character is limited, your reader must be also.

Some point-of-view choices — third-person objective, omniscient, and head-hopping — don't limit you to a single POV character. In that case, you still need to choose some location for your imaginary camera. Don't give your reader vertigo by jumping the camera around at random.

Add description economically, without unnecessary references to the POV character. The example could've started out this way:

> You see a guy with long, greasy black hair . . .

The extra words "You see" add nothing to the scene, so they're wasted words. The reader knows that she's inside the head of the POV character, so she doesn't need to be told who's doing the seeing. Only one possible character could be seeing. You almost never need to tell the reader who is doing the seeing, hearing, smelling, tasting, and touching. No person ever thinks, "I'm seeing a tiger." Instead, they just *see the tiger.*

Looking in: *Showing a character's attitude toward what she sees*

Modern novelists weave snippets of description right along with action, dialogue, interior emotion, and interior monologue into a tightly woven emotive tapestry that's highly personalized — it reflects a character's inner state, not the actual state of the world.

Filter your description through the brain and emotions of your POV character (if you have one), noting only the details the character cares about (as we explain in Chapter 6, which discusses story world). What words would he use to describe what he's seeing? Use those words. What value judgments would he place on what he's seeing? Use value-loaded words that reflect those judgments.

For instance, if Jack is looking at the tiger that killed his daughter, then this might be what the reader sees: "The tiger's malevolent eyes gleamed yellow in the moonlight." The word *malevolent* is Jack's value judgment of what he's seeing. Jack hates this killing machine, and the reader does, too, without having to be told.

If you don't have a POV character, then you need to make a decision about how you'll filter those descriptions. Will you filter them through the brain and emotions of the focal character? The author? Some omniscient narrator? These days, it's not so popular to let the author or a narrator intrude into the story, so think carefully about your choice.

On the surface: Revealing characters by their appearances

As a novelist, you can't get directly inside your non-POV characters to tell their thoughts and feelings using interior monologue or thoughts. But you *can* use description to still give the reader some insight into those thoughts and feelings, not to mention the character's backstory, current behavioral patterns, personality, and more.

For instance, a person's way of dressing tells you a lot about him. Likewise, his personal grooming or lack of it. His facial expressions tell you even more. Look at the example in detail and see what readers find out from the unhappy writer who attacks you at the conference:

- ✔ The long, greasy black hair tells you that he either doesn't care much about his appearance or he's making a statement about who he is.

- ✔ The scar tells you he's a guy who's been in a fight.

- ✔ The scruffy sideburns shout that he's not concerned about his looks, and the gray speckles place him roughly in his forties.

- ✔ The black leather and chains are a statement. Context matters: At a writing conference where most writers are trying to look professional, the statement is pretty sharply worded.

- ✔ The nunchakus are an implied threat.

- ✔ The dilated pupils warn of drug abuse and a high likelihood of violence.

- ✔ The stream of tobacco reinforces the message that he's a tough customer.

- ✔ The stubble on his chin screams "unprofessional."

Note that description often plays to stereotypes. We've chosen to highlight every possible stereotype. But of course, we have options. If we were to replace the black leather and chains with a flamingo-pink three-piece suit, we'd be merrily muddying the waters by sending conflicting messages. As a writer, you choose what sort of message you want to send your reader. (For advice on avoiding stereotypes, flip to Chapter 7.)

We recommend the chapter titled "Particularity" in *Stein on Writing,* by Sol Stein (St. Martin's Griffin), for some insights into description.

Some authors who excel at description of the physical environment include Sir Arthur Conan Doyle in his Sherlock Holmes series; Tom Clancy in *The Hunt for Red October* and its sequels; and James Swain in *Grift Sense* and its sequels. Some novels that use description of characters very well are: *Outlander*, by Diana Gabaldon; *The Godfather*, by Mario Puzo; and *A Tale of Two Cities*, by Charles Dickens.

Flashback

A *flashback* is a container for a scene set earlier in the story. A flashback shows what happened "back then" in real-time, just as if it were happening now. You show it using exactly the same techniques you use anywhere else — action, dialogue, interior emotion, interior monologue, and description. The only thing distinctive about a flashback is that it has two transition points, one at the beginning and one at the end.

A flashback is not narrative summary. It is not a character reminiscing about the past. Despite what some writing teachers might tell you, flashback is not a crime against humanity. You don't want to overdo flashbacks, but they can be a useful tool.

You use a flashback when you have a definite need to show some backstory using all the showing tools at your disposal — action, dialogue, interior emotion, interior monologue, and description. (See Chapter 7 for a discussion of backstory and why it's important for your characters.) You have other options, of course. You could use narrative summary. You could have one character pull the backstory out of another using dialogue. You could even have a character piece it together from evidence discovered — an old book or newspaper clipping.

If you use flashbacks, you need a reason. Your reader will naturally wonder why you didn't simply start your story earlier if the flashback is so important. Make it clear within the story why the flashback is necessary. For example, if some event happened 20 years before the story started, that's a good reason to use a flashback instead of starting the story 20 years early.

Readers won't care about backstory until they care about your characters, so hold off on using flashbacks until you have your readers firmly inside the skin of your POV character. However, after you've done that, then a flashback is a workable way to show backstory, so long as you don't overdo the technique.

Here's an example that gives several paragraphs of flashback. Notice the transitions in and out of the flashback. Also notice, that in the first paragraph of the flashback, we switch to past tense. In all following paragraphs, we revert to present tense.

> That tobacco juice triggers a memory of this same writing conference, a year ago. You were pacing under a tree, checking your watch every five seconds, waiting for your appointment with a big-shot editor. Your sample chapters were damp with sweat.
>
> "Dude, you look wasted," says a voice behind you. "Waiting for an editor?"

You turn and see a guy who looks like Central Casting's clichéd idea of a Hell's Angel wannabe. You give him a weak grin. "Yeah, I'm kind of nervous."

"What's your story about?" he spits a slug of tobacco juice onto the tree right next to you.

You flinch at the reek of the juice. "I'm writing a suspense novel about a bus driver having dreams about an impending terrorist attack on Disneyland, just like the ones he was having right before 9/11."

His eyes light up. "Yeah? Dude, that's like *exactly* the kind of dreams I been having lately. You got North Koreans in your story? And ATF goons?"

"ATF?" You know you've heard that acronym somewhere, but your mind isn't quite in gear right now.

"Alcohol, tobacco, firearms." He spits again. "Watch out, dude. They're here at the conference. Watching. Don't look now, but there's one on the balcony with binoculars zooming on us now."

You spin around to look. There isn't any ATF agent on the balcony. When you turn back to your new friend, he's gone. Disappeared completely. Was he real? The only evidence is that stream of tobacco juice on the tree.

Now, a year later, he's back, and he's stepping toward you on cat-quick feet, swinging his nunchakus slowly, his face twisted into a scowl.

The tricky parts of a flashback are the entry and exit points. Your goal is to make a seamless transition each way.

Getting into a flashback

To get into a flashback, you have to do three things in the correct order:

1. **Make an explicit reference to a memory.**

   In our example, we do this with the sentence "That tobacco juice triggers a memory of this same writing conference, a year ago." Note that we're going to use the tobacco juice as a sensory device on both ends of the flashback, a common technique.

2. **Immediately begin the new scene as if it were any other scene, using a different verb tense than you were using before the flashback.**

   In our example, we follow up immediately with this sentence: "You were pacing under a tree, checking your watch every five seconds, waiting for your appointment with a big-shot editor." This is the same POV character, but now temporarily using the past tense, instead of the present tense that we were using in the main scene.

3. **After you've established the transition to the past, switch back to the original tense.**

   This rescues you from using past-perfect tense for an entire flashback, if your original scene was in past tense.

That's really all there is to getting in. Continue the flashback until it's over.

Getting back to the main story

To get out of a flashback, reverse the steps you used to get in:

1. **If possible, tie back in to whatever sensory device you used to get into the flashback.**

   In our example, we use the one sentence "The only evidence is that stream of tobacco juice on the tree."

2. **Bring the reader back to the present with a time reference.**

   In our example, we do this as follows: "Now, a year later, he's back, and he's stepping toward you on cat-quick feet, swinging his nunchakus slowly, his face twisted into a scowl."

You're now fully back in the scene that you interrupted and ready to move forward to complete the scene.

Flashbacks provide you with an excellent way to show large amounts of backstory. Be creative in your transitions. The *Harry Potter* series uses a Pensieve — a magical container that holds memories — to transmit a number of essential memories of Professors Dumbledore and Snape to young Harry Potter. Each foray into the Pensieve is a flashback that gives Harry crucial insights into a world he is too young to remember.

Sol Stein devotes a chapter to flashbacks in his book, *Stein on Writing* (St. Martin's Griffin).

We recommend that you be cautious in using flashbacks, especially near the beginning of your story. Some examples in which flashbacks play an important role are: *The Man From St. Petersburg*, by Ken Follett; and *Harry Potter and the Deathly Hallows*, by J. K. Rowling. Both books delay showing the flashbacks as long as possible, making sure that the reader is well into the story first.

Narrative summary and other forms of telling

Narrative summary, exposition, and static description are tools for telling, rather than showing. Here's how they compare:

- **Narrative summary:** *Narrative summary* is the telling of part of a story by summarizing events that happen over a stretch of time instead of showing events moment by moment. You can use narrative summary to summarize actions, dialogue, feelings, thoughts, and description. An example of narrative summary is

    "George Smiley walked six miles through London in the fog, pondering how to trap his nemesis, Karla."

- **Exposition:** Writers distinguish narrative summary from *exposition,* which is an explanation of some set of facts. Here's an example of exposition:

    "Karla was the wily head of Moscow Centre, a man who had lured Smiley's colleague, Bill Haydon, into becoming a double agent."

- **Static description:** Writers also distinguish narrative summary from *static description,* which is the description of a scene, person, or thing shown from outside any character's head. An example of static description is

    "A lone streetlamp glowed in the fog on a deserted street on the outskirts of London."

Because listing all these techniques for telling is tedious, we often use the catch-all term *narrative summary* when we really mean any or all of them.

One important thing to keep in mind about narrative summary is that it violates the rule "show, don't tell." Why would you ever do such a thing? After all, showing is your golden key for giving your reader a powerful emotional experience by putting your reader directly inside the skin of a POV character.

What does narrative summary accomplish that would justify using it? Here are some answers:

- Narrative summary is a quick and efficient way to give your reader information or opinion. You don't really want to show everything going on in the lives of your characters; you want to compress those things that don't advance the story so you can focus on those things that do.

> Narrative summary allows you to quickly cover a substantial amount of time (and distance) and summarize a long sequence of events. Some things that would be tedious to show can be told quickly and painlessly.

> ✔ You need to vary the pace of your storytelling, and narrative summary gives your reader a breather after an intensely paced scene.

Our example contains two closing paragraphs of narrative summary, which serve as a bridge to take us from a fairly absurd story into a serious discussion of the main tools that you have for writing your scenes. Here are the closing paragraphs of the scene we've been composing through this chapter, both of which are narrative summary:

> As he approaches, it occurs to you that you've just experienced every one of the main tools that a writer has for "showing" a scene. You began with some action, followed by dialogue, interior emotion, interior monologue, and description. Then you transitioned in and out of a flashback. Now, finally, you're summarizing your scene with a bit of narrative summary.

> As the nunchakus scream toward your head, it occurs to you that only a fiction writer would analyze his life in terms of the basic units of fiction while he's getting beat up by a crazy thug. Apparently, you're a real writer.

Here are some guidelines for writing narrative summary:

✔ **Keep it short.** The fewer words of narrative summary that you can get by with, the happier your reader will be. Your reader is not reading for facts. She's reading for feelings. Give her what she paid for.

✔ **Convey interesting information.** If you're going to make your reader wade through narrative summary, make it as interesting as possible. Odd or surprising facts are always interesting, and so is critical information that explains mysteries about your characters or the story world. Vivid, concrete details that create strong sensory images are always welcome to your reader.

✔ **Use a strong voice.** If the way you string together words and phrase your sentences is strong and distinctive and entertaining, it'll keep your reader with you.

✔ **If possible, be brilliant.** Readers don't mind reading narrative summary when it's dazzlingly wonderful. Literary novelists typically use larger blocks of narrative summary than commercial writers. They get away with this because they do it beautifully. Yet remember that many readers don't care for literary fiction, precisely because they don't want to bother with narrative summary, no matter how brilliant.

Beginning writers tend to overuse narrative summary, which is why we continually caution you against it. It's just plain difficult to give your reader a powerful emotional experience using narrative summary. Most of the time, you'll find it more valuable to focus on the emotive experience using action, dialogue, interior emotion, interior monologue, description, and flashback. But you'll find narrative summary useful when you need to bridge gaps in space or time, to give your reader information, to express opinions, or simply to break up the pace. When you do, make those words count.

Numerous novels include a healthy dose of well-done narrative summary. A few of our favorites include: *The Godfather*, by Mario Puzo; *The Curious Incident of the Dog in the Night-time*, by Mark Haddon; *The Kite Runner,* by Khaled Hosseini; *Girl With a Pearl Earring*, by Tracy Chevalier; and *The Day of the Jackal*, by Frederick Forsyth.

We recommend the chapter titled "Show and Tell" in *Self-Editing for Fiction Writers,* by Renni Browne and Dave King (Harper), for some additional advice on when and when not to use narrative summary.

The Secret of Showing

Earlier in this chapter, we take the art of showing to bits and study every part in detail. But fiction is more than the sum of its bits — there's a right way and a wrong way to put Humpty together again. You must put the parts together in a way that is

- ✔ **Understandable:** In real life, everything happens at once. You have to disentangle this into a stream of words that focus first on one character and then another so that the jumble of action makes sense to the reader.

- ✔ **Emotive:** You must create the illusion that your reader is your POV character (or your focal character, if you have no POV characters or several).

- ✔ **Believable:** You need to make the reader believe that cause and effect are operating in your universe, yet you must avoid predictability.

All this is hard, which is why writing fiction is a difficult craft to master. In this section, we show you what we consider to be the most important techniques in all of fiction writing. If you master nothing else in the craft of fiction, master these techniques.

Sorting it all out

Modern fiction writers don't show or tell fiction willy-nilly. There's a pattern to storytelling, one which you already know from dialogue. In dialogue, you show one person speaking, then another, then another. Each speaker gets his own paragraph, and no other person is allowed to speak in that paragraph. If one character interrupts another, then the words of the first speaker get cut off abruptly — you simply can't show the words of both speakers over-printed on top of each other.

That's different from real life. In real conversations among real people, having two or even three people speaking simultaneously is common. Your brain can often sort this all out and keep track of the separate speakers, but even if your brain gets confused, your ear still hears all the sounds simultane-ously. You can't do that in writing dialogue, and that's why writers use the convention of putting the words of each person into a separate paragraph. The reader simply wouldn't tolerate "everyone talking at once" in a novel. Likewise for the other methods of showing.

The modern writer doesn't try to show "everything happening at once." Nor does she show "everyone feeling at once" or "everyone thinking at once." Instead, she focuses on different characters in turn, giving each character one or more paragraphs in which to act, talk, feel, think, and look.

That paragraph or group of paragraphs forms a unit in fiction — the lowest layer of plot complexity. We need a technical term for this unit of fiction. Since there doesn't seem to be such a technical term, we're going to create one. We'll use the analogy of a film clip, which is a sequence of video frames.

We define a *clip* to be a sequence of sentences focused on a single character that contains any mix of action, dialogue, interior emotion, interior mono-logue, and description.

Here is an example clip that contains only dialogue: "You must throw the Ring of Power into the Cracks of Doom," said Gandalf.

Here is an example clip that combines action with dialogue and interior monologue: Frodo staggered up the sides of Mount Doom. "Sam, we're almost there." Was that the entrance to the Cracks of Doom?

Here is an example clip that combines description with action and dialogue: Gollum stared out of the cave, shading his eyes against the sun with long, gnarled fingers. Snarling, he lunged at Frodo. "Precious!"

A clip can contain as many paragraphs as you need. In scenes with more than one character, clips rarely continue more than about three paragraphs, because a clip focuses on a single character. (That's our definition of a clip.) As soon as you switch focus to a new character, you're writing a new clip.

Most scenes therefore have dozens of clips, because most scenes have two or more characters interacting with each other dozens of times.

The key thing to remember is that *each clip focuses on a single character*. When you switch focus to a different character, one clip has ended and a new one has begun. This idea is crucial to writing focused scenes.

Understanding the two kinds of clips

Writers use two different kinds of clips, depending on whether they focus on the POV character or a non-POV character. Remember that the reader sees the POV character from *inside*, and has access to that character's private thoughts and feelings. The reader sees the non-POV character from the outside, and therefore sees only the "public face" of that character. So we distinguish these two kinds of clips:

- **Private clip:** This type of clip focuses on a POV character and has access to that character's private thoughts and feelings. In a private clip, your reader sees the world through the POV character's eyes. The reader sees the POV character's actions, dialogue, interior emotion, and interior monologue privately — from the inside.

- **Public clip:** This type of clip focuses on a non-POV character and has access only to the publicly viewable part of the character. The reader sees the character's actions, dialogue, and description publicly — from the outside. The reader may be able to guess the character's thoughts and emotions from facial expressions and body language, but the reader can never know for sure what's going on inside that character.

After many years of writing and teaching fiction, we believe that the single most important secret to writing great fiction is to master the knack of writing clips well — both private clips and public clips. When you alternate between private clips and public clips in your scene, the reader experiences life the way the POV character does. The private clips show the reader what's going on inside the POV character. The public clips show the reader what the POV character sees the other characters doing.

This is exactly the way you experience the world. You have a rich private life with a whole complex of thoughts and feelings that you can't share with the world, even though you try to do so through your actions and your words. You can try to understand others by the information they make publicly available — their actions, words, and facial expressions, but you don't always succeed.

If you have a POV character, then by writing fiction using alternating private clips and public clips, you give the reader the uncanny feeling that she is the POV character. If you don't have a POV character, then you show your reader only public clips of all your characters, giving your fiction a cinematic feel.

Writing public clips

Writing a public clip is straightforward. A public clip shows the reader anything the POV character is able to see, hear, smell, taste, or touch. Because the reader knows that the POV character is the person doing the seeing, hearing, smelling, tasting, and touching, you don't have to say so. All you have to do is show the sensory input.

You can use any combination of the following three tools in your public clips:

✔ Action

✔ Dialogue

✔ Description

We pick up our example scene immediately after the flashback and write a public clip that focuses on your nemesis. Up till now, our example scene has generally used only one or two tools at a time, first action, then dialogue, interior emotion, interior monologue, and description. Here, we mix and match to get a more typical public clip. It begins with dialogue, switches to action, then shows some description — all of the typical elements in a public clip:

> "Nobody steals ideas from me." Your opponent glides toward you on cat-quick feet, swinging his nunchakus slowly, his face twisted into a scowl. His conference name-tag says, "Hi! My name is: Hack Moore."

Writing private clips

Writing a private clip is more complex, because you're showing the reader what's going on both inside and outside your POV character. A private clip shows the reader anything the POV character does, says, feels, or thinks. It does *not* usually show anything the POV character sees, hears, smells, or tastes. (Those normally come in a public clip that focuses on some other character.)

The way private clips work depends on the point of view (POV) you've chosen. See Chapter 7 for a discussion of POV. Look at how the different POV choices work (or don't work) with private clips:

✔ **First person:** This is a common choice of POV, and it's a good one if you're just discovering how to write private clips. Staying inside the head of the POV character is easy in first person. You just show the reader "everything I do, say, feel, and think."

✔ **Third person:** This is the most common choice of POV because readers seem to prefer it. This works very well with private clips. You need to discipline yourself to tell the thoughts and feelings of only the POV character, and nobody else, but it's an easy discipline to master.

✔ **Third person objective:** This is not such a common POV choice, because you can't get inside the focal character's head. You're restricting yourself to what the focal character does and says and to the descriptions of his facial features. This means that you can't write private clips at all in third person objective. You have to write your entire story using public clips for all characters. This is a tight constraint, and you may find yourself wishing for regular third person.

✔ **Head-hopping:** Writing teachers routinely try to discourage writers from using this POV choice. The reason is that you're now allowed to use private clips for any character you like. There's no special character in your scene that your reader can exclusively identify with. This can quickly destroy any illusion that your reader actually is one of the characters. You have to work extra hard as a writer to make your reader identify with your lead character. Is it worth it, when you could choose a different POV that limits you to one character? You decide.

✔ **Omniscient:** Many writing teachers absolutely loathe this POV choice, for all the same reasons that they hate head hopping. Not only can you write private clips for any character, but you also can switch to a god-like point of view. Not many readers suffer from the delusion that they're gods, so now you have a really tough job. Furthermore, you're tempted in this POV to use lots of narrative summary — telling, rather than showing. We remind you that it's possible to write a powerful novel in omniscient POV — if you have the skills to handle it.

✔ **Second person:** This is the rarest POV choice, because it requires you to convince the reader at every point that he or she would do what the POV character does. If you can manage it (we take a stab at it in this chapter), then it has all the advantages of first person. Maintaining discipline and writing private clips that show "everything you do, say, feel, and think" is easy.

You can use any of the following four tools in your private clips:

✔ Action

✔ Dialogue

✔ Interior emotion

✔ Interior monologue

You must get one complication right in your private clips: the order. Action, dialogue, and interior monologue normally take a bit of time in real life — usually at least half a second and often more. These are rational activities, and getting your rational brain in gear takes time. The one exception is reflexive or instinctive actions or dialogue, which can happen much faster (touch a burning stove — your hand jerks back in roughly a tenth of a second and you make an unintelligible cry of pain an instant later). These are nonrational responses, so they can happen more quickly. Interior emotion often happens even faster. If a wild tiger leaps through your window, you feel a lightning bolt of fear much sooner than you can respond either rationally or nonrationally.

Here's a simple rule to use: Show first whatever happens fastest. Most often, this means that you show interior emotion first, followed by various instinctive actions or dialogue, followed by the more rational kinds of action, dialogue, and interior monologue.

Continuing with our example scene, we now show a private clip that mixes all the tools at our disposal. We begin with a sentence of interior emotion, follow it up with an action, then some interior monologue, then another action, and finally close with two sentences of dialogue:

> Your heart is hammering in your throat. You raise your leather portfolio to chest height. Maybe a little negotiation will calm things down. You put on your chummiest smile. "Hack, can we talk about this? We had a great time chatting last year, didn't we?"

Putting cause and effect together

In the preceding sections, we explain how to write public clips and private clips. The only thing left is to keep stringing them together through a full scene.

Here's a critical rule: Always get the time sequence correct and always put the cause before the effect. Normally, each private clip will be at least partly the cause of the public clip that follows it. Normally, each public clip will be at least partly the cause of the private clip that follows it.

Here we continue our scene for a few more clips to see how this plays out in practice. Study the following example and identify each public clip and each private clip. Which tools do we use in each one? Could you change the order of any of the parts within the internal clips?

> Hack lunges forward, swinging his nunchakus in a great arcing circle at your head.

You twist to one side, throwing your portfolio up as a shield.

The nunchakus crash against it, sending a shock wave through your shoulder.

Pain slices into your neck like a hot knife. "Aughhh!" You keep twisting your body sideways, grab Hack's hair in your right hand, yank it viciously down, and raise your knee.

Hack's momentum carries him into a face-plant against your kneecap. The nunchakus fall out of his nerveless hands and he sags to the floor.

A dozen people begin screaming at once. Four guys jump on Hack's arms and legs, pinning him to the ground. "Somebody call the cops!"

You stagger backward. Your stomach feels horribly queasy and your collarbone is screaming — probably broken. What must your editor be thinking?

Friendly hands guide you back into your chair. "Are you all right?" your editor asks. "Wow, that was amazing! You . . . did great. You people, call an ambulance!"

A soft, muzzy blackness begins oozing down over your eyes. You fight the darkness as long as you can, knowing that someday, somehow, you're going to work this into a novel.

In the preceding example, we count five public clips (three focusing on Hack, one on the numerous bystanders, and one on your editor). We also see four private clips. Showing more than one public clip in a row, each focusing on different characters, is fine. In scenes with a number of characters, it's common to show two or even three public clips for each private clip.

You may be wondering if you must change paragraphs every time you transition to a new clip. No, you can paragraph your scenes however you want. We prefer to break paragraphs between clips for clarity. That's the way everybody paragraphs dialogue, and we think it makes sense to do so, even when we add action, interior emotions, interior monologue, and description into the mix. Paragraph your scenes in a way that feels natural to you. The only unbreakable rule in writing fiction is that there are no unbreakable rules.

Your reader experiences the scene from inside the skin of the POV character, so you want to give as much air time as possible to your POV character. But you have to balance that with the needs of the scene. When a lot is happening outside your POV character, you need to show the important parts.

Notice that nowhere do we get inside Hack's head nor try to show interior emotion or interior monologue for him. We don't need to. The reader wants the thoughts and feelings of only one character — the POV character.

We owe a great debt to Dwight Swain's classic book, *Techniques of the Selling Writer* (University of Oklahoma Press), which contains a long discussion of "motivation-reaction units." Swain's term "motivation" is nothing more nor less than a public clip. His term "reaction" is identical to what we call a private clip.

Balancing showing and telling tools

We find certain books indispensable in understanding the craft of writing. We've referred to several of them in this chapter. For your convenience, we gather them all here:

✔ *Techniques of the Selling Writer* **(University of Oklahoma Press), by Dwight Swain:** Great info on "motivation-reaction units."

✔ *Empowering Characters' Emotions,* **by Margie Lawson:** A terrific resource on nonverbal communication in actions and on showing interior emotion. This online course is available on Dr. Lawson's Web site at www.margielawson.com.

✔ *Stein on Writing* **(St. Martin's Griffin), by Sol Stein:** Great advice on showing and telling, dialogue, flashbacks, and much more.

✔ *Self-Editing for Fiction Writers* **(Harper), by Renni Browne and Dave King:** An essential guide to editing, with strong chapters on dialogue, interior monologue, and narrative summary.

✔ *Getting Into Character* **(Wiley), by Brandilyn Collins:** The information on subtexting in dialogue is worth the price of the book all by itself.

Chapter 11

Thinking Through Your Theme

. . . .

. . . .

Fiction is art, and all art carries a message of some sort. We call that message the *theme* of your story. A theme is the deep meaning of your novel, and many great novels pack powerful themes. Of course, a novel can have a thin or ambiguous theme and still be a fine story. Themes are important, but they're not as important as giving your reader a powerful emotional experience.

In this chapter, we take a stab at analyzing the themes of a number of best-selling novels. Our purpose here is not to do a deep literary analysis. We just want to demystify the idea of theme by giving you some examples of themes for novels that you're likely to have read.

Also, although theme is important, we believe that building your novel around a theme is hazardous. That feels too much like a sermon, not entertainment. Far better to let your theme grow naturally out of your story. You may not know what the theme of your novel is until you've revised it several times, so part of your problem as an author is to figure out what your story means. Later in this chapter, we give you several techniques to help you do that.

Understanding Why Your Theme Matters

People mean different things when they talk about theme, so we give our definition of it here: *Theme* is the deep meaning of your book. It's the central message you're trying to get across to your reader. It may be "the moral of the story," if you wrote your story to have a moral. It may be your own vision of how the world works, your philosophy of life, or your recipe for the perfect brownie. Your theme is whatever you want it to be.

You may be wary of "message-driven art" and rightly so. We're extremely wary of it ourselves. But you should also be wary of meaningless art. Art has meaning, just as food has flavor. It's a mistake to make that flavor either too strong or too weak.

In this section, we discuss the usefulness of having a theme, explain what a theme looks like, and provide sample themes of 20 best-selling novels.

Looking at why writers include themes in their novels

Different readers will read your story through their own mindsets, so they may come away from your novel with a different theme than the one you intended. Furthermore, truly great fiction may well contain a number of themes. Therefore, the theme of any novel is always ambiguous and open to debate. That's part of what makes reading fun.

Unless readers plan to analyze your novel for a report or book club, they probably won't be too concerned about getting the "right" interpretation of your story — they'll care more about what the story means to them. For the writer, theme is important because your story is the only contact most readers will have with you. The novel is your chance to show others how you view the world.

Consider this: You're reading an online review of your first novel, which has just been released. It's a good review, all things considered. The reviewer's summary of the storyline follows the one you provided your editor years ago. And the reviewer loves your characters, calling them "strong and true." He also praises your fast action and snappy dialogue. Generally, he likes your novel. You're holding your breath when you get to the closing paragraph, which runs like this: "In the end, though, the author's vapid vision of nihilistic existential despair leaves the reader feeling both exhausted and depressed."

Your jaw bounces a few times on your desktop. Huh? Since when do you have a vapid vision of nihilistic existential despair? What does that even mean? This reviewer doesn't get your vision at all. He's an idiot.

It's entirely possible that the reviewer *is* an idiot. However, it's also possible that the reason that he doesn't get your vision is that you haven't given him enough evidence to figure it out. Lacking any idea of what your vision may be, the reviewer latches onto minor things you never intended to be central symbols. Hence that pesky "nihilistic existential despair" — probably taken from a throwaway line by a side character in a minor scene.

What went wrong? That's easy. Your story has a weak theme or none at all.

Examining the features of a theme

We like to summarize a theme in one sentence. It doesn't have to be a deep sentence (although it's nice if it is). But we'll be blunt: If your novel isn't deep, the theme sentence for it can't be deep, either. Not everyone likes deep fiction, and that's okay. The purpose of fiction is to give the reader a powerful emotional experience. The theme is an extra. If the emotional experiences you arouse in your reader are powerful enough, then she'll probably buy into your theme. Otherwise, she probably won't.

Your theme should have these features:

- ✔ **True:** Your theme sentence should express some truth about the world.
- ✔ **Important:** Your theme should be about the significant stuff in life.
- ✔ **Short:** Your theme should be a single sentence, not a manifesto.

Example themes for 20 novels

A good way to figure out how to write a theme sentence is to look at some examples. Be aware that every reader is going to take away something slightly different from your novel. If it's a deep novel, different readers may take away very different things. Most of the novels we analyze here are pretty deep, so what we took away from them may be different from what you take away from them. We may even be wildly off. Try your own hand at defining the themes for these books and then compare your themes to ours. Is there some common ground? That's likely to be part of the author's intended message. We're going to resist the urge to find as many themes as possible in these. Our theme sentences will give the main message that we personally took away from each of these novels.

We'll admit right away that we had to guess at some of these themes. Not all of the authors felt it necessary to give their works a clear theme. Some authors prefer simply to entertain, without creating a message for their fiction. You may object that we're assuming that it's actually possible to discover the author's intent. Yes, we do. If we thought an author's intent was impossible to discover, we wouldn't be writing this book. The author *always* runs the risk of being misunderstood, but we believe he also runs a very reasonable risk of being understood. We hope you'll understand:

- *The Lord of the Rings,* **by J. R. R. Tolkien (fantasy):** "Good ultimately conquers evil, because evil defeats itself."

  We've rephrased a famous sentence from the book: "Oft evil will shall evil mar." The novel is an epic tale of the battle between good and evil.

- *River God,* **by Wilbur Smith (historical action-adventure):** "Genius and guile are a match for raw strength."

  The theme for this novel is nowhere spelled out, so this is what we took away from the novel. It's an adventure tale set in ancient Egypt, with the genius slave Taita as narrator and lead character. Adventure novels typically put little importance on theme.

- *The Clan of the Cave Bear,* **by Jean Auel (historical):** "Neanderthals are real people, too."

  The lead character Ayla is a young human girl who grows up in an adoptive family of Neanderthals. The story makes clear how genetically close the Neanderthal lineage is to the human.

- *The Pillars of the Earth,* **by Ken Follett (historical thriller):** "No man stands above the law."

  This novel is a saga spanning half a century, ending about the time of the murder of Thomas Becket, archbishop of Canterbury. Although we can't be sure that we've captured Follett's intent for the theme of this story, it's certainly plausible in view of one of the final scenes. But another theme may be, "What goes around, comes around." That's a cliché, but clichés often work nicely as themes, even for deep novels.

- *Outlander,* **by Diana Gabaldon (time-travel romance):** "Love conquers all."

  This is a romance novel, a genre not noted for deep themes. Perhaps our theme sentence actually applies to *all* romance novels. That's perfectly okay. Themes need not be unique or profound. Fiction is not philosophy. Fiction is about creating a powerful emotional experience. We think *Outlander* is an outstanding story and that this theme sentence applies especially well to it.

- *My Name is Asher Lev,* **by Chaim Potok (literary):** "A great artist cannot avoid experiencing great pain — and inflicting it."

  The themes of literary novels are often profound. This is a deep novel by a deep novelist, and the theme is correspondingly deep. We think this novel is especially interesting to fiction writers, who may well identify with the lead character, Asher Lev. It's one of the best fictional portraits of an artist that we've seen.

✔ ***The Kite Runner,*** **by Khaled Hosseini (literary):** "There is a way to be good again."

We've quoted a sentence from the first chapter which represents well the core truth of this book.

✔ ***The Lovely Bones,*** **by Alice Sebold (literary):** "There is justice in this universe."

This novel is a bit hazy in its theme, and we've had to guess as to its intended meaning. Literary novels can be very ambiguous in their themes.

✔ ***The Speed of Dark,*** **by Elizabeth Moon (literary):** "To thine own self be true."

Taking a quotation from literature as your theme sentence is perfectly okay. This one is a quote from Shakespeare's *Hamlet,* and it seems particularly appropriate for this novel. The lead character is a high-functioning autistic who is offered a chance to be cured. But will the cure change his fundamental identity? It's a hard choice, and who's to say which is the right answer?

✔ ***The Time Traveler's Wife,*** **by Audrey Niffenegger (literary):** "There is a love that transcends time."

This romantic literary novel is unforgettable. The lead character Clare is married to Henry, a man with a genetic defect that causes him to time-travel during moments of high stress. Can their love survive this wrinkle in time? Yes, but . . .

✔ ***Girl with a Pearl Earring,*** **by Tracy Chevalier (literary historical):** "A great artist will sacrifice everything for his art."

The theme for this novel is similar to that of *My Name is Asher Lev.* In both cases, a great artist is at the center of the story. In *Girl with a Pearl Earring,* the lead character is a young servant in the home of Johannes Vermeer, and the story provides a possible backstory for a famous painting by Vermeer.

✔ ***Pride and Prejudice,*** **by Jane Austen (romance):** "A man's character is more important than his money, looks, or good humor."

Austen is a deep writer, and her novels can be assigned any number of themes, but we think ours is as good as any. Heroine Lizzie Bennet would like to fall in love with the man she marries, but not just any man. More than anything, she wants a man of strong character. A pleasant, pliable man like Mr. Bingley won't do for Lizzie; she needs a man like Mr. Darcy.

✔ ***Contact,*** **by Carl Sagan (science fiction):** "God is a mathematician."

Carl Sagan's novel about the first contact between humanity and aliens provides him with a platform to sound any number of themes, and it's not easy to decide which may have been most important to Sagan. The novel speculates on a possible truce in the long-running feud between science and religion.

✔ *Gorky Park*, **by Martin Cruz Smith (mystery):** "No good deed goes unpunished."

We've chosen a well-known aphorism as the theme for this story about an honest cop who does his job in a dirty world.

✔ *Blink*, **by Ted Dekker (Christian thriller):** "God is in control, whether you think so or not."

This is a fairly common theme in Christian fiction and it resonates well with Dekker's core audience.

✔ *The Da Vinci Code,* **by Dan Brown (thriller):** "Everything you thought you knew about Jesus is wrong."

The storyline essentially stops in the middle for three chapters while one of the characters expounds on this theme at length. The novel is heavily theme-oriented, which helped drive sales among those who liked the theme. The book drew sharp attacks from historians, who argued that everything Brown thinks *he* knows about Jesus is wrong. Those attacks made for great publicity, which also helped drive sales.

✔ *The Man From St. Petersburg,* **by Ken Follett (historical thriller):** "The most dangerous man is the one who cannot fear, because then he is impervious to everything except love."

Thrillers don't normally spend much ink on developing themes, but we think we're close to the truth. The assassin is one of the most likeable and reader-identifiable villains we've seen — incapable of fear until he finds a reason to love.

✔ *The Firm,* **by John Grisham (legal thriller):** "Be careful what you wish for."

Grisham's protagonist Mitch McDeere is a poverty-stricken law student who only wants to get a decent job. He gets a fabulous one, but it comes with conditions that he doesn't imagine until it's too late.

✔ *The Spy Who Came In From the Cold,* **by John le Carré (spy thriller):** "Espionage is a dirty, dirty, dirty, dirty, dirty business."

When this novel was published in the early 1960s, spy novels typically featured shallow James Bond-like characters. Le Carré rewrote the rules on what you could do in a spy novel. We think this is still the best spy novel ever written.

✔ *The Hunt for Red October,* **by Tom Clancy (military technothriller):** "The Evil Empire will destroy itself through its own incompetence."

The theme for this novel is quite similar to the one we've assigned to *The Lord of the Rings*. Military technothrillers are often driven by strong principles of justice. Readers in this genre have an unbending sense of right and wrong and they want to see the good prevail and the evil vanquished.

Deciding When to Identify Your Theme

Theme is important, no doubt about it. But if you let it, a strong theme can take over your novel. If you write your novel mainly to advance your theme, here are the main hazards awaiting you:

- ✔ **Your characters may be shallow.** If you know your theme before you create your characters, then you'll be mightily tempted to create them specifically to illustrate the theme. You'll be tempted to avoid giving them conflicting values, because one of those values may contradict your theme or confuse your reader.

- ✔ **Your plot may be contrived.** If you already know your theme before you construct your plot, you'll find it all too easy to tailor the story exactly to fit the theme. You'll fear getting sidetracked in story threads or sub-plots that may detract from the message of the story. You may even cheat on the plot because you need to in order to make the story work out right.

- ✔ **You may write a sermon.** Of course, if your readers agree with your theme, they won't consider it a sermon. But the readers who disagree with your theme will definitely consider your story a sermon — a heavy-handed and unwelcome one. A heavily theme-based novel is going to polarize your readership. It may also draw a firestorm of criticism from reviewers, who usually believe that a novel should be about entertainment first.

Regardless of which creative paradigm you use (see Chapter 4), we believe you should develop your theme last in your story, when you've already worked out the main details of your story world, your characters, and your plot. That way, your story doesn't take a back seat to your message. It's not uncommon for novelists to write the entire story without really nailing down what it all means. They may in fact write several drafts before they figure it out. We think that's good. We believe that the strongest themes are those that arise organically out of the story. In the next section, we help you discover the theme of your story.

Despite our advice, you may feel that you want to build a story from the ground up around some theme. You may not be worried at all by the prospect that readers will think you're preaching a sermon. Is that okay? Yes, it's your book, so you can write it however you want, but be aware that it's a high-risk approach. (To be fair, it may also be a high-reward approach).

If your story appears to be designed solely to promote a theme, agents and editors are going to be deeply suspicious of your work. Editors generally don't like sermons masquerading as fiction. If that's the kind of book you want to peddle, they're going to be much tougher on you than you may have expected.

Because we're wary of heavily theme-based fiction ourselves, we hate to admit this, but it's a fact — if you build your novel from the ground up on a theme and if you can get it published, you may possibly see a very high reward for your labors. Many readers *love* theme-based novels that confirm their own beliefs. If readers fall in love with your theme, they may tell everyone they know, giving you extraordinary word-of-mouth publicity.

Most readers only hate theme-based novels that appear to them to be promoting the "wrong" message. If some of your readers hate your message, they'll definitely tell everyone they know, and they may even trash you in public — giving you even more word-of-mouth publicity. You can probably think of several recent massively best-selling novels that you consider pure tripe — dreckish sermons from first wretched word to last. And yet they sold like fire, because there's no such thing as bad publicity for a fiction writer. Bad publicity just makes a novel that much more likely to wind up in the hands of people who don't consider it a sermon at all — they think it's straight, common sense.

If you're going to go this route, you need a boatload of humility, because you may well get wildly undeserved praise from your admirers and at the same time get a hellishly undeserved roasting from your critics. Don't kid yourself that either your admirers or your critics are telling the truth. They're reacting to your message, not to you.

Writing a heavily theme-based novel is high-risk/high-reward. Before you write one, think three times about whether the rewards justify the risks.

Finding Your Theme

How do you find your theme? There isn't any foolproof way to get there, but this section identifies some possible roads you can take.

Faking it till you make it

You probably have some idea of what the deep meaning of your story is, even from the very first day the idea for the story leaps into your mind. The theme may be fuzzy in your mind, but it's there. When somebody asks what your theme is, being a little vague is perfectly okay.

If you're writing a romance, for example, you may say, "My story is about the enduring power of love." Nobody is ever going to criticize that theme, for the simple reason that theme isn't that big of a deal in a romance novel.

Likewise, if you're writing a thriller, you could say, "My story is about the power of _____." Fill in the blank with any handy word that fits your story. "Fear" would work. So would "ambition." So would "ignorance," "knowledge," "the little guy," "multinational corporations," "religion," and "technology." You really can put just about anything in that's remotely related to your story, and you'll have a decent working prototype for your theme.

Mystery readers typically are less interested in theme than in a good, original puzzle, so you probably won't be asked about the theme if you're writing a mystery. But if you are, you can play the same game as for a suspense novel.

If you're writing a fantasy novel, you can always say, "It's about the battle between good and evil." This probably also works for many horror novels.

You can be vague for a good long time using evasions like the preceding ones. The nice thing is that they aren't really evasions. The theme of your novel most likely will be pretty much along the lines you're claiming. As you work on your story, there may come a day when your theme springs brilliantly into focus. When that happens, you'll know it. Don't rush that day. Keep faking it with platitudes until you get there.

Is that okay? Of course it is. You're doing the best you can, working from the abstract to the concrete. Fiction is hard, and figuring out your theme is one of the hardest parts of it. It's not your fault if you haven't worked out something deep and profound yet. Nobody has the right to stampede you into coming up with a theme before its time, any more than they have the right to dictate to a vintner when the wine will be ready.

Depending on your category and your target reader and your own goals as a writer and the particular story you're writing, there may *never* come a day when a powerful theme emerges. In that case, your theme will always be whatever vague platitude you started with. You aren't required to have a unique and dazzling theme for your story. The examples that we show earlier in this chapter should make it clear that some novels have clearly defined deep themes, and some are much fuzzier.

Reading your own novel for the first time

Assume that no voice from heaven has given you an inspired theme for your story. You've finished the first draft. You've edited it several times. Your story world feels as real as rain. Your characters are strong. Your plot zings at all six layers. And you still don't quite know what your story's about.

Set your novel aside for a bit. Read somebody else's work, preferably one with a strong theme. It doesn't have to be terribly similar to your book; it just needs to be something fresh, preferably a book that many people agree is a really good book. Write a theme sentence for that other book.

Now you're in the frame of mind to come back to your novel. Sit down and read your entire book in one sitting. Pretend that this is the first time you've ever read it. Ignore any wording problems or plot choices or character glitches. Just read — fast. When you get to the end, close it and ask yourself, "What's the author trying to say here?"

That may sizzle your synapses enough to come up with a profound theme sentence. It may. Then again, it may not.

Listening to your characters

If you've been careful to build real, three-dimensional characters, then you may want to try listening to them to see what they have to say. Read through some of their best scenes. At any point, do they get on their soap box and start shrieking? Did they surprise you? Did they say something you never would have said yourself? That may make a very nice theme.

You may also want to try interviewing your characters to find your theme. Imagine you're a journalist doing a profile of your characters for *Time* magazine. Ask each character what she learned from her experiences in your story. Write down the answers. Is there anything surprising that you hadn't really thought about? If so, grab it.

Using test readers

Most writers have any number of friends who love to read. When your novel is fairly well polished, give out copies to a few of your friends and ask them to read it. Promise that you'll list them in the acknowledgments but only if they finish reading it by a certain deadline. If they meet your deadline, take them out for coffee and debrief them. Ask them what the novel meant to them. Did any of the characters say anything particularly striking? It's just possible you'll hit a nerve with one of your readers. If you've already got a theme in mind, your test readers will tell you if that theme is resonating with them.

Must you have a theme?

What if, despite your best efforts, you still can't come up with a strong theme for your novel? What's the worst that can happen?

The worst that can happen is that some readers may read in a theme where none exists. They may accuse you of having a "vapid vision of nihilistic existential despair," whatever that means. Being misunderstood can be painful, but you won't die from it.

Other readers will see that you have no theme and will accuse you of being shallow. This is less bad than being misunderstood, but it's still not fun. Very few writers want to be known as shallow. Again, it won't kill you, so don't take it personally.

Many readers won't even notice if your novel is missing a deep theme. Readers read for entertainment first, and plenty of them are looking for a nice beach read, not something profound. These readers won't care if you don't have a deep theme.

Refining Your Theme

If you do find your theme, the odds are very high that it won't be perfectly developed in your story. The reason is that you didn't write the story merely to illustrate some sappy theme. You wrote the story to move your readers emotively, and in the process, a theme emerged. Now you need to buff that out a bit in your story. Read through your entire novel again, marking places where you could highlight the theme a little. The key word here is a *little*.

Strengthen your theme but resist the urge to explain. Your reader is smart. Trust her to figure out what you have to say.

What you're looking for is places in your novel where the theme emerges naturally but it comes out fuzzy or distorted. Clarify those — that's what we mean when we say you should strengthen your theme.

You're also looking for places where the theme pokes its head up rather unnaturally — where it seems intrusive, forced, or just plain heavy handed. Trim it back there or take it out. The theme needs to advance the story, not weigh it down. Some of the litmus tests we use are the following: If the theme comes up in narrative summary, then it's probably the author intruding into the story. If the theme comes up in a character's dialogue or interior monologue, then it's probably legitimate, especially if it advances the story. If the theme is hinted at by concrete actions in the story, then it's almost always legitimate.

Be on the alert for places in your story where you contradict your theme. If you find them, then you can either resolve them so there's no contradiction, or you can just acknowledge them with a line or two that makes it clear that you know that paradoxes abound and there aren't any easy answers. Readers are smart and will spot contradictions that they think you missed. But if your characters acknowledge the contradiction — or wrestle with it — then your readers know that you know about it, and you're off the hook.

Part III
Editing and Polishing Your Story and Characters

The 5th Wave   By Rich Tennant

"If you must know, the reason you're not in any of my novels is that you're not a believable character."

In this part . . .

Being able to produce perfect prose in your first draft every time would be great. However, the reality of writing is that great fiction always requires editing and polishing before it's ready for prime time. In this part, we show you how to analyze your characters, scrutinize your story structure, and edit your scenes.

Chapter 12

Analyzing Your Characters

· ·

In This Chapter

▶ Reading through your story with an eye toward characters

▶ Keeping track of character details

▶ Analyzing motivations

▶ Evaluating your choice of narrator and POV character

▶ Improving characters

· ·

*A*fter you've written your story, you need to put on your editing hat and make sure it's as strong as possible. This begins with a careful analysis of your characters. Great fiction needs great characters, so don't be afraid to rework your characters until they're fully alive and three-dimensional.

At some point, you should develop a *character bible* that spells out in one place everything there is to know about each character. You need this to maintain story consistency and to help you create fully rounded characters. It's wise to start building your character bible before you start writing, even if you don't know much about your characters. It's also wise to keep adding to it as you write your story and when you do your high-level read-through after you finish the first draft. However, virtually all writers analyze their characters only after writing the first draft, so we present this tool in this chapter.

In Chapter 7, we discuss the importance of character *motivations,* which we define as the sum total of a character's values, ambition, and story goal. You can't have a story without a *story goal* — the one concrete thing that your lead character wants to have or to do or to be. Normally, a story goal comes from some abstract ambition of the character. Ambitions ultimately arise from a character's *values* — core truths that he believes are so obvious that they can't and shouldn't be explained. And where do values come from? That's a mystery. Values can't be fully explained, but you can give a good reason for them through your character's backstory.

You may have written your story in a point of view that seems obvious to you. When you're ready to edit your story, you need to reexamine that choice, verify that it makes sense for your story, and then check that you've been consistent in your POV choices throughout your manuscript.

In this chapter, we take you through the process of analyzing and improving the characters in your story. We discuss keeping track of fine details, revisiting your character's motivations, making sure your choice of POV works, and strengthening your characters.

The High-Level Read-Through: Preparing Yourself to Edit

Before you start editing your manuscript, you need to get the big picture. We strongly recommend that you do a high-level read-through to give you that big picture. At this point, you don't do any actual editing. Instead, you just take notes on what you need to do, using the ideas we cover later in this chapter.

Read through your complete manuscript, taking notes on every scene. You can take notes on paper, or you can insert comments into your document, using the *comment* feature on your word processor. Don't edit anything; your goal is to make sure your characters work. As you read each scene, mentally answer the following questions:

- ✔ Who is the POV character for this scene? Is this the best POV character for this scene?

- ✔ If you're writing in standard third person, first person, or second person, are you showing only what your POV character sees, hears, thinks, knows, feels, smells, tastes, or touches?

- ✔ If you're writing in third person objective, do you ever accidentally use interior emotion or interior monologue? Does this mean that you'd secretly like to use the more usual third person?

- ✔ Do your characters have unique and distinctive voices in their dialogue and interior monologue?

- ✔ Are your characters boring, shallow, unbelievable, or unlikeable?

After you finish your high-level read-through, you still have to do a lot of work to fix your characters. Go through these steps in order:

1. **Review all your notes, looking for patterns.**

   What are the main problems with each of your characters?

2. **Spend some time meditating on your characters.**

   What changes do you need to make to bring your characters up to snuff?

3. **Revise your character bible for each character to make each one better.**

   See the following section for info on how to develop a character bible.

 Don't make any changes in your manuscript yet. You may have some problems in your story structure and scenes that you also need to fix. Because character and plot are intertwined, you really need to think through them both before you begin making changes. When you make the edits we describe in Chapters 13, 14, and 15, also take into account everything new you discover about your characters in this chapter.

Developing a Bible for Each Character

You're reading your e-mail from your fans and find one that looks promising. The subject line reads, "Loved your novel!!!!" You open the e-mail and scan it:

> Dear Author:
>
> I was up all night reading your novel and loved every word of it. You had me fooled all the way, so congratulations, because I read a lot and it's hard to pull one over on me. I'm working on a novel of my own. Not that you have to read it, so don't feel obligated, but are you interested?
>
> By the way, can I offer my services as a proofreader? I noticed that Katie Sue has green eyes on page 17, but on page 323, her eyes are brown. And Jonas is 180 pounds on page 3, but three chapters later, he's up to 210, even though I never noticed him eating a thing. And how is it that his maternal grandmother is Irish the first time we hear about her, Hungarian the second time, and back to Irish at the end?
>
> Other than that, great story! Let me know about the proofreading. I'm cheap because I'm only 12.
>
> Your fan,
>
> Jim Bob

The fact is that mistakes happen. You'll never write a perfect book. (If you do, you'll be insufferable and other authors will treat you the way the other reindeer treated Rudolf.) But your goal should always be perfection, even if you know you'll never reach it. You'll be punished for every mistake with letters from a few Jim Bobs, and not all of them will be nice.

One of the most embarrassing mistakes you can make is inconsistency in your characters. Shifting eye color, rapid weight gains or losses, and drifting ethnic heritages are just three of the many inconsistencies that can sneak into your story. When you have only one or two main characters in your book, or when you've written only one book, you're not likely to make many mistakes. But as your characters and books proliferate, they all start blending together.

Your protection against all such errors is to write up a *bible* for your characters. In your character bible, you keep a record of all the details that you need to remember for each character. Your character bible doesn't need to be fancy. It just needs to get the job done, and you need to save it where you can always find it.

Writers use character bibles for two distinct purposes:

- ✔ **As a creative tool:** Writing a character bible is a terrific exercise to get to know all the characters in your story. It's a powerful tool that sparks your creativity in unpredictable ways. You can't know in advance which details will affect your story and which won't, so record everything in your character bible, even details you're sure won't matter to the story.

  Even if you don't create your character bible until after you've finished your first draft, writing it may suggest new, creative ideas for the second draft. We've often seen some of those insignificant details suggest plot developments later in the story. For instance, even if you think you'll never need to know what your character's first dog was named, writing down the fact that it was a greyhound may later suggest to you that your character knows all about dog racing and the gambling world.

- ✔ **As an editing tool:** If you record all the myriad details about each character, you can consult your bible when you have a question about consistency. At 3 a.m. on the night before your book is due, it's a lot easier to browse through a ten-page character bible looking for Katie Sue's eye color or Jonas's weight than it is to search through your entire manuscript.

We recommend that you have a special folder on your hard drive named something like "Books Written." There, make a folder for every book that you write, named with your working title or an abbreviation of it. In the folder for your book, make another folder named "Research" and save your character bible there. You can create a document named "Characters" that contains all the critical information on all the characters in your novel.

What goes into your character bible? Just about anything that helps you understand your characters better or that helps you remember the myriad details that you need to keep straight. We recommend that you consider at least the following main categories:

- ✔ Physical traits
- ✔ Emotional and family life
- ✔ Intellectual life
- ✔ Backstory and motivation

This section describes these elements in detail.

Physical traits

Physical traits are the easiest things to track and the most embarrassing to get wrong, because there really can't be any decent explanation when those eyes drift from blue to brown. You should record anything you consider important. Here are a few of the specific traits we recommend that you track:

- ✔ Date of birth and age
- ✔ Height and weight
- ✔ Ethnic heritage
- ✔ Hair and eye color

Include a detailed physical description, including scars or physical handicaps, along with the character's usual style of dressing.

Emotional and family life

Your readers want to know what your character's private life is like. This is a bit more open-ended than the physical traits. Here are some points to get you started. Consider these and any other issues that seem appropriate for your characters:

- ✔ What's your character's personality like? Describe it in 25 words or less.
- ✔ What kind of sense of humor does your character have?
- ✔ What's your character's religious faith? Explain where it came from.
- ✔ What political party does your character belong to and why?
- ✔ What's the character's family like? Describe it, including parents, siblings, and children. You may include grandparents, cousins, a spouse, or anyone else relevant.

- ✔ What are the character's friends like? Describe them, including your character's best male friend and best female friend.

- ✔ Who are your character's enemies? Explain how they came to be enemies.

- ✔ What is in your character's pockets, wallet, purse, or backpack? Describe the contents in detail.

- ✔ What's your character's home like? Describe it in detail.

- ✔ What is your character's happiest childhood memory? His worst?

- ✔ How would your character describe himself?

- ✔ How would your character's friends describe him?

Intellectual and work life

Your character has a public face, including education and possibly a career. Here are some things that you may need to describe in your character bible:

- ✔ Your character's educational background

- ✔ What sort of employment your character has and his work history

- ✔ Your character's favorite music, books, and movies

- ✔ Any interesting hobbies

- ✔ Your character's personal philosophy (and where it came from)

Backstory and motivation

Spelling out your characters' backstory and motivation in writing somewhere is critical, and your character bible is a fine place to put this info so you'll always have it handy. Your character bible needs to cover backstory and motivation at some length. If you haven't worked them out for your main characters, we highly recommend that you work through the exercises in Chapter 7 for each character. There's simply no substitute for doing these exercises.

In your character bible, aim for a page or more of backstory on each of your main characters and a bit less for the minor characters. You also need at least a few sentences to spell out the values, ambitions, and story goals of your main characters.

You can work on backstory and motivation at any time, depending on your creative paradigm. (See Chapter 4 for a discussion of your creative paradigm and how it influences the order in which you do your creative work.) If you're a seat-of-the-pants writer or an edit-as-you-go writer, you may well write the entire first draft of your book first, before you ever think much about back-story or motivation. If you're a Snowflaker or an outliner, then you probably enjoy developing backstory and motivation first, so that your first draft will be as close as possible to your last draft. Whatever works for you is fine, but do the work!

In the next section, we ask you to psychoanalyze your character and probe his motivations more deeply.

Psychoanalyzing Your Characters

The biggest problem writers have with characters' motivations is not giving them any. The main solution is to make a conscious effort to name the follow-ing core pieces of motivation for each main character (which we introduce in Chapter 7):

- ✔ **Values:** What are the core truths for your character? You can have sev-eral of these.
- ✔ **Ambition:** What one abstract thing does your character want most in the world?
- ✔ **Story goal:** What one concrete thing does your character believe she needs to do or have or become in order to achieve her ambition?

If you have these worked out for your characters, that's great! Then your goal in editing is to make them better to deepen your character, sharpen the con-flict of the story, and make it all reasonable to your reader. This section can help you do so.

Are values in conflict?

Every character has values, and great stories thrive on conflicts between values. *Values* are core truths — things your character believes to be true without examining them. When your main character's core truths are in con-flict, then he can't be predictable, and neither can your story.

Consider two conflicting values of Don Corleone, the Mafia leader in Mario Puzo's *The Godfather:*

- ✔ "Nothing is more important than respect."
- ✔ "Nothing is more important than family."

Don Corleone's troubles begin when a rising young Mafioso comes to him with a proposal for a joint venture in narcotics. Corleone believes that this sort of crime is bad business, and he'll have nothing to do with it. But Sonny, the oldest son of Don Corleone, exposes his interest in the matter by questioning his father's judgment in front of the drug-dealing Mafioso, an act of blatant disrespect. Afterward, Don Corleone reprimands his son, but he doesn't oust him. His love of family has come into conflict with his need for respect.

It's a fatal mistake. The spurned Mafioso, sensing weakness, tries to assassinate Don Corleone so he can negotiate a deal with Sonny. This leads to a terrible war of attrition between the Corleones and the Five Families of New York.

As you read your story, ask whether the values of your lead character are in conflict. If not, can you revise them to be in conflict? Can you add a new value that will conflict with the existing ones?

Do the values make sense from the backstory?

Your characters generally can't give any reasons for their values. A value is a truth so sacred, so true, that it simply can't be explained. If a character can explain his values, then you haven't taken him far enough — some core truths beneath those values explain them. In that case, those underlying core truths are his real values.

You are not your character. You are the god of the universe that you're creating as your story world. You are omniscient, and you *can* explain your character's values — at least to some degree — from his backstory. Somewhere in the half-remembered mists of time lie the reasons for your character's values.

Searching for the source of Don Corleone's values

Why does Don Corleone value respect so much? Why does he call himself a "man of respect"? He can give no reason, because it's obvious to him. But the answer is that Don Corleone is a Sicilian, raised in an honor culture. In such a culture, honor is worth more than money. Corleone's criminal enterprises in the U.S. depend critically on holding the respect of his friends and his enemies.

Why does Don Corleone value family so much? Again, it's part of his Sicilian culture. Blood loyalty is everything; no explanation is needed. None is possible, and Don Corleone would be astonished that anyone would ask for one.

But not all Sicilians become Mafia dons. What explains Don Corleone's rise to power as the head of one of the most vicious crime families in the country? Don Corleone holds another value that we haven't discussed yet: "A man is responsible to use power in every possible way to benefit his family and those who respect him."

This value becomes clear in the first chapter of *The Godfather,* when Don Corleone receives four different visitors on the wedding day of his daughter. Each visitor needs something from him, but his responses to each one show his values clearly. Those who have a history of showing respect to Corleone get what they want; those who don't have such a history must learn respect first and then reap the benefits of knowing the Godfather.

Where did Don Corleone develop this value? Readers don't discover the answer until a number of chapters into the book, when Mario Puzo provides a number of pages of the backstory, showing how a quiet, humble Sicilian young man transformed into the powerful Godfather by a series of choices that he made in a world that treats quiet, humble Sicilian young men with contempt and injustice. By the end of this long backstory sequence, the reader still doesn't consider Don Corleone a moral man. However, the reader *understands* how Corleone justifies his actions to himself.

Making sense of your characters' values

Some of your characters will inherit cultural values; others will create their values based on early life experiences. You should be able to give some justification for each value; however, don't expect to be able to make an ironclad case that these "core truths" are in fact true. Values are intensely personal and by their nature can't be proven. The best you can do is to make a reasonable case that your character's values make sense to him, given his culture, personality, genetic traits, and life experiences. That's all you need.

As you read through your manuscript, ask the following questions:

- ✔ Do the values of your characters make sense to you? Even if you don't agree with those values, can you understand how your characters came to believe them?

- ✔ If the values don't make sense, then can you find a way for each character to justify the values that currently seem implausible?

- ✔ If your justification for any of the values seems weak, can you strengthen it? If you can't, then those values are broken and you need to come up with something more plausible, because your reader isn't going to believe that anyone would hold those values.

Every character thinks he's the hero of the story; no character believes he's evil incarnate. Characters justify their behavior by their values, core truths that they consider "obviously true." The more likely your reader is to reject your character's values, the more you need to work to show a backstory that explains how those values came to exist. Your reader must believe that your character believes his values to be absolutely true — that's the secret to creating three-dimensional characters.

Does ambition follow from values?

Each character has an *ambition* — one abstract thing that he wants more than anything else in life. Some characters know this early in their story; others only gradually develop an ambition. Regardless, that ambition needs to spring from the character's values.

The Godfather is the story of how Michael Corleone, the youngest son of Don Corleone, develops an ambition to be like his father. At the beginning of the story, that seems like an unlikely ambition for Michael. The year is 1945, and he's a clean-cut Army veteran and college boy who has apparently renounced his family's criminal connections and has a non-Italian girlfriend who thinks he's kidding when he talks about his father's dark past.

Yet Michael Corleone is made of the same steel as his father, with the same ferocious will and the same icy control over his emotions. He shares his father's values — family ties and respect — without being able to explain them any better than his father can. When Don Corleone is critically wounded by a rival Mafioso, it's Michael Corleone, the white sheep of the family, who volunteers to kill the man who ordered the hit. This is Michael's first step toward an ambition he only dimly realizes — to be a man like his father.

That ambition arises directly from Michael's values. Until his father was shot, Michael could afford to distance himself from the family business. But Michael can't simply walk away without avenging this hit. He can't. His blood ties demand it. Having decided to take vengeance, Michael chooses to do it in a way that earns him respect, even from his older brothers and his father's tough *caporegimes*. Michael has other options, but none of them would command respect. Michael is more his father's son than he knew.

As you read through your story, ask whether you've defined an ambition for each of your main characters. Does that ambition spring directly from at least one of the character's values? If not, you have two options:

 ✔ Find a new value to give your character that will explain this ambition.

 ✔ Change the ambition to be in line with the character's values.

Will the story goal satisfy the ambition?

Every lead character needs a *story goal* — a concrete wish to get something, achieve something, or become something. Until your primary character has a story goal, you have no story; you have only a set of incidents that mean nothing to the reader. After you have a story goal, your reader *invests* in the story. You've set the hook: Will the lead character reach his story goal or not?

A story goal must be objective, simple, important, achievable, and difficult (see Chapter 7 for details). But in the editing stage, you need to verify one other thing: Would reaching the story goal actually achieve your lead character's ambition? If not, then that's a problem.

Achieving Michael Corleone's ambition

In *The Godfather,* Michael Corleone feels impelled to kill the man who ordered the hit on his father, along with the dirty police captain who's in league with him. Corleone shoots them in a restaurant where the three have met to negotiate a peace. Twenty minutes later, he's on a boat headed for Sicily, where he'll lie low until the heat dies down.

That ends Act 1, and it's a disaster for Michael. He had planned to marry his WASP (white Anglo-Saxon Protestant) girlfriend and settle down to an ordinary life outside the shadow of his family's criminal ventures. Now he's banished to hide out in Sicily, and his story goal is apparently very simple: to come home.

However, it's more complicated than that. Yes, Michael wants to come home, but come home as what? Michael knows, and the reader knows, that Michael can never come home and resume his former life as a law-abiding citizen. Michael Corleone is a murderer, with a death sentence over his head from five rival Mafia families. He's a cop-killer with a long prison sentence awaiting him, courtesy of the American justice system.

If Michael Corleone comes home again, he'll need the help of his father and family and the alternative system of power that they maintain. Michael Corleone can never come home clean. He'll have to come home as a member of the Corleone syndicate or not at all. By virtue of his bloodline, he'll be in competition with his two older brothers. Who will become the new Godfather when Don Corleone eventually retires or dies? If Michael Corleone comes home, he has no choice but to aim for that position. He's the smartest of the three sons, but is he the toughest? After showing his strong moralistic leanings early, can Michael come home as the new Godfather? That's the story question that carries the story for the rest of the book.

Michael Corleone's ambition is to become a man like his father, an ambition that he could achieve in many ways. But the path he chooses is to *become* his father.

Evaluating your main characters' story goals and ambitions

You can define your story goal at any point in Act 1 of your story (which usually takes up the first quarter of your story — see Chapter 8 for details on three-act structure). The earlier you do it, the clearer your story will be to your reader. But many great stories don't clearly specify the story goal until the disaster at the very end of Act 1.

Ask the following questions as you read through your story:

- ✔ Does each of your main characters have a story goal? If not, then you need to define one; otherwise, that character exists only to advance the story of one of the other characters. Every character must have a life of his own.

- ✔ Does each story goal spring directly from the character's ambition?

- ✔ Is the story goal objective, simple, important, achievable, and difficult? If it fails on any of these points, can you recast it?

- ✔ Does each main character have a story goal that you've clearly spelled out by the end of Act 1? If not, can you nudge that character to develop a story goal sooner?

The Narrator: Fine-Tuning Point-of-View and Voice

Which kind of narrator you use and how that narrator tells the story can have a big impact on whether your characters and your story work. In this section, we help you reevaluate your choice of both point of view (POV) and POV character, ensure that your writing's consistent, and consider character voice.

Does your POV strategy work?

Every story needs a point-of-view strategy (see Chapter 7 for a review of six common choices for POV). The three most common of these, in order, are

- ✔ **Third person:** You show the scene from inside the skin of one character, using third-person pronouns such as *he* or *she*.

- ✔ **First person:** You show the scene from inside the skin of one character, using first-person pronouns such as *I* and *me*.

- ✔ **Head-hopping:** You show the scene from inside the skin of several characters, hopping from one head to another, in each case using third-person pronouns.

What POV choice did you make in your manuscript? In this section, you revisit your decision and make sure it's working, because a wrong choice can sink your story.

Evaluating your POV

In this section, we help you make sure you use your POV choice to your best advantage. For more information on the advantages and disadvantages of each POV, see Chapter 7.

Third person

Third person POV is accepted in all categories, so if you're using it, then you really don't need to worry any more about your choice. Third person is a good, safe bet.

Here are some questions to help you make sure that you're using third person to its best effect:

- ✔ Is it clear in every scene who the *POV character* (the character you want readers to identify with) is? Do you establish the POV character as early as possible in the scene?

- ✔ Do you accidentally slip out of the POV character's head to tell readers things he doesn't know or to show readers things he can't see?

- ✔ Do you tell the reader information in narrative summary that you could slip in as dialogue or interior monologue (with suitable subtlety)?

- ✔ Have you made sure you filter description through the emotional lens of the POV character?

First person

Some readers don't like first person POV, and we're not sure why, because there's no good technical reason to dislike first person. It's at least as good as third person POV for giving your reader a powerful emotional experience. But the fact remains that some readers refuse to read a book in first person.

Ask the following questions to help you make the most of first person POV:

- ✔ Is your POV character — the narrator — able to be present for most of the action? One problem with first person can arise when your narrator can't physically be on the scene for all the action; then you have to resort to having other characters tell what happened in those scenes. Would it make sense to use multiple POV characters so you can have another narrator be at those scenes?

- ✔ Are you giving too much airtime to the narrator's interior monologue and narrative summary? Both of these are valuable techniques, but the question is whether they're out of proportion.

✔ Are you taking full advantage of the intimacy that first-person narration gives you?

✔ If your narrator has a unique voice, does it permeate the entire story, including the actions and descriptions of other characters?

Head-hopping

Most editors we've talked to hate the head-hopping POV and will ignore your protests that "Margaret Mitchell did it in *Gone With the Wind.*" Editors who don't like head-hopping will cut you off at the knees with a comment like, "You're not Margaret Mitchell. Come back when you are."

If you're using a head-hopping POV, ask the following questions:

✔ Do you have a good reason every time you switch to a new POV character within each scene?

✔ Do you hop heads so often that the reader can't identify strongly with the focal character in each scene?

✔ Can you reduce the amount of head-hopping without damaging the emotional impact of your story?

Omniscient

Using omniscient POV isn't common these days. It's very hard to do well. Many editors consider omniscient a red flag. Complaining that this or that author whom you like uses omniscient POV doesn't help — that argument doesn't carry much weight unless you can write as well as that author.

If you're using omniscient POV, ask yourself the following:

✔ Do you have a compelling reason for giving information that none of the characters can know?

✔ Do you give your reader a fair share of time inside the heads of your important characters? If not, can you increase the time you spend there?

✔ Can you reduce the number of transitions in and out of the heads of characters?

✔ Are your omniscient segments as strong as possible?

Second person

Second person POV is difficult to do well, and many readers simply rebel at the notion of reading a story in second person. It can work if you know what you're doing, but it's going to be a strike against you in any novel — and two strikes against you in your debut novel. So think very long and hard before choosing this option, and get some opinions from published authors or editors or agents to make sure it's working for you.

If you're using second person, ask yourself a few questions:

- ✔ Is there a compelling reason to use second person rather than first?
- ✔ Do you have problems getting your POV character into every scene? If so, would it make sense to use multiple third person POV characters instead?

Third person objective

Third person objective isn't easy to do well, because you're giving away the two main advantages that you hold over screenwriters: your ability to write interior emotion and interior monologue (see Chapter 10 for details on these two powerful tools). Therefore, this POV is technically challenging: You have to show all those thoughts and feelings of your lead character using only action, dialogue, and description. Yet the third person objective POV is doable, and it can have a cinematic feel if you do it exceptionally well.

Here are some questions to ask if you're using third person objective:

- ✔ Does your novel have a strong cinematic feel?
- ✔ Does your reader identify well with the focal character in each scene, even though you can't use interior emotion and interior monologue?
- ✔ Are you occasionally drifting inside the character's head, even though you intended not to? If so, would it make sense to choose third person instead so you can get inside the character intentionally rather than accidentally?

Asking whether your POV choice fits your category

Look at other recent novels in your category (anything published in the last 20 years counts as "recent"). How many of them use the POV choice you made, and how many use a different one? Do reviewers criticize them for this choice, or do they ignore it? Do online customer book reviews mention the choice of POV, and if so, what do they say about it?

If you know some published authors in your category, ask them for their opinion on your choice of POV. Will your choice be a show-stopper for your project? (If so, then change your choice of POV, even if it seems unfair.) Will your choice be a problem for readers? (If so, then think hard about your choice, but don't feel absolutely obligated to change.)

If you can talk to editors or agents at a writing conference or elsewhere, show them a sample chapter of your manuscript and ask them whether your POV choice is going to be a problem.

Have you chosen the right POV character?

Even novels with only a single POV character may require some careful thought: which character is the best POV character for the story? For example, nearly all the Sherlock Holmes stories have Dr. Watson rather than Sherlock as the POV character. Why? Holmes has supreme confidence in his own skills and could easily come off as arrogant if he were the POV character. Because Watson frankly admits that he's put off by Holmes's strong ego, the reader doesn't have to wonder whether the author knows that Holmes is conceited. Watson is then free to praise Sherlock's more likeable features. If Holmes were the POV character, he could hardly do that without seeming even more egotistical.

If you have a larger-than-life central character like Sherlock Holmes, you may find it useful to use a sidekick who can give you a little distance as a POV character.

In novels with multiple POV characters, then you need to decide on a POV character for each scene. That's a hard question, and you often can't find any easy answers. You don't need a sidekick, because each of the POV characters can give that objective look at the others.

Your choice of POV character may depend on whether the scene is an active scene or a reactive scene (see Chapter 9 for a discussion of the two main kinds of scenes):

> ✔ **If it's an active scene, who has the most to lose in the scene, and who is the actual loser in the scene?** These may be the same character. Either of them may make an excellent POV character, because they're most likely to have a powerful emotional experience during the scene.

> ✔ **If it's a reactive scene, who is suffering most keenly in the reaction part of the scene, and who has the best analytical skills in the dilemma part of the scene?** Again, these may be the same character. They both make good choices for the POV character. The reaction part of the scene is a great place to give your reader emotive hits; the dilemma part is a strong opportunity to get your reader inside the thought processes of the POV character.

Any of the characters in a scene is fair game to be the POV character. Consider each of them and ask which is the most entertaining choice for your reader. This is no light choice. The scene will likely have a very different feel as seen through the eyes of the different characters.

Is your POV consistent?

After you've decided for certain that the POV strategy you've chosen is the right one for your novel, you still need to make sure that you're actually using that POV consistently throughout your story. Your reader wants to know that you aren't going to change the rules on her. If you're going to use first person POV for a certain character, use first person for that character everywhere in the book.

Normally, if a book is written in first person, the whole story is written in that POV, but we've seen novels that worked well with first person for one character and third person for the other characters. An excellent example is Diana Gabaldon's *Dragonfly in Amber.*

Consistency is important. If you're going to use third person POV for a character in one scene, then don't use first person or objective third person for that character in other scenes.

Does your character have a unique voice?

Some of your characters may have a unique and distinctive way of speaking and thinking, which comes across in their dialogue and interior monologue. It also flavors their observations of the other characters. You aren't required to give your characters a strong voice (which we discuss in Chapter 10), but doing so makes your writing more compelling. Much of the charm of Mark Twain's *Huckleberry Finn* comes from the voice of the narrator, Huck, who is none too reliable as a narrator. Huck is an innocent, ignorant country boy. The reader isn't intended to believe everything Huck says, and the reader is expected to understand things that Huck doesn't.

To develop strong character voice, you need to have an ear for dialogue. Some authors do this naturally, and some don't. The key is to listen to real people, constantly asking what makes someone's voice unique and what it reveals about her personality. After listening to a person for a few minutes, try writing a few paragraphs that mimic her word usage, sentence structure, thought patterns, and personality (you may use some slang, but don't overdo it). This is hard, but with practice, you can figure out how to mimic people on paper. After you've mastered this skill, try writing one of your characters in the voice of someone you've met. You may find your character coming alive as you try this.

Be wary of trying to carry too much of the story with voice. Characters with a strong voice are great, but don't try to inject too much interior monologue to show off that voice. Even worse, don't get sloppy and overuse narrative summary, just because you have a great narrative voice.

Fixing Broken Characters

Your characters are not written in stone. If you find a problem with one of your characters, then fix him! You can rework your characters to make them deeper, more believable, and more interesting. But first you need to diagnose the problem. This section tells you how to change boring, shallow, unbelievable, or unlikeable characters — we can guarantee you'll have more success changing them than real people!

Boring characters

Characters are interesting when they have a strong and compelling goal. When they lack a good goal, they're boring. If your characters are boring, give them something to desperately want.

If it's early in your story, your characters may not yet have a clearly defined story goal. That's okay. Remember that your story is an interruption in the lives of your main characters. Before the story broke in on them, they were each living lives and pursuing goals. Modest goals, maybe, but they had something they wanted to do or have or become. Those modest goals keep your reader interested while you lead your character to his story goal.

In George Lucas's *Star Wars*, for example, Luke Skywalker really doesn't have a strong story goal until the very end of Act 1, when Storm Troopers murder his aunt and uncle. After that happens, his story goal gels quickly: To go with Obi-Wan Kenobi to help the Rebel Alliance. But well before the massacre at his home, Luke has been nursing a desire to go to military school and become a pilot. And he's been following the Rebellion with keen interest, hating the Empire with a deep hatred. Luke's hope, at the beginning of the movie, is that the new droids will free up his uncle enough so he can go for military training as soon as possible. That's not a huge goal, but it's enough to make Luke reasonably interesting. When he meets up with Kenobi and develops a much larger and more important goal, he becomes that much more interesting.

Shallow characters

We call characters *shallow* when there just isn't much to them: when a reader can predict what they'll do or say, when they come across as one-dimensional, or when their interests seem trivial and unimportant.

What's the cure for a shallow character? Most of the time, the character just needs some values. Either you haven't given the character any values at all, or you've given her only one. Give her another value, and make sure it's in conflict with the first one. In some cases, the values you've given the character are simply shallow in themselves.

For example, say you have a major character who's a beach bunny. All she really cares about is hanging out at the beach, working on her tan, and smiling at the surfer guys. She has only one value: "Hanging out at the beach is better than anything else in the world." When you write it out like that, her vapidity springs into sharp relief, doesn't it? But adding some depth to her isn't so hard. Interview this bunny and find out what makes her tick. Why does she spend so much time at the beach?

Maybe her mother's dead and her father's a rageaholic. Home is a hellhole, so she escapes by going to the beach. But the beach isn't her real value. Her real values are "Family is important to me" and "Peace and stability are important to me." These two values create conflict for your bunny, because her family violates her peace and stability. That's why she goes to the beach. Suddenly, Miss Beach is a bit deeper, isn't she?

Unbelievable characters

You'll almost always think your characters are believable, because to you, your characters are real people. So it comes as a bit of a shock when one of your critiquers insists that "Fredhelm wouldn't torch the mayor's house. He's just not that kind of person." You can argue all you want that Fredhelm really would torch the house, but if your reader doesn't buy it, then you have a problem.

When you hear that your characters are doing something unbelievable, congratulate yourself that you've at least created a character who's real enough that readers think they know what Fredhelm is actually like. That's an accomplishment. But how do you convince your readers that Fredhelm could commit arson?

If your characters are unbelievable, connect the dots more clearly from backstory to values to ambition to story goal. The answer is usually that you have to do one of three things:

- ✔ **Make it clearer that the character's story goal follows directly from his ambition.** Is the story goal obviously the best way to achieve the ambition? Is there a simpler or more plausible way to get there?

- ✔ **Make it clearer that the character's ambition follows from at least one of his values.** Which value most strongly supports his ambition? Does

> another value just as strongly oppose the ambition? Can you find a way to tip the balance so that the ambition seems more believable?
>
> ✔ **Make it clearer just why the character's values are so important to him.** Do the values have a plausible explanation in the character's backstory?

Earlier in this chapter, we discuss the curious case of Michael Corleone, an honest young man with a good future who comes from a family of gangsters. At a crucial point in the story, Michael agrees to avenge the attempted murder of his father by killing a rival Mafioso and a crooked police captain. That's a huge change in direction for Michael, but author Mario Puzo makes it believable by laying the groundwork, showing the reader Michael's family background, his values of family and honor, his iron will, and his ability to think like his father — "it's not personal; it's business." Few readers would agree with Michael's decision, but they *believe* that Michael would make it.

In some cases, after thinking hard about your character's backstory, values, ambitions, and story goal, you may realize that she really has done something out of character. In that case, either change her actions or find yourself a new character capable of doing the job.

Unlikeable characters

Some characters are just plain unlikeable. When your test readers tell you that they don't like a particular character, you don't have many options. Either you can make the character more likeable, or you can make him stronger. Here's how to fix an unlikable character:

1. **Figure out why the character is unlikeable.**

   Is he annoying? Stupid? Arrogant? Klutzy? Cruel?

2. **Ask whether that behavior was intentional; then improve your character.**

   Here's how to fix him:

   - If it was an accident, make him less annoying, stupid, arrogant, klutzy, or cruel.

   - If your character is intentionally unlikeable, make him more interesting, deep, and believable (as we discuss in the three preceding sections).

Consider the assassin in Frederick Forsyth's thriller *The Day of the Jackal*. By anybody's standards, the Jackal is thoroughly unlikeable. He's a contract assassin, hired to kill Charles de Gaulle. He casually kills a photographer who tries to blackmail him. He seduces a married woman and then murders her when she becomes inconvenient.

What makes the Jackal a compelling character? A number of things. First, he's immensely competent, as the reader discovers when his thuggish employers interview him and he reveals that he knows more about them than they know about him. Second, he has an impossible task: to assassinate the world's best-protected man. Third, he has a strong motivation: completing the contract will make him rich enough to quit the assassination business. Fourth, he prepares meticulously, never revealing to the reader his reasons for doing things, leaving them to puzzle out how he's going to kill de Gaulle. Fifth, he acts decisively in the face of enormous obstacles. All these factors earn the Jackal the reader's respect and fascination.

Chapter 13

Scrutinizing Your Story Structure

In This Chapter

▶ Fixing common storyline problems

▶ Analyzing the three-act structure

▶ Using your scene list to restructure your story and write your second draft

---

We recommend that when you're ready to begin editing your manuscript, you first analyze your characters (as we discuss in Chapter 12) and then analyze your story structure (the subject of this chapter). Regardless of your creative paradigm, figure out these big-picture problems with your story and fix them first, before you dive into the detailed edits (which we cover in Chapters 14 and 15).

Story structure is nothing more than a very high-level summary of your story. In this chapter, we show you how to edit your story structure at three levels: your *storyline* (a one-sentence summary of your story), your *three-act structure* (a one-paragraph summary of your story), and your *scene list* (a list that summarizes every scene in your novel).

Your storyline is a powerful selling tool that you'll use forever in selling your story to your editor, her publishing team, the bookstore people, and readers. It's more than just a selling tool, though — it's also your strategic vision of what your novel is about. A good storyline radically simplifies your editing process by forcing you to define what's important and what isn't.

Your three-act structure allows you to map out the big pieces of your book. If you have a satisfying three-act structure, then you have a leg up on making your readers happy, because modern readers are wired to expect a three-act structure — whether they know it or not. If your three-act structure is weak or wandering, your reader may feel that the story isn't going anywhere, even if she can't quite explain why. It's your job to figure out what's wrong and make it right before your reader ever sees it.

Your scene list gives you an overview of your story and makes it easy to plan the revisions of your manuscript. You can make decisions on adding, deleting, and moving scenes using your scene list. You can also add notes to yourself on key revisions you intend to make. When you finish revising your scene list, you can use it to quickly create the second draft of your novel.

Editing Your Storyline

We strongly believe that the very first step in editing your manuscript should be to define your strategic vision for your novel — your storyline. The storyline can guide you in every decision you make as you edit your novel. Why do you need a storyline? Because if you really understand your story, then you can boil it down to a single sentence of 25 words or less. If you can't boil it down that far, then you don't understand your story yet.

Randy often runs storyline clinics online, asking his blog readers to post one-sentence summaries of their novels. Storylines of 30, 40, or even 50-plus words are common. Often these involve numerous characters and plot threads. Randy then challenges his blog readers to cut the fat out of these long, convoluted storylines. Sometimes the surgery gets pretty severe. When you slice a 50-word storyline down to 15 words, you've cut to the bone!

Have you written your storyline yet? If not, read through the section on how to write a storyline in Chapter 8 and then write one that describes your story. Don't read further until you do, because this section looks at some of the most common problems that we see in storylines and suggests ways to fix them. You can't fix what you don't have.

Removing all unnecessary weight

The purpose of the storyline is *not* to tell the story; the purpose of the storyline is to define the direction of the novel. Most storylines are too long, so the first question you should always ask is this: "What else can I cut out of my storyline?" Here are the three numbers we look at in a storyline:

- **The number of words:** If it's more than 25, then make every possible effort to cut some words.
- **The number of characters:** If the storyline mentions more than three, that's too many. Two is better than three. One may be all you need.
- **The number of story threads:** If it's more than one, then strongly consider cutting it to one.

A storyline is your reader's first contact with your story. It's also your strategic vision of the story. Make it simple and memorable, not merely for your reader's sake, but also for your own.

Keeping your characters anonymous

When you tell someone your storyline, it's probably the first thing they've ever heard about your novel. Your hearer has no context at all for your characters, so you have to give all the context right there in the storyline. So look at your storyline and focus on the characters, describing them in a few words without telling their names.

Giving the names of the characters in a storyline wastes words. After all, which is shorter: "Frodo the hobbit" or "a hobbit"? "Vito Corleone, godfather of a Mafia family" or "a Mafia godfather"? "Lizzie Bennet, an unmarried young woman" or "an unmarried young woman"?

Tell your character's uniqueness, not her name. Your storyline helps you sell the concept of your story, and unless you're writing historical fiction with famous characters, you don't need to give out names of characters to sell a concept. You just need one or two or a few words that define the characters. Hobbits and godfathers and unmarried young women are intrinsically interesting (to the right readers). Frodo and Vito and Lizzie are fine names, but they just aren't that interesting without a context.

Staying focused

Trying to sneak just a bit more into a storyline is all too easy. If you have a storyline down to 13 words, you may think it really doesn't cost you much to add five words that allude to a second plot thread or a third character. But think again. Does the addition really help? Or will it complicate things and make it easier for someone in your selling chain to bungle the message?

An adage from writer and editor Sol Stein applies to your storyline: "One plus one equals a half." If your storyline covers the most important plot thread in your story, then why would you want to dilute it with the second most important plot thread?

Cutting down some example storylines

You may feel that you're writing such a complex story that you simply can't cut your storyline down. Cut it down anyway.

Be clear about one thing: Complexity in a story is good. We're all for complex stories — big, powerful tales that require a wide stage: fantasies like *The Lord of the Rings,* by J. R. R. Tolkien; thrillers like *The Godfather,* by Mario Puzo; timeless romances like *Pride and Prejudice,* by Jane Austen. However, each of these novels involves a central plot thread and central characters — an overall focus for the book. This section looks at each of these novels in turn and shows how to cut down a big, complex storyline into something far easier to handle.

Example: The Lord of the Rings

The Lord of the Rings is a massive story that covers hundreds of leagues of travel, scores of characters, numerous people groups, a dozen-plus languages, half a dozen sentient races, and several major plot threads. Here's a long, convoluted storyline that still doesn't do justice to the story:

> Gandalf the wizard wants to defeat the Dark Lord Sauron for all time, so when he learns that Frodo the hobbit has Sauron's Ring of Power, he persuades Frodo to travel to Rivendell to confer with the elf lord Elrond about how best to destroy the Ring, and the best way turns out to be to send a small party of hobbits, men, elves, and dwarves to go toward Mordor, but their team is attacked by orcs and two of the hobbits are kidnapped, forcing three of the survivors to pursue them, leaving Frodo and his servant Sam to journey on toward Mordor with the unlikely guide Gollum, who tries to betray them to Shelob while Aragorn, Legolas, and Gimli fight a major battle at Helm's Deep and then spur on the Rohirrim to go to battle in Gondor, while they themselves take the Paths of the Dead and meet them at the decisive battle that saves Gondor but nearly kills Faramir, who falls in love with Eowyn, who is in love with Aragorn, who is betrothed to Arwen, whom he can't have until he is king, which can't happen until Frodo destroys the Ring.

And that isn't the half of it. That isn't the tenth of it. We've used 195 words, mentioned 13 characters by name and still left out essential characters such as Merrie, Pippin, Tom Bombadil, Galadriel, Boromir, Theoden, Denethor, Treebeard, and numerous others. How can we possibly cut more?

The answer's simple: The critical character is Frodo the hobbit. However well the other characters in the story fight their battles, all is for nothing if Frodo fails to throw the Ring of Power into the Cracks of Doom. This is Frodo's story. Therefore, cut the storyline down to Frodo:

> A hobbit learns that destroying his magic ring is the key to saving Middle Earth from the Dark Lord.

Nineteen words, two characters, one plot thread. This isn't nearly enough to tell the story, but a storyline isn't supposed to do that; it's supposed to tell you what's most important in the story. If you were J. R. R. Tolkien and your publisher demanded you cut the word count in half, this storyline would tell you what to keep and what to cut.

Example: The Godfather

The Godfather is a big story featuring dozens of characters in New York City, Las Vegas, Hollywood, and Sicily. The novel weaves together numerous story threads into a complex tapestry. Consider the following sprawling storyline:

> When Don Corleone, the head of a New York Mafia family, is shot in the street and nearly killed, his middle son Freddie collapses emotionally and is shipped off to Las Vegas while his eldest son Sonny takes charge of the business and tries to beat the family enemies into submission through a war of relentless brutality until he is murdered by the opposition, while the third son Michael avenges the attempted assassination and then has to hide out in Sicily until the heat dies down and he can come back to help take over the reins of the family.

This storyline leaves out quite a number of characters — hitman Luca Brasi, Mama Corleone, Michael's girlfriend Kay Adams, Sonny's girlfriend Lucy Mancini, the famous singer and movie star Johnny Fontane, Johnny's sidekick Nino Valenti, the family *consigliori* Tom Hagen, the twisted movie mogul Jack Woltz, the brilliant surgeon Jules Segal, Michael's wife Appollonia, Michael's sister Connie and her no-good husband Carlo Rizzi, and the two *caporegimes*, Tessio and Clemenza. Most of these are POV characters, and all of them are important to the story. We've left out all these vital characters, and we still have a 100-word storyline with four characters. We still have far too much. How can we possibly cut more?

That's easy: We cut more. Only two characters are essential to our storyline — the Godfather Don Corleone and his youngest son Michael, who will replace him. Everybody else is secondary. Because Michael is the central character of the story, we focus our storyline on him:

> When a Mafia godfather is shot in the streets, his youngest son quits college to avenge him.

Seventeen words, two characters, one plot thread. It's not perfect. It can't capture the bigness of the book; only reading it will capture that. But this storyline keeps you focused on the main story. If you had to edit the original manuscript into published form, this storyline would guide you all the way.

Example: Pride and Prejudice

Jane Austen's novel isn't quite as big as the examples in the preceding sections, but it's plenty big for a romance novel, a genre that usually keeps the stage tightly focused. Take a look at a possible storyline for the novel:

When Lizzie Bennet and her sisters learn that wealthy young bachelor Mr. Bingley has moved into nearby Netherfield Hall, they hope that one of them will marry Bingley, opening the way for the other sisters to marry wealthy young men, and luckily the eldest sister Jane does catch Bingley's eye and there are high hopes of a wedding until Bingley suddenly abandons country life for London, leaving Jane heartbroken and her sisters to pursue the likes of Mr. Wickham, a charming soldier who tells Lizzie that he's poor on account of Bingley's friend, the wealthy Mr. Darcy, a brusque man who shows no interest in Lizzie until he unexpectedly proposes to her, which she refuses and then begins to regret, the more so as she learns that Darcy is a far better man than Wickham, who ultimately seduces Lizzie's youngest sister Lydia, dashing the hopes of all the sisters for marriage to decent men until Darcy steps in and solves all the problems anonymously.

Whew! That storyline is simply awful, isn't it? It includes 164 words, features six characters by name, and covers three story threads. Again, it's all too much. We haven't even mentioned Mama Bennet, Papa Bennet, Mary and Kitty Bennet, Mr. Collins, Charlotte Lucas, Lady Catherine de Bourgh, Georgiana Darcy, or Colonel Fitzwilliam. We've said nothing about that dreaded entailment, which is the cause of the Bennet girls' predicament. We've said almost nothing, yet we've said far too much.

The solution is to focus on the primary characters, Lizzie and Mr. Darcy, along with their story thread. Everything else has to go. Everything. All that remains is this:

> A young Englishwoman from a peculiar family is pursued by an arrogant and wealthy young man.

Sixteen words, two characters, one story thread. Nothing in this storyline reveals the fact that the novel will endure for two centuries. No storyline could tell you such a thing. Don't try to make your storyline support too much weight.

A storyline is a sound bite, nothing more. Yet it guides your thinking through the entire revision process, so get it right before you begin detailed editing of your manuscript.

Testing Your Three-Act Structure

When you have a solid storyline, you're ready to move on to the next step in revising your story: editing your three-act structure. In Chapter 8, we describe the three-act structure and augment it with what we call the three-disaster structure. The main ideas are these:

- ✔ Each act covers a long chunk of the story, and each disaster is a single point of time in the story.

- ✔ Act 1 covers roughly the first quarter of the story and introduces the main characters.

- ✔ The first disaster comes at the very end of Act 1 and forces the lead character to commit irrevocably to the story. If the main character doesn't yet have a story goal by this point in the story, this disaster forces him to choose one.

- ✔ Act 2 covers roughly half the story and includes many obstacles and setbacks.

- ✔ The second disaster comes at the midpoint of Act 2 and solves the problem of the sagging middle by changing the direction of the story.

- ✔ The third disaster comes at the end of Act 2 and forces the lead character to commit to ending the story. Normally, this means committing to some sort of final confrontation, which appears likely to fail but may succeed. *Success* means that the lead character achieves his story goal; *failure* means he doesn't.

- ✔ Act 3 works through the final confrontation (which includes the *climax*, the high point of the story and its resolution), shows the aftermath, and finally wraps things up.

If you haven't written your three-act structure yet, now is the time to work it out for your story. Read through the section on how to write a three-act structure in Chapter 8 and then write one. (If you find your story has more than three acts, see the nearby sidebar "Handling extra acts.")

Handling extra acts

You may wonder what to do if your story doesn't have only three acts. What if it has four? Or five? Or twenty? Remember that the three-act structure is popular because it works, but it's not the only possible high-level structure for a story. If your story structure works, then it works.

If you have a four-act structure, then your four acts may be equal in length. If so, then your Acts 2 and 3 are nothing more than what we've been calling Act 2 here, and your Act 4 is what we've been calling Act 3. That's just a difference in terminology.

However, if you have a five-act structure, then that may well be fundamentally different from a three-act structure. That's fine, so long as it works. If thinking of your story as a three-act structure doesn't make sense, then don't.

If you have a twenty-act structure, then we suspect you've spread your story too thin. If you look hard, you can probably clump those acts into three big chunks, with major disasters at the usual places for a three-act structure.

In this section, we take you through the process of testing every aspect of your three-act structure. We do this by testing the three-act structure for *The Godfather* and for *Pride and Prejudice* — are these books up to snuff? We also include some questions to help you analyze your own story. As you answer those questions, don't make changes yet — simply make notes for the changes you want to make; then make all your structural changes at once. At the end of this chapter, we discuss writing your second draft.

You may wonder whether your secondary story threads should also have a three-act structure. They can, and analyzing your other story threads using the three-act structure often makes sense. Don't feel obligated to make the three disasters of each story thread all fall at the same time as the corresponding disasters in the main story. The timing of the three disasters that we give is only an approximation.

What are your three disasters?

Your first step is to identify your three disasters — one that makes the main character commit to the story, one that changes the direction of the story, and one that forces the final confrontation.

Here's our analysis of the three-act structure for *The Godfather,* with the three disasters in italics:

> When Mafia godfather Vito Corleone is nearly killed by his enemy Virgil Sollozzo, the powerful Corleone Family is thrown into chaos. Vito's youngest son Michael, a goody-goody college boy, avenges the hit by killing Sollozzo and his police guardian, but then *Michael is forced to flee the country.* Sonny Corleone, Michael's oldest brother, wages war on the other Five Families for months, until at last *his enemies catch Sonny in the open and murder him.* Hiding in Sicily, Michael falls in love and marries a local girl, *who dies in an assassination attempt aimed at him.* At last, Michael comes home, becomes the new godfather of the Corleone family, and finds a brutally effective way to make a lasting peace with his enemies.

Here's our analysis of the three-act structure for *Pride and Prejudice* (from Chapter 8), with the disasters in italics:

> When Lizzie Bennet and her sisters meet some wealthy young men at a ball, Lizzie takes a keen dislike to one of them, Mr. Darcy. Lizzie's sister Jane falls in love with Darcy's friend Mr. Bingley and Lizzie takes an interest in Mr. Wickham — whom she then learns *has been financially ruined by Darcy.* When Lizzie visits her married friend in Hunsford some

months later, Mr. Darcy seeks her out and proposes marriage to her, but *she rejects him flat out.* Lizzie soon learns that Darcy is a better man than she thought, and she is beginning to regret her rejection when her sister *Lydia runs away to live in sin with Mr. Wickham.* When Lizzie learns that Mr. Darcy rescued her sister's reputation and when he learns that she no longer hates him, the two realize that they were made for each other.

Now check out some diagnostic tests on these three-act structures.

Are your acts balanced in length?

The three disasters mark the end of Act 1 and the middle and end of Act 2. Your reader has certain expectations on the length of the various acts:

- ✔ The first act should cover roughly the first quarter of the story.
- ✔ The second act should take up about half the story.
- ✔ The third act should cover the final quarter.

These are approximations. Many excellent stories bend these guidelines quite a bit.

Noting act length in The Godfather and Pride and Prejudice

The Godfather is internally divided into seven books of unequal length. Our edition of the novel has 446 pages. Act 1 ends on page 153, about a third of the way into the story, and Act 2 ends on page 354. So Act 1 is quite a bit longer than usual, whereas Act 2 and Act 3 are both quite a bit shorter than is common. The reason for this is simple: *The Godfather* is a very complex book with many characters. Setting up this chessboard takes quite a few pages. The ending is short, because most of the story threads are wrapped up earlier, leaving only the main thread (Michael's story) to resolve.

Pride and Prejudice is a book of 61 chapters, with 332 pages in our edition. The first act goes through Chapter 16, which ends on page 73, roughly a fifth of the way into the novel. The second act goes through chapter 46, which ends on page 237, nearly three-quarters of the way through the book. The acts are therefore very well balanced, but the ending is a bit longer than normal. The reason the ending needs to be longer than usual is that Austen must wrap up several major story threads, which are all strongly tied to each other — first the thread with Lydia and Wickham, then the thread with Jane and Bingley, and finally the thread with Lizzie and Darcy. Each story thread demands substantial page count to wind down.

Checking the balance of acts in your story

Look at the three-act structure for your novel and answer these diagnostic questions:

- ✔ Are you comfortable with the relative lengths of the acts?

- ✔ Are any of your acts substantially longer or shorter than normal? If the act lengths are abnormally proportioned, do you have a good reason for it?

- ✔ Would it make sense to substantially cut or add pages in one of the acts?

- ✔ Would it make sense to move either the first disaster or the third disaster to get more normal proportions for the acts?

Make notes for yourself on any structural changes you think you may need to make for your story, but don't make any changes yet! You still have plenty of other things to think about. You address the balance of acts in the later section "Scene List: Analyzing the Flow of Scenes."

The beginning: Does it accelerate the story?

Your beginning — Act 1 — begins with the reader knowing nothing about your characters, their backstories, values, ambitions, and story goals. However, you can't bog down your story by spending the first 50 pages bringing the reader up to speed on on all that. You need to start your story with motion on page one.

Your story doesn't have to be moving very fast at first, nor does it have to be going in the "right direction." It just needs to be moving in some clear direction. As Act 1 continues, you accelerate the story and change direction as your lead character's story goal comes into focus. By the end of Act 1, you need to be heading at full speed in the right direction.

Looking at acceleration in the example novels

The Godfather begins with the wedding of Vito Corleone's daughter. Readers meet many characters in this wedding, all of them important to the story. Shortly after the wedding, Corleone rejects a business proposal from Sollozzo, making him an enemy. Not long afterward, Corleone is nearly murdered in the streets, and already the story is running at full speed. The acceleration is very fast, but it's smooth and clean.

Pride and Prejudice begins with the news that Mr. Bingley has leased Netherfield Hall and with Mrs. Bennet's insisting to her husband that they simply must meet the young man so that he can fall in love with one of their five daughters. Within a few pages, the young women have met Bingley and his friend Darcy at a local ball. Bingley is a hit with the Bennets, and Darcy is off to a horrid start. By page 10, Austen has hit her stride and the story is well-launched.

Checking your own beginning

Read through the first five chapters of your story and consider these diagnostic questions:

- ✔ How many pages of backstory do you have in the beginning of your story? How much narrative summary? If the answer surprises you, can you reduce backstory and narrative summary in the first five chapters?

- ✔ How many pages must the reader work through to meet all the key players? Would it make sense to introduce these characters earlier?

- ✔ Does the lead character have some sort of goal right away, even if it's not the ultimate story goal of the story?

The first disaster: Is the call to action clear?

Your reader wants to know that your characters are truly committed to the story. The lead character may well know his story goal early on, but usually that story goal is not yet fire-tested. That changes at the first disaster at the end of Act 1. If it's a real disaster, it's going to force the lead character to rethink things. Just how badly does he want what he thinks he wants?

A good first disaster makes the lead character commit by presenting him with a choice between backing out or going on with the story. In short, the first disaster gives the lead character a call to action.

Committing Michael Corleone and Mr. Darcy to the story

In *The Godfather,* Michael Corleone's call to action actually comes before his first disaster — at the meeting of the Family when he volunteers to kill Virgil Sollozzo and his renegade cop bodyguard. This is out of character for Michael, but it's believable because the reader has seen that Michael is truly his father's son. From Michael's point of view, his decision is not mere personal vengeance; it's sound business logic. Somebody needs to kill Sollozzo, and the only person who can get close enough is the seemingly innocent Michael. Michael could walk away from his family; until now, he's held them at a distance. Now he chooses to join his fate with theirs, and this decision is irrevocable, because it includes killing a uniformed cop.

In *Pride and Prejudice,* the first disaster comes on Lizzie's hearing from Mr. Wickham that he's been ruined by Mr. Darcy. This is a lie, but Lizzie doesn't know it and Darcy isn't yet aware of the rumor. But soon thereafter at Mr. Bingley's ball, Darcy asks Lizzie to dance, and she's as rude as she can be behind a mask of politeness. Darcy is already in love with Lizzie, but she doesn't know it yet, and he's far too wary of gossip to tell Lizzie what a cad Wickham really is. His call to action is clear: If he doesn't ramp up his pursuit of Lizzie, a scoundrel like Wickham may get her. But Darcy will be fighting this battle with one hand tied behind his back, because he can't humiliate his sister Georgiana by exposing Wickham as the scoundrel who nearly seduced her.

Presenting your call to action

Read the chapter containing your first disaster, which ends Act 1. Think hard about these questions and take some notes:

- ✔ Does your disaster come bundled with a *call to action* — a demand for a commitment to the story goal?

- ✔ What are the risks of your call to action? What are the rewards? Can you raise the stakes by increasing either the risks or the rewards?

- ✔ Why can't your lead character refuse the call to action? What in his backstory, his values, or his ambition forces him to commit to the story? Have you developed that reason enough so that your reader will believe your lead character's decision to commit to the story? (For details on character motivation, see Chapter 12.)

The second disaster: Does it support the long middle?

Act 2 of your story — the middle — is the longest act, and therefore it's the most susceptible to settling into a dull routine that may lose your reader's interest. Your lead character will have setbacks and minor victories, but after a while, they may start all melding together. By the middle of Act 2, your reader wants and needs a change of pace. That's why you need a second disaster.

The second disaster needs to be big, and it needs to change the direction of the story. It may be a surprise, or it may be merely the plausible result of your lead character's decision to take risks.

Changing direction in The Godfather and Pride and Prejudice

In *The Godfather,* the lead character Michael is hidden safely away in Sicily. Life goes on in the U.S., but the Corleone family is on a long slide toward oblivion under the not-so-great leadership of the eldest brother, Sonny. He's a brutal killer, lacking the cunning and finesse of his father. Just past the midpoint of the book, one of Don Corleone's clients, an undertaker named Amerigo Bonasera, receives a request from the Don for a favor. Bonasera goes to his funeral parlor and receives the Don . . . who's brought the savagely shot up body of Sonny Corleone. It's a shock to the reader, but it's necessary, because it makes clear that Michael Corleone must come home to take the reins of the family.

In *Pride and Prejudice,* Lizzie Bennet is visiting her friend Charlotte, who has married Lizzie's boring cousin, Mr. Collins. Collins is a sycophant to Lady Catherine de Bourgh, the aunt of Mr. Darcy, who is visiting her. Lizzie hates having to see Darcy, and she assumes he despises her. Precisely at the middle of the story, Lizzie is thrown for a knockout, along with the reader, when Darcy proposes to her. His proposal is clumsy, patronizing, and insulting. She's blunt and insulting in her refusal, apparently burning all her bridges. But her refusal is a turning point for Darcy, because he now sees himself for what he is. Darcy realizes that he needs an attitude adjustment. Is he man enough to make it?

Considering your own second disaster

Read the chapter containing your second disaster. Then answer these questions in your notes:

- ✔ Is your disaster roughly in the middle of the story? If not, would it make sense to move things around to put it more in the middle?

- ✔ Is this disaster the worst thing to happen so far in the story? If not, can you make it worse?

- ✔ Does the disaster create a turning point, forcing some important internal change in your lead characters or some change of plans on how to reach their story goals?

- ✔ Is the disaster as surprising as possible? Can you make it more surprising without ruining its plausibility?

The third disaster: Does it force the ending?

The purpose of Act 2 is to delay the ending by giving your lead character a series of obstacles and setbacks. This builds tension as the reader worries more and more about whether the lead character can ever reach his story goal. The purpose of your third disaster is to force your lead character to switch into his endgame. He must make a decision to pursue some action or some final confrontation that will end in either total victory or total defeat. No more dithering!

Leading to final confrontations in the example novels

In *The Godfather,* Don Corleone reacts to the death of Sonny by apparently throwing in the towel. He calls a meeting of the leaders of the Five Families and makes an end of hostilities. He agrees to the request that caused the war — he'll provide political and legal cover for their drug-smuggling enterprise. He vows to forego vengeance for Sonny's murder but warns that he will tolerate no assault on his youngest son Michael, whom he still hopes to bring back to America. Meanwhile, in Sicily, Michael has married a local girl and is living in newlywed bliss. He and his wife decide to switch to a new location where he'll be less known. But on the day they're to leave, a car bomb intended for him kills his wife. It's another shocking disaster, and it raises a question: How will the Corleones respond to this violation of the Godfather's one condition for a truce?

In *Pride and Prejudice,* Mr. Darcy responds to Lizzie's cold refusal of his proposal by writing her a letter telling the truth about Mr. Wickham. Over the rest of Act 2, Lizzie's eyes slowly open to the truth that Darcy is a man of character — a man who does not gossip about others, who is warm and true to his friends, a man who loves art and inspires love in those who know him best. What was she thinking to refuse him? A chance meeting between her and Darcy leads to enormous awkwardness. Both of them have changed, but how can they return to where they were before the disastrous proposal? It seems impossible. Then word arrives that Mr. Wickham has run off with Lizzie's youngest sister Lydia — without a marriage license. Now Lizzie must return home to a family disgraced and destroyed. Darcy feels responsible, because he has kept Wickham's deceit silent to protect the reputation of his sister Georgiana. Can Darcy do anything to make amends?

Evaluating your third disaster

Read the chapter containing your third disaster, which marks the end of Act 2. Consider these questions:

> ✔ Is this disaster unexpected and yet plausible? If the reader could've seen it coming, can you tweak your story a bit to make it more of a shock? If it's not quite believable, can you lay in a bit more foreshadowing to make the reader accept it more easily? (For more on foreshadowing, see the later section titled "Foreshadowing: Planting clues to prepare your readers.")
>
> ✔ Is this disaster the worst in the story so far? Does the disaster make the situation appear to be hopeless? Can you make this dark moment even darker for your lead character?
>
> ✔ Does the disaster force the lead character to pursue some all-or-nothing course of action that will lead to an ending? Or could your lead character walk away and do nothing? If so, can you box him in tighter so that he has no option but to risk everything on one last desperate throw?

The ending: Does it leave your reader wanting to tell others?

You aren't required to make your reader like your ending; the reader reads your story because the beginning was enticing and the middle kept her engrossed. Plenty of books end with a thud, including many bestsellers and classics. But the ending is the last thing your reader reads before she returns to daily life and her friends. If your ending satisfies her, then she'll talk you up. If it doesn't, she won't. Your best marketing plan is to write a great ending, because it encourages word-of-mouth, which is the most powerful marketing force in the universe.

In Chapter 8, we discuss the three kinds of endings: happy, unhappy, and bittersweet. Any of these can be a great ending, depending on what kind of book you're writing. Don't assume that a happy ending will be the one that satisfies your reader most. Don't assume that you have to kick your reader in the teeth with an unhappy ending to be appropriately artsy. Your ending should fit your story. Your lead character needs to get what he deserves, in a way the reader doesn't expect.

Wrapping up the example novels

In *The Godfather*, Vito Corleone at last finds a way to bring his son Michael home while evading the electric chair that the system has waiting for him. So Michael is off the hook. And yet, somebody tried to assassinate Michael in Sicily — who did it? How will Michael and Vito respond? Can Michael ever live and work in America when the truce has been violated by the Five Families? Is Michael a man like his father, a brute like his brother Sonny, or a wimp like his brother Freddie?

If you've read the book, you know that the ending fits the story perfectly: After his father dies of a stroke, Michael takes the reins of the family, lulls his enemies into complacence with a show of weakness, and then orders a series of hits that avenge his dead wife and make him the most powerful man in the New York underworld. In ordering a hit on his own brother-in-law, Michael proves he's even more ruthless than his father. It's a bittersweet ending. Michael has achieved his story goal — at the cost of searing his conscience. He's achieved greatness but lost his goodness, and that's enough to make you grab your friends and tell them, "I just read the most amazing book . . ."

In *Pride and Prejudice*, Lizzie Bennet is astonished when her uncle somehow rescues the situation. Her sister Lydia and Wickham are found; Wickham's debts are cleared; they're married, erasing the family disgrace that would've prevented the older sisters from marrying. And yet, there's something odd about the whole thing. When Mr. Bingley returns to court Lizzie's sister Jane, Lizzie puts aside her thoughts about this strange turn of luck. If only she'd been less rude when Mr. Darcy proposed to her so many months ago, her own future might be as bright. Darcy is a far better man than she'd ever dreamed, but he's beyond her reach. Or is he?

When Darcy's aunt, Lady Catherine de Bourgh, arrives at Lizzie's home, furious about a strange rumor that Lizzie has set her cap on Darcy, Lizzie can only wonder where such a rumor came from, but she refuses to deny it. Lady Catherine is outraged, and her account of Lizzie's impudence gives Darcy the hope he needs to propose to Lizzie once again. If you like that sort of thing, it's a happy ending that can make you tell a few friends — and for the last couple of centuries, a fair few million readers have liked that sort of thing.

Assessing your own ending

Read the entire ending of your story — all of Act 3 — and think about these questions:

- ✔ Does your lead character reach some final confrontation that focuses the story tension to a peak?

- ✔ Is the resolution of your story happy, unhappy, or bittersweet? Is this ending an acceptable one for the category of book you're writing?

  - If it's a happy ending, can you make the victory more complete?

  - If it's an unhappy ending, can you make the defeat more terrible?

  - If it's bittersweet, can you sharpen the contrast?

- ✔ Does your ending fit your story? Does your lead character get what he deserves? Is it surprising?

- ✔ What particular feature of your ending may encourage your reader to tell a few friends? Can you strengthen this feature? If it isn't there, can you work one in without sacrificing your artistic integrity?

Scene List: Analyzing the Flow of Scenes

After you have a solid storyline and you've nailed down your three-act structure, we recommend that you analyze your scenes to make sure they're all working well together. A *scene list* shows you at a glance every scene in your novel. If you haven't written a scene list yet, see Chapter 9 for help in creating one. It doesn't take long, and you'll find it a powerful tool in editing the middle layers of your plot.

In this section, we talk about how to revise your scene list — reordering, adding, deleting, and retargeting scenes — so that you can edit the scenes as quickly as possible (we talk about editing the scenes themselves in Chapters 14 and 15). We also discuss foreshadowing and explain how to use your scene list to quickly create the second draft of your novel with all the large-scale revisions.

Rearranging your scenes

The first thing to do is to make sure that your scene list has an entry for every scene in your manuscript. We recommend using either a spreadsheet or 3-x-5 cards to make a scene list. Each entry should have one to three sentences that summarize the scene. Ask these diagnostic questions:

- ✔ **Are the three main disasters about equally spaced through the story?** Scan your scene list and identify the three scenes that contain the three disasters of your three-act structure. Mark these scenes in some way (for example, color these three lines of your scene list in a spreadsheet or mark 3-x-5 cards with a red pen). Are you happy with the spacing of these disasters? If not, can you move some of the other scenes around to make the spacing more pleasing? Can you add or delete new scenes?

- ✔ **If you're using multiple POV characters, do some of them get too much air time while others get too little?** If you color-code each POV character, you can see at a glance how many scenes each character has the POV. Expect that each lead character will be the POV character more often than the minor characters. If you see patterns you don't like, can you change the POV character for some scenes to get a nicer distribution? (For tips on choosing a POV character, see Chapter 12.)

- ✔ **Does the story logic work for each thread of the story?** If not, can you add, delete, or reorder scenes to make the logic work better? Does the timeline make sense?

- ✔ **How does the emotional intensity of your scenes vary?** Not all scenes need to be equally intense; that would bore your reader. You need to establish a rhythm in emotional intensity for your scenes. Each scene should reach the level of intensity appropriate for its place in the story.

If it falls short of that intensity, consider a new placement for that scene or look for ways to increase that scene's emotional punch (see Chapters 14 and 15 for tips on editing scenes).

✔ **Can you add suspense by delaying a scene?** Can you withhold information from a character by removing him from certain critical scenes?

We find that working with a scene list helps make the revision process go much more smoothly. Moving lines around in a spreadsheet is much easier than cutting and pasting multi-page scenes in a word processor.

Foreshadowing: Planting clues to prepare readers

You must walk a fine line between making your three main disasters believable and making them surprising. That's hard, because the reader may see a believable disaster coming long in advance. On the other hand, the reader may think that a surprising disaster is just a bit too unbelievable. The same is true of your story's climax, or resolution, which should also be both believable and surprising.

One key to striking a good balance between surprise and believability is to foreshadow your disasters and story climax long in advance by throwing in small clues and other bits of information that the reader may overlook. When you spring a surprise twist, your reader will instantly realize that she should've seen it coming, because you gave her all the information she needed. Your scene list is an ideal way to keep track of these clues and hints.

For example, if you were writing *Pride and Prejudice,* you'd want to make the third disaster as believable as possible (Mr. Wickham persuades 15-year-old Lydia to run off with him to live in sin) and yet still be a surprise. If Jane Austen had a spreadsheet with a list of scenes, she could've added notes to herself to insert the following clues into specific scenes:

✔ Show Lydia going gaga over officers early in the book.

✔ Include a scene showing Lydia dancing with Wickham at a party.

✔ In Mr. Darcy's letter to Lizzie revealing that Wickham tried to elope with Georgiana Darcy, add a comment that she was 15.

✔ In some other scene, mention in passing that Lydia is 15.

Of course, you don't need a scene list to remember to insert all these clues. A scene list is simply a convenient way to decide where to put the clues when you're getting ready to edit your manuscript. The scene list shows you your story at a glance, helping you space out the bits and pieces of foreshadowing as widely as possible.

Putting it all together as a second draft

If you've revised your scene list, you're now ready to make the first real set of edits to your manuscript. We assume you have your entire manuscript in one single document in your word processor. If you don't, then you can modify the steps here to create one document that contains the entire second draft of your novel. Work through the following steps:

1. **Make a copy of your document, giving it a new name that tells you it's the second draft.**

   If your original document was named "MyNovel.doc," then you can name your new copy something like "MyNovel2.doc." Keep your original in a safe place. From now on, work only on the second draft.

2. **If you've deleted scenes from your scene list, delete the corresponding scenes in your new document.**

   We discuss deleting scenes in Chapter 14.

3. **If you've added scenes to your scene list, make notes at the appropriate places in your new document.**

   Adding a sentence or two in square brackets explaining what should happen in the new scene is enough. You don't have to write the new scene yet, but you can if you want to.

4. **If you've moved scenes in your scene list, cut and paste the corresponding scenes into their new locations in the new document.**

5. **If you've marked any scenes for major revisions, insert a note in square brackets at the beginning of the scene that explains what changes need to go into the scene.**

   You don't need to make these changes yet.

6. **If you haven't yet written all your new scenes, write them now.**

   Your second draft is now complete.

7. **Make a new copy of your document to serve as the third draft of your novel.**

   Give it a name something like "MyNovel3.doc." Congratulations! You're now ready to edit each scene in your third-draft document, using the methods we explain in Chapters 14 and 15.

Chapter 14

Editing Your Scenes for Structure

· ·

· ·

*A*fter you've verified that your characters are solid (see Chapter 12) and you've made your storyline, three-act structure, and scene list as strong as possible (see Chapter 13), you're ready to edit the structure of every scene of your novel. The basic unit of fiction is the scene, so getting its structure right is critical. Your novel may have 50 to 100 scenes or even more, and all your scenes are important. They all need to contribute to your story.

In this chapter, we give you some specific diagnostic questions to ask about the two fundamental kinds of scenes: proactive scenes and reactive scenes. Each question exposes a particular kind of problem, and for each problem type, we suggest a plan of attack to fix it.

Examples are important, so this chapter also shows you some examples of broken scenes and how to buff them into shape. We don't care to embarrass other authors by pulling up scenes from published novels that we consider weak and trying to fix them; instead, we've looked through published novels for strong scenes. Then we imagined hypothetical earlier versions of those scenes that have problems of our own devising. We tell you how you can go about fixing those hypothetical problems. Finally, we sketch out how the author actually wrote the scene in the real novel.

If you decide that a scene can't be fixed, then you have to put it out of its misery. Be merciless with scenes you can't save and gentle with those you can.

Note that this chapter deals only with *structural* problems; the next chapter explains how to fix problems in action, dialogue, and the other tools you use to create scenes. We recommend that you fix the structural problems in all your scenes first.

Triage: Deciding Whether to Fix, Kill, or Leave a Scene Alone

Editing scene structure begins with a process we call *triage*. To triage your scenes, you read each scene, analyze its structure, and make one of three decisions:

- ✔ **The structure works.** Don't mess with it.

- ✔ **The structure doesn't work, but it can be fixed.** Revise it.

- ✔ **The structure doesn't work, and it's never going to work.** Kill it.

In Chapter 9, we describe the two types of scene structures: proactive (which follows the pattern goal, conflict, and setback) and reactive (which follows the pattern reaction, dilemma, and decision). In this section, we help you determine whether the structure of a scene works.

Identifying ailing scenes

Here are some basic diagnostic questions that you should ask of every scene. Before you ask these questions, read through the scene carefully. Don't skim. Read at your normal pace without editing or making any notes. Then ask the following:

- ✔ Has your POV character moved closer to her story goal in this scene or been pushed further away from it?

- ✔ Is your POV character better off or worse off at the end of the scene?

- ✔ If you were reading this story for the first time, would you feel compelled to turn the page to find out what happens next?

We say that a scene's structure *works* if the scene has moved the story forward. If you answered yes to any of these diagnostic questions, then the structure of your scene likely works. If you answered yes to all three, then you can be pretty sure it works.

If your scene's structure works, then leave it alone. We don't mean that you'll never edit this scene; we mean you should leave the structure of the scene alone. Chapter 15 shows you how to edit it for dialogue, action, and more.

If the scene's structure doesn't work, then your life is considerably more complicated. The real question is why the scene doesn't work. Here are the most common structural problems:

✔ The scene is neither a proactive scene nor a reactive scene.

✔ The scene is supposed to be a proactive scene, but some of its parts (goal, conflict, or setback) are missing or weak.

✔ The scene is supposed to be a reactive scene, but some of its parts (reaction, dilemma, or decision) are missing or weak.

Evaluating a scene's chances of recovery

If you do have a structural problem with the scene, then you still need to decide whether to fix it or kill it.

Think hard about how to fix a scene before you declare it dead. Only if the scene is an incorrigible, hopeless drain on your story should you kill it. Consider the following questions to help you decide whether you can fix the problem:

✔ **What changed in the scene?** If nothing changed, and if there's no chance of anything changing, then this scene is in big, big trouble. Why would you have a scene in which nothing changes? We're going to guess you put it in there to feed a big lump of backstory to your reader. If so, do you really need all that backstory? Is it necessary in order to drive the story, or is it merely information that your reader could live without?

✔ **Does the scene offer new information to your characters, or is it just new to your readers?** If it's not new to your characters, then look for a way to make it new and interesting to at least one of them:

   • Can you find a way to turn that new information into bad news for a character? If so, that's a setback, which is a terrific way to end a proactive scene.

   • Is there a way to use that new information to help a character move toward her story goal? If so, that's a decision, which is a terrific way to end a reactive scene.

✔ **Does the scene end with either a setback or a decision?** If not, then the scene fits neither of the standard patterns — proactive scenes or reactive scenes. That's probably why you feel it isn't working. Can you imagine a way to add either a setback or a decision at the end of the scene? Would that amp up the emotional effect of the scene?

If a scene looks fixable, see the upcoming sections "Fixing Proactive Scenes" and "Fixing Reactive Scenes" for some guidance on strengthening your scene. If you can't find a way to introduce change into your scene, preferably as either a setback or a decision, you may have to kill the scene. We discuss unfixable scenes later in "Killing an Incurable Scene."

Fixing Proactive Scenes

A proactive scene needs to involve a goal, a conflict, and a setback. Ask yourself the following questions to find ways to strengthen a proactive scene:

- ✔ **Do you clearly define a goal at the beginning of the scene?** Is the goal simple, objective, worthwhile, achievable, and difficult (see Chapter 9 for details on these criteria)? If it fails in any of these, can you find a way to make it so?

- ✔ **Is the main part of the scene directed toward achieving that goal?** Does the POV character meet resistance? Every proactive scene needs conflict — repeated steps toward the goal, with each attempt hitting resistance. Is the resistance in your scene weak, making the scene boring? Does your character get what he wants too easily? Can you think of ways to firm up the resistance? Can you make life tougher for your POV character?

  Is the length of the scene appropriate to its importance? Should you shorten it or lengthen it?

- ✔ **Does your scene end in a strong setback?** Is the setback a complete reversal of the goal? Does it leave the POV character in a worse situation than if he'd never pursued that goal in the first place? Can you tweak your goal for this scene so that the setback fits it better?

In this section, we start with a flawed example scene and show you how asking diagnostic questions can help you fix a proactive scene.

Imagining a proactive scene: The Day of the Jackal

The example we take is a hypothetical proactive scene set early in the thriller *The Day of the Jackal*, by Frederick Forsyth. (We know, of course, that Forsyth based his actual scene on a real historical event, so we aren't trying to reconstruct how he actually came to write his scene; our purpose here is to show how you can take a weak, spineless scene and give it bones and muscle by asking the right questions.)

Here, in summary form, is how our imaginary flawed version of this scene runs: A dozen Frenchmen are standing beside a busy street in Paris on August 22, 1962. It's a bit past 8 p.m. and dusk has fallen. Visibility is poor, but the roar of two Citroën cars and several police motorcycles catches the attention of the characters. They turn and see the motorcade of President Charles de Gaulle flash past.

The men beside the road are angry when they see de Gaulle. All of them are veterans of the Algerian War, and all feel betrayed by de Gaulle's violation of his campaign promises to keep Algeria. They spend a few minutes cursing de Gaulle's name and then head off to the local tavern to drown their sorrows in beer.

Checking for change

What's wrong with the structure of the hypothetical scene in the preceding section? Everything! Nothing changes here. Our characters are neither better off nor worse off at the end of the scene. The 12 Frenchmen hate de Gaulle at the beginning of the scene, and they hate him at the end.

The reason nothing changes is that our characters come into the scene without any particular goal. Because they have no goal, they do nothing about their rage, other than vent a few curses. Although this may be the way you'd behave toward some hated political figure, it makes terrible fiction. Nothing happens. This scene doesn't work.

You may complain that no writer would ever write a scene like this. Surely a writer has some purpose going into every scene, right? The answer is no, not always. For many writers, the joy of fiction is discovering where the story is going as they write it. If they don't get it right on the first draft, then they need to fix it in the editing stage.

How can we make our hypothetical scene work? We'll consider our diagnostic questions and see whether we can improve it.

Choosing a powerful goal

For a proactive scene, first consider the characters' goal. Is a goal clearly defined at the beginning of the scene? Is that goal simple, objective, worthwhile, achievable, and difficult? If not, can you make it so?

Our characters don't have any goal at the beginning of the example scene, but we can easily give them one. What goal might these gentlemen choose? To shake their fists at a motorcade? To yell insults at a man who can't hear them? No and no. Those are insignificant goals, unworthy of our attention. We need to give them a big goal, the biggest we can imagine. Shoot for the moon here.

The goal we'll give them is to assassinate Charles de Gaulle. This is pretty extreme, but our characters are men of strong passions. Extreme goals make good thrillers. Now check to see whether this goal meets our requirements:

- ✔ **Is it simple?** Yes. *Simple* means that explaining the goal is simple. The reader needs no complex proofs that a bullet to the brain will kill a man.

- ✔ **Is it objective?** Yes. At the end of the scene, de Gaulle will be either dead or alive. Any observer will be able to tell whether he is or isn't.

- ✔ **Is it worthwhile?** Yes, in the minds of our characters. This is a key point.

  Your reader doesn't need to believe that the goal is worthwhile; the reader only needs to believe that your characters think the goal is worthwhile.

- ✔ **Is it achievable?** Yes. Charles de Gaulle is mortal. Shoot him enough times, and he'll die. ***Note:*** You may argue that this isn't achievable, because the reader knows that de Gaulle wasn't assassinated in 1962. True, but the reader is always willing to suspend disbelief and consider an alternate history of events.

- ✔ **Is it difficult to achieve?** Yes. The French security forces are well-trained, tough, and disciplined. Getting to de Gaulle is not going to be as easy as a tiptoe through the Tuileries.

As a result of setting up a clearly defined goal, the scene must become a bit longer. The beginning of the scene won't merely show the men standing on a street corner doing nothing; it'll show them moving into position according to a plan they've spent months rehearsing.

Stretching out the conflict

Suppose we've rewritten our hypothetical scene with a new and improved goal as follows: Our intended assassins wait for de Gaulle's motorcade to come by. They've planned everything meticulously. They have a lookout on station to signal them when de Gaulle's Citroën is getting close. They have a team of riflemen on foot to stop de Gaulle's car in a barrage of bullets. They have other men ready to swoop in by car to administer the *coup de grâce*. They have getaway cars and an exit strategy. The plan goes off perfectly. The men kill de Gaulle and then stroll away to the nearest tavern, where their joyful countrymen buy them drinks until the wee hours.

What's wrong with *this* scene? From a structural point of view, the gaping problem is that there's no conflict. Take a look at our diagnostic questions: Does the POV character meet resistance? Is it too easy for your character to get what he wants? Can you make life tougher for your POV character?

This scene has gone far too easily for our assassins. The solution is simple: We need to make the plan go awry. The killers have made meticulous plans, but even so, something must go wrong. Then more things have to go wrong, and more. Conflict needs to go on and on until the scene is over. Our characters won't face just one obstacle; they'll face several.

Say we design some conflict into this scene. First, the assassins fail to anticipate how dark it'll be when de Gaulle's car arrives at their killing zone. Their lookout fails to see the motorcade approaching in the dusk until it's passing by, so he fails to send the signal.

That's an obstacle, but it's not enough. Our characters don't slink away when things get tough. Even though they've missed the signal and are caught unprepared, the instant they see de Gaulle's car, they begin firing anyway, taking as many shots as they can while the motorcade flashes past. They're marksmen, and some of their bullets hit the car and shred the tires.

That's conflict, but it's still not enough. French security forces don't take all those bullets lying down. De Gaulle's driver takes evasive action as he's trained to do. His bodyguards begin shooting back. On and on the action goes, as each side makes desperate moves. The second team of killers in cars takes their shots at de Gaulle. His driver evades again, while the security men fight back. We show all this conflict detail, instant by instant as it unfolds.

Desperately seeking setbacks

Say that we've rewritten our hypothetical scene as we detail in the two preceding sections: Our dozen assassins have made a careful plan to kill Charles de Gaulle. However, they've failed to take account of the timing for dusk, so they're caught unprepared. They fire anyway, shredding the tires of the presidential car. French security forces fire back, and a massive gun battle follows. De Gaulle's car is disabled and rolls to a halt. The leader of the assassination team fires his last bullet and kills de Gaulle.

Now what's wrong with this scene? The structural problem is that our characters get what they want. Nothing could make them happier than what they achieve, so the novel is over on page 10. Does that strike you as a wee bit early?

Look over our diagnostic questions: Does your scene end in a strong setback? Is the setback a complete reversal of the goal? Does it leave the POV character in a worse situation than if he'd never pursued that goal in the first place?

Early in the story, characters don't need a victory; they need a setback. They need a major failure. They need a reason to come back and fight again in the next chapter, and the next, and the next, all the way to the end of the book. Early successes make dull stories. Early setbacks make exciting ones.

The solution is to have de Gaulle survive this attempt but also to let the assassins escape in the confusion, furious at themselves and determined to do better next time. That's a complete reversal of their goal. They're worse off than they were at the beginning of the scene, because now French security is after them with all its fury. The intended assassins are now men on the run.

Examining the final result

Here's how the scene actually plays out in the novel: The assassins have a lookout posted 100 yards up the avenue to signal them by waving a newspaper when de Gaulle's Citroën DS approaches. That should give the gunmen several seconds to concentrate their firepower on the car.

The flaw in their plan comes when they consult the table for dusk for the previous year, 1961, rather than for the current year, 1962. In 1961, dusk on August 22 fell at 8:35 p.m. But in 1962, it falls 25 minutes earlier, at 8:10 p.m. (Forsyth doesn't explain the astronomical reason for this apparently impossible event, but it appears that few readers have ever challenged it.)

As the scene plays out, de Gaulle's car approaches at 8:18 p.m. The lookout signals as it speeds by, but he's almost invisible to the gunmen 100 yards down the avenue. They see de Gaulle just as he races past and they rush a few shots at the retreating Citroën, blowing out its tires, shattering its windows, and missing the presidential nose by inches but failing to disable the car or even wing the General. The second mobile team of killers then engages de Gaulle's security forces in a high-speed gun battle, but they also fail. The motorcade reaches the airport safely and de Gaulle sneers, "They can't shoot straight."

The mission has failed, and now the assassins are on the run and French security is forewarned and doubly cautious. That's a setback that sets up the entire novel that follows.

Frederick Forsyth didn't develop his scene they way we've sketched it out, because he based it on an actual assassination attempt. But if he hadn't had a historical event to work from, he still could've developed it from a lame scene like the one we began with — simply by asking the right questions.

Fixing Reactive Scenes

A reactive scene contains a reaction, a dilemma, and a decision. Ask the following diagnostic questions to help you nurse reactive scenes to health:

✔ **Does the scene begin with a reaction appropriate to the setback from a previous scene?** Is it emotive and visceral? Is the reaction reasonable, given the POV character's emotional state and personality type? Does it run too long or too short?

✔ **Do you segue from the reaction to a dilemma that gives the POV character no good options?** Is the dilemma appropriately difficult for the scene you're writing — neither too easy nor too hard? Is there some obvious solution kicking around that your character is too dense to see? Have you boxed in your character well enough? Does the character spend the appropriate amount of time trying to solve the problem?

✔ **Does your character come to a decision at the end?** Is the decision simple, objective, worthwhile, achievable, and difficult? Will your reader respect your character's decision? Will your reader feel compelled to turn the page to see whether the character can execute that decision?

In this section, we imagine a hypothetical reactive scene that doesn't work and change it by stages to make it work.

Imagining a reactive scene: Outlander

We take inspiration for our example reactive scene from the time-travel romance novel *Outlander,* by Diana Gabaldon. The scene is set roughly a quarter of the way into the book, and it forms the end of Act 1 in the novel's three-act structure, so we first need to talk about the story setup.

It's late 1945. World War II is over, and the heroine, Claire Randall, is an English nurse getting reacquainted with her husband Frank after several years of wartime separation. While visiting Scotland with Frank, Claire accidentally passes through a time portal and finds herself in 1743 Scotland with no way to get back. The clan MacKenzie takes her in, but they suspect her of being an English spy. When Claire's been there about a month, the local English captain "Black Jack" Randall (an ancestor of Claire's husband Frank) interrogates her and disbelieves the lies she tells him about where she came from. Captain Randall ends the interview by slugging Claire in the belly and ordering her Scottish friends to deliver her into his custody on the following Monday for further questioning. This is the setback that Claire must now recover from. It's a major setback — it's the first disaster in the book's three-disaster structure.

How should we follow this disaster? Before we tell you how Diana Gabaldon did it, we imagine a poorly structured reactive scene that runs as follows: Claire has a chat with Dougal MacKenzie, one of the clan chieftains, and his nephew Jamie Fraser, a swashbuckling young giant whom Claire has a crush on. They agree that it's rotten luck that she'll have to turn herself in on Monday, but because they can't do anything about it, Claire and Jamie might as well get drunk and then retire to a private place for the smooching scene that every romance novel needs.

Checking for change (again)

What's wrong with the reactive scene in the preceding section? It's horrible. Nothing has changed by the end of the scene. Claire is in mortal danger at the beginning, and she's still in mortal danger at the end.

The reason nothing changes is that Claire doesn't seem to care. She doesn't react at all after being slugged, and she doesn't worry about her future. Because Claire doesn't seem to want change, she doesn't pursue it, and therefore nothing happens. You may know some people who'd give up in that kind of situation and go get drunk with their friends, but our fictional characters need to be tougher than that. In fiction, characters need to fight back. The scene as we've described it doesn't work.

You may argue that nobody would ever write such a weak scene. Yes, they would. Writers write weak scenes all the time — but remember that writing a weak scene is often just a stepping stone to writing a strong one. The solution is to ask the right questions and then use the answers to strengthen the scene. We show you how in the following sections.

Fitting the reaction to the setback

Start with the diagnostic questions about the reaction part of the reactive scene: Does the scene begin with a reaction appropriate to the setback from a previous scene? Is it emotive and visceral? Is the reaction reasonable, given the POV character's emotional state and personality type? Does it run too long or too short?

In our hypothetical scene, Claire doesn't seem to feel any pain or any emotion after being slugged in the stomach. That's not appropriate. We're going to give her time to feel the pain; give her time to let the shock run through her and then out of her; give her time to burn with rage at her attacker, chew herself out for her helplessness. She'll take time to feel.

Claire would seem like a weakling if we drag this out too long, but she'd seem inhuman if we cut this reaction short. We'll set the length of the reaction to fit its importance. We'll let her work through the pain, and then she'll be ready for the next phase of the scene.

Working through the dilemma

Say we've added an appropriate reaction to our hypothetical scene, which now runs like this: For a few minutes, Claire can hardly breathe because of the pain in her belly. She thinks she may throw up, and her mind feels numb at the thought that a man who looks like her husband could be so evil. Then she has a chat with Dougal MacKenzie and his nephew Jamie Fraser. They agree that it's rotten luck that she'll have to turn herself in on Monday, but because they can't do anything about it, Claire and Jamie might as well get drunk and then retire to a private place for the smooching scene that every romance novel needs.

This is slightly better than our first cut at the scene, but it's still wretchedly unrealistic. The structure is still weak. Claire has now worked through the pain from the past scene, but she doesn't seem to worry about her future.

Look at our next set of diagnostic questions: Do you segue from the reaction to a dilemma that gives the POV character no good options? Is the dilemma appropriately difficult? Is there some obvious solution kicking around that your character is too dense to see? Have you boxed in your character well enough? Does the character spend the appropriate amount of time trying to solve the problem?

We need Claire to face up to her problems by working through her options in detail. They're bad options, all of them, but Claire must spend some time talking or thinking about them to convince the reader that she's truly boxed in.

For starters, Jack Randall doesn't trust her, and if she turns herself in to him next Monday, then he could do anything — flog her, rape her, hang her. Given Randall's horrible reputation, these are not only possible; they're likely. Turning herself in is a terrible idea.

What else can Claire try? Can she run? Not a chance. The English soldiers control the roads. Furthermore, she's not free to leave the Scottish men she's traveling with, because they still suspect her of being an English spy. Everybody suspects Claire, and the only person who really likes her is Jamie.

Jamie's uncle Dougal finally hits on a terrific idea that will solve all their problems. If Claire marries Jamie, then she'll no longer be subject to English law. Instead, she'll be a Scot and therefore under the control of the local laird.

The marriage will also make it impossible for Jamie ever to usurp his uncle's place as laird, because the MacKenzie clan would never accept a leader with an English-born wife. This plan solves everybody's problems, but for Claire, it's a terrible idea. She likes Jamie, to be sure. She's even attracted to him. But she's married, and she's the kind of person who takes her marriage vows seriously. Her husband is still in 1945, and she hopes to get back to him through the time portal as soon as possible. Claire can't possibly marry Jamie.

Coming to a decision

Given the revisions in the preceding sections, our scene is coming along reasonably well, with a strong reaction and a sharp dilemma that we can summarize this way: For a few minutes, Claire can hardly breathe because of the pain in her belly. She thinks she may throw up, and her mind feels numb at the thought that a man who looks like her husband could be so evil. Now she needs to figure out what to do next Monday. She can't turn herself in to Captain Randall — he might kill her. She can't escape — the English control the roads. She can't take Dougal's advice and marry Jamie — she's already married to a man she loves. Unable to decide, she spends the weekend in a drunken stupor, smooching with Jamie.

What's wrong with this? The structural problem is the fact that Claire can't stop dithering, so this dilemma is never going to end.

Look at our diagnostic questions: Does your character come to a decision at the end? Is the decision simple, objective, worthwhile, achievable, and difficult? Will your reader respect your character's decision? Will your reader feel compelled to turn the page to see whether the character can execute that decision?

Claire needs to decide, which means taking her least-bad option. That turns out to be marrying Jamie. This decision fits all our criteria. Getting married is both simple and objective. Is it worthwhile? Yes, Jamie's one hot guy, and Claire already has a crush on him. Is it achievable? Yes, because Jamie's willing and a parson is available. Is it difficult? Yes, because Claire is married already — to a man who isn't born yet — but she's still committed to him.

Coming to the final result

Here's how the reactive scene actually works in *Outlander:* After Captain Randall slugs Claire in the stomach, she spends several paragraphs feeling her pain and recovering from the shock to her system. Jamie's uncle Dougal confronts Captain Randall in his office and vents his outrage, but Claire can't hear the details.

When Dougal finishes ranting at Randall, he escorts Claire out of the fort and takes her to a sulfurous spring known as the liar's spring because a local legend says that anyone who drinks from it and then tells a lie will have her gizzard burned out. After Claire drinks, Dougal questions her and confirms in his own mind that she's no English spy. He still has no idea who she is or where she came from, but he's convinced that he can let her into the clan by marrying Jamie.

Dougal then tells Claire in excruciating detail the story of how Captain Randall flogged Jamie a few years ago — twice in one week — nearly killing him. Dougal lays it on thick, making it clear that Randall is far worse than Claire had imagined and that Jamie has incredible courage.

Why has Dougal told her all this? He wants to impress on Claire just how evil Captain Randall is and also what an excellent man Jamie is. Then Dougal tells her that he's decided she must marry Jamie. She protests, of course, and puts up quite a lot of opposition, but turning herself in to Randall would be too horrible to imagine. Jamie is a strong, courageous, and kind man who'll protect Claire with his life.

The reader, by this point, is desperately hoping she'll agree. Claire continues to protest, looking for any way out. She runs through every argument she can, first with Dougal, then with herself. Finally, she demands to talk to Jamie, who has no qualms at all about marrying her. Slowly, her resistance wears down and she finally realizes she has no choice. She's going to marry Jamie. This is the decision that commits Claire to the rest of the story.

Killing an Incurable Scene

A weak scene can become a strong scene if you just ask the right questions and then use the answers to find ways to improve it, as we show you in the preceding sections. Some scenes, however, just don't pull through, despite your best efforts.

Every scene needs to pull its own weight by advancing your story. Every scene is a mini-story that must give your reader a powerful emotional experience. Every scene. No exceptions.

If you have a scene that simply can't be helped, then you already know you should kill it — you probably just don't want to. You feel that this scene is your baby. You labored over those words. You sweated blood to create that scene. Now you should kill it just because it isn't doing its job?

If you're struggling with this idea, you're being shackled by the wrong metaphor. Scenes are not your babies; scenes aren't people at all. Scenes are records of conflict in your story. That's it — just records. They're black ink on white paper. Bits on a hard drive. Inert matter.

We don't recommend that you delete any scene, of course. It'll be there on your computer for all eternity, sitting in your previous draft, should you ever need to go look it up. When you *kill* a scene, all you're doing is refusing to pull it forward into your next draft. That scene is deadwood, a failed idea that's now sucking the life out of your story. Leave it behind.

If losing a scene leaves a small gap in your story, then make a note for yourself to salvage whatever bits of it you need. If you were using the scene to give the reader some necessary information, then find some other scene that works and wedge in the information there.

Don't waste your emotional energy grieving for scenes that can't be fixed. You need that energy for injecting new emotive life into the scenes that can.

Chapter 15

Editing Your Scenes for Content

• •

In This Chapter

▶ Deciding whether to show or tell

▶ Editing clips

▶ Following special notes on flashbacks

▶ Editing telling

• •

*I*n this chapter, we focus on the one editing task that's most important in creating a powerful emotional experience: editing your scenes to improve both your *showing* and *telling*. (See Chapter 10 for a discussion of showing and telling.)

Editors often advise writers to "show, don't tell." That's especially good advice for beginning writers, who tend to show far too little and tell far too much. The problem is that intermediate writers sometimes show too much and tell too little. You need to strike the right balance, showing your story well during the high-intensity parts and telling the story well when you need to compress time or pass along important information to your reader.

Here's the secret of showing: Write each scene as a sequence of *clips* — the smallest unit of conflict in fiction. Clips are made up of action, dialogue, interior emotion, interior monologue, and sensory description. (See Chapter 10 for an introduction to clips.) If editors tell you that you aren't showing enough, then discipline yourself to write in clips and to edit them the way we show you in this chapter.

There isn't any such simple secret for telling. You have a variety of ways to tell: Narrative summary, exposition, and static description all qualify. These are all potent tools in the hands of a skilled writer, but giving you rules on how best to use them is extremely difficult. However, we do give you some guidelines on telling and how to edit your segments of telling.

Deciding Whether to Show or Tell

Showing can be high on emotive force, but it's usually low on information content. Telling rarely carries much emotional punch, but it can efficiently pass on information. You need to use whatever works best.

Edit your scene sentence by sentence, keeping the following questions in mind:

- ✔ Is the sentence showing or telling?

- ✔ How much emotive punch do you need for this sentence? How much emotive punch does it pack?

- ✔ Is the sentence helping to move the story forward?

- ✔ How much information do you need in this sentence? How much information does it carry?

In this section, we help you take the answers to these questions and decide how best to present your story. We then work through an example that shows how to apply our guidelines for showing and telling.

You won't always make the decision to switch a segment from telling to showing; sometimes, telling just makes more sense. But whether you decide to show or tell, you should know the reason for your decision. As you edit each sentence and paragraph of each scene, weigh your options and switch if you need to.

Knowing when clips, flashbacks, or telling techniques are most appropriate

In this section, we provide some practical guidelines to help you decide whether to show something using clips or flashback or whether to tell it using narrative summary and similar tools.

When to use clips

Use clips whenever all of the following are true (which should be most of the time):

- ✔ Whatever is happening is going on right now.

- ✔ Something emotively important is happening in your scene. If it's a proactive scene, this means that your lead character is defining his goal, facing down conflict, or experiencing a setback. If it's a reactive scene, it means that your lead character is having an emotive reaction, working through a dilemma, or reaching a decision. (For more on scene types, see Chapters 9 and 14.)

When to use flashback

Use a flashback when all of the following statements are true:

✔ Something emotively important happened in your lead character's backstory, and your reader needs to know about it right now.

✔ You can't reveal the events in clips (in the present) using dialogue or interior monologue or some combination of them.

✔ You can insert the flashback without breaking the tension in the present story.

Remember that a flashback is a container for a series of clips set in the past. The flashback needs to have a transition at each end to take the reader back in time and then bring her forward again.

When to tell

Tell your story — using narrative summary, exposition, or static description — when

✔ You need to pass on some information that doesn't move the story forward, but it's essential for your reader to know. That info may be about the story world or a character's backstory or some mundane events that bear on the story. (If the information isn't essential, cut it altogether; see the later section "Knowing when to kill a segment of telling" for details.)

✔ You need to show a transition from one time to another or one place to another.

✔ You want to compress time, express a value judgment, or speed up actions that you don't need to show in detail.

✔ The information has little emotive impact.

✔ Showing the information using clips would take too long or be too boring or tedious.

Following an example of decision-making

We now apply the show-and-tell guidelines in the preceding section to an example paragraph. Here's the paragraph we want to edit:

> You're at your first book signing, and you're nervous because you're going to have to speak to a crowd of strangers. To get your mind off your fears, you start thinking about the reason you wrote your book in the first place. After 9/11, you used to have nightmares about it. Gradually, you got to wondering what might've happened if you'd had those nightmares before the tragedy. Could you have prevented it? You like to think that you could have. That's what prompted the idea for your first novel.

That paragraph is all telling, and it's pretty dull. Part of it is happening right now. Part of it is backstory. Does the paragraph carry any emotive punch? Not much. Does it need to? Yes, because we intend this to be the beginning of a fairly high-action scene that we want to continue developing through this chapter.

Our first goal is to tap into some emotion. The obvious choice is the anxiety that the lead character is feeling. We need to dramatize that, and the best way is to use some interior emotion and possibly some interior monologue.

Our other goal is to show some of that backstory, because it's important for the rest of the scene that we're developing. Can we use flashback? No, that's a bad idea at the start of a scene. Can we use either dialogue or interior monologue? Yes. Which should we use? Dialogue is often better, as long as we don't have one character telling another what they both know and as long as it advances the story. In this example, the lead character is about to speak to a crowd of people who are intensely interested in the author's backstory, so we have a good reason to mention the past. Furthermore, we can make this backstory lead immediately into conflict.

Now we rewrite the paragraph, expanding it into three paragraphs. We could choose any number of styles, but we've chosen a style appropriate for an action novel, because it lets us illustrate our main points clearly:

> You're at your first book signing. Hands slick with sweat, you barely hear the store's PR director introducing you. Your heart is thumping in your chest at warp speed and your ears are ringing. Applause from the crowd cuts through the curtain of fear that surrounds you. It's show time, whether you're ready or not. You stand up and wobble toward the lectern.
>
> You take a last swig of cold water, inhale deeply, and smile at the crowd. "For years after 9/11, I used to dream about what happened," you say. "Then one day, I got to wondering what it would've been like if I'd had those dreams *before* 9/11. What if I'd suspected something was coming . . . but did nothing? What if I had to live with the guilt of wondering if I could've changed things? What if I began having dreams about some new impending disaster? What would I do?"
>
> "Bull$#*&!" bellows a voice from the back of the crowd.

Now consider what we've done in this revision. We've expanded from one paragraph to three. Ending up with extra text is common when you switch from telling to showing, because showing is less efficient. Here's how the new passage breaks down:

✔ Paragraph one

- We trimmed the first sentence, though it still tells rather than shows. Why tell here? Why not use a more vivid sentence? We could've used some evocative, sensory description, but we chose to establish the setting quickly and get straight to the emotive part.

- The second and third sentences give the reader three hits of *interior emotion* — physiological reactions that show the POV character's feelings. We aren't going for subtlety here. We're showing sweaty hands, a thumping heart, and ringing ears.

- The next sentence shows applause and tells about fear. It's not a strong sentence. We're lowering the intensity with this sentence because it's important to vary the intensity within a scene.

- The next sentence is indirect interior monologue — a cliché about its being show time. The cliché works here because that's how the POV character thinks.

- The last sentence is action — the character stands and wobbles. Again, we're not trying to be subtle here. *Wobble* is a strong verb.

By the end of the first paragraph, the POV character already has a clear goal for the scene: to conquer the anxiety of a first book-signing speech.

✔ **Paragraph two**

- The next paragraph begins with three actions that all show the POV character trying to get a grip: sipping water, breathing deeply, and smiling. We don't need to tell the reader that the POV character is battling anxiety. The actions say so.

- The rest of the second paragraph is all dialogue, spoken by the POV character. It's filling in some backstory, which is fine here because the audience at the bookstore doesn't know this information but is definitely interested in hearing it.

The first two paragraphs make up one long *private clip* (see Chapter 10 for a full explanation of this term). A private clip focuses on the POV character.

✔ **Paragraph three**

- The last paragraph is a *public clip* — it switches focus to a non-POV character.

- This sliver of dialogue also introduces more conflict into the scene. Now the POV character not only has anxiety to deal with but also some unknown antagonist. The stakes for this scene have gone up.

A Good Show: Editing Clips

If you've decided that a given segment of your scene needs to be showing rather than telling, then the first thing to do is to make sure the segment uses clips. You write *clips* using the five basic tools for showing: action, dialogue, interior emotion, interior monologue, and sensory description. (See Chapter 10 for a full explanation of how to combine these basic tools into the two kinds of clips, public and private.)

If you have a segment composed of clips, you still may have some editing work to do. Here are the most common problems we see in clips:

- ✔ **Paragraphs don't focus on a single character.** This is a problem because a paragraph should be as unified as possible.

- ✔ **The scene has more than one POV character.** Unless you intended to write in head-hopping or omniscient POV, this is a problem.

- ✔ **The reader sees things that the POV character can't.** This is a problem unless you intended to write in third person objective or omniscient POV.

- ✔ **The reader sees the cause after the effect.** This can disorient the reader, because in the real world, causes happen before effects.

- ✔ **The time scales are muddled so that slow processes finish before fast ones.** This can disorient the reader.

In this section, we give some guidelines to help you fix these problems, and we show you examples of each solution.

You'll bend these clips-editing guidelines often and violate them on occasion — when it works to do so. But we encourage you to test everything you write against these guidelines and see whether they suggest ways to improve your writing. If they do, then use them and be ahead of where you were. If not, then ignore them and lose nothing.

Guidelines for editing clips

We recommend that you follow a pattern when you write your clips to give the reader cues about the story. Here's how to evaluate the pattern when you edit your scenes:

1. **Identify each clip as either a private clip or a public clip, and add a paragraph break between each clip.**

   A *private clip* focuses on the POV character. A *public clip* focuses on any other character. Eliminate narrative summary if you can.

2. **Make sure each clip uses the right tools.**

   Each private clip can use action, dialogue, interior monologue, or interior emotion, but it should usually avoid description, which almost always shows things external to the POV character.

Each public clip can use action, dialogue, or description, but it should avoid interior monologue and interior emotion, because your reader can't know what non-POV characters are thinking and feeling.

3. **Make sure each clip gets its timing right.**

Here's how to manage the timing of two events in a clip:

- **If they happen at roughly the same time:** Show them in the order in which they begin.

- **If they begin at the same time:** Show them in order from quickest to slowest.

- **If they begin at the same time and take the same length of time:** Show them in whatever order you like best.

In this section, we look at a number of cooked-up examples of poorly done clips and show how to whip them into shape by applying this pattern.

Fixing mixed clips

Consider the following example paragraph, which continues the scene we begin earlier in "Following an example of decision-making":

> A big guy in black leather steps out from where he's been hiding in the Cookbooks section. He's got a scar on his left cheek and scruffy gray side-burns, and he's holding a *chainsaw.* He starts it up and revs the engine as he strides toward you. "You stole one idea from me, dude, and you ain't going to steal any more!" "What's your name?" Your heart is hammering in your chest as the guy in black leather moves toward you. You grab two copies of your book, thinking they might be some protection. "Throckmorton," he says. "But my friends call me Hack." *Throckmorton?* What kind of a parent names their kid Throckmorton? "Dude, I'm sure we can talk this out." Throckmorton stops and points the chainsaw directly at your face. "I'll let Mr. Stihl do my talking."

Ouch. That paragraph contains seven clips, three of them private clips and four, public clips.

We're not religious about never mixing public and private clips within a paragraph. Occasionally, it can make sense. But we do it as rarely as we'd put the dialogue for two different characters in the same paragraph — and for the same reason: Starting a new paragraph for each clip helps readers keep things straight.

This issue is particularly obvious with the sentence, "Dude, I'm sure we can talk this out." After you've read the entire sentence, you can work out from the context that the speaker is the POV character, not Throckmorton. But there's no way you can know that when you start reading the sentence. As a result, when you begin reading that sentence, part of your mind is shrieking, "Who's talking here?" The mixed-up nature of the paragraph is forcing you to work harder than you should, taking you partly out of the story. No author should do that to a reader.

Now split this passage out into one clip per paragraph. It becomes a fair bit easier to read. It also creates more white space on the page, leading the reader's eye to whiz through the story faster, creating the illusion that things are happening more quickly.

> A big guy in black leather steps out from where he's been hiding in the Cookbooks section. He's got a scar on his left cheek and scruffy gray side-burns, and he's holding a *chainsaw*. He starts it up and revs the engine as he strides toward you. "You stole one idea from me, dude, and you ain't going to steal any more!"
>
> "What's your name?" Your heart is hammering in your chest.
>
> The guy in black leather keeps moving toward you.
>
> You grab two copies of your book, thinking they might be some protection.
>
> "Throckmorton," he says. "But my friends call me Hack."
>
> *Throckmorton?* What kind of a parent names their kid Throckmorton? "Dude, I'm sure we can talk this out."
>
> Throckmorton stops and points the chainsaw directly at your face. "I'll let Mr. Stihl do my talking."

This reads better. We've changed hardly any words at all, yet we've gained quite a lot in clarity. Every little improvement helps. You may argue that this is a trivial change. Yes, it's a trivial change, but it's well worth your time, because you get so much improvement for such a little bit of effort. We recommend separating all clips with paragraph breaks first, before you do anything else.

Fixing unintentional head-hopping

You may choose to use multiple POV characters in a given scene. If you're writing in either the head-hopping or the omniscient POV, then you've made a conscious decision to have more than one POV character in each scene. That's your artistic choice, and you're free to make it. (For advice on choosing a POV, see Chapters 7 and 12.)

The problem comes if you intended to stick to a single POV character for a scene but you got inside the head of some other character. Head-hopping mixes the emotive messages you send your reader, so you need to fix it if it's not part of your chosen POV.

Read the following series of paragraphs, which hop in and out of the heads of multiple characters:

> Your audience is backing away from Throckmorton, screaming. One of the women, reminded of her husband, faints dead away on the floor. Two guys grab her and haul her to safety. It occurs to the taller of them that he could've thrown a body tackle on Throckmorton from behind and taken him out, but now that he's a safe distance away, he doesn't have the guts to go back into danger.

> Throckmorton studies you with a malicious grin. He's remembering the way his father tortured him when he was a boy. He's remembering how his mother wrung her hands and screamed and never intervened. He's thinking how much you look like his seventh grade English teacher, who did nothing when he wrote poems about being flogged with a whip.

> You can see in Throckmorton's eyes that he's going to lunge at you. You slam the book in your left hand hard on the lectern, watching for Throckmorton's eyes to flick down at the movement. Then you fling the book in your right hand straight at his face.

The problem here is that the reader is getting mixed emotional messages. First, the reader dips inside the head of a woman, who promptly faints. The next instant, the reader is a guy who shows a little courage by helping rescue the woman but not enough to attack Throckmorton. Then, for a full paragraph, the reader becomes Throckmorton and starts to empathize with him because of his brutalized childhood. Finally, the reader returns to the real POV character and now has to fight Throckmorton.

Your reader wants to know whom to root for. When you let her hop from head to head at random, she's rooting for everybody, which means she's rooting for nobody. By trying to do too much, you accomplish too little.

Can you hop between heads effectively? Of course. Margaret Mitchell did it in *Gone With the Wind*. Mario Puzo did it in *The Godfather*. But neither of them did it at random. If you're going to allow yourself into the heads of multiple POV characters in a scene, you need to have a reason for it. You also need to do it carefully and manage your reader's emotions.

If you've caught yourself head-hopping unintentionally, the solution is simple: Write your POV character using only private clips. Write all other characters in the scene using only public clips.

Here's a rewrite of the example passage. We have to do radical surgery, and we can't take our reader as deeply inside the non-POV characters, but she'll be far more firmly rooted in the real POV character:

> Your audience is backing away from Throckmorton, screaming. One of the women faints dead away on the floor. Two guys grab her and haul her to safety.
>
> Throckmorton studies you with a malicious grin, but his eyes are tortured, staring at you with a glazed look, as if you're somebody he knows. Sweat stands out on his forehead, and an artery throbs in a patchwork of old scars on his wind-burned neck.
>
> You can see in Throckmorton's eyes that he's going to lunge at you. You slam the book in your left hand hard on the lectern, watching for Throckmorton's eyes to flick down at the movement. Then you fling the book in your right hand straight at his face.

We've lost some of the emotive power of Throckmorton's childhood here. That simply can't be helped if we're going to use a single POV character in this scene. But we've gained something, too — we've given our reader one definite POV character to root for.

You may be wondering whether this scene would work better if you were to write it from Throckmorton's POV. It might. But if you rewrote it that way, the reader would expect you to put her exclusively in Throckmorton's mind. We provide tips on choosing a POV character in Chapter 12.

Fixing out-of-body experiences

You may choose to show your reader things your focal character can't see or know. If you're writing in third person objective or omniscient POV, then that's the artistic choice you've made. However, if you've chosen any other POV, that, too, is an artistic choice, and you need to stick to it consistently.

This next series of paragraphs shows what happens when you show something that the POV character can't see:

> Throckmorton jerks his head to one side, and the book whizzes past his right ear. Rage lights up his eyes, and he steps toward you, revving the chainsaw.
>
> You grab a handful of copies of your book and back away from him, holding them up as a shield. You don't see that you're about to step on the store's PR director, who has just fainted behind you.

Things are going well here until we show the reader something the POV character can't see: the bookstore lady lying passed out on the floor.

What's wrong with that? Doesn't it heighten tension? Perhaps. *Tension* is the expectation of something bad. Showing your reader that the POV character may step on the bookstore lady can ramp up tension. But there's a cost: Showing this reminds the reader that she's not the POV character, and one of your primary goals is to persuade your reader that she is the POV character.

Don't destroy the fictive dream just for the sake of a little extra tension. Instead of taking your reader outside the POV character, increase tension by giving your POV character some hint of what's going on.

If you've accidentally wandered outside the head of your POV character, the solution is simple: Write your POV character using only private clips; write all other characters in the scene using only public clips. Show your reader only what your POV character can see, hear, smell, taste, or touch. Here's a rewrite of the example scene:

> Throckmorton jerks his head to one side, and the book whizzes past his right ear. Rage lights up his eyes, and he steps toward you, revving the chainsaw.

> You grab a handful of copies of your book and back away from him, holding them up as a shield.

> "Sweet Jesus, help me!" moans the store's PR director behind you. An instant later, a dull whump on the floor tells you she's fainted.

Fixing cause-effect problems

Always, always, always show a cause first, and then show the effect. Here's an example paragraph that breaks this rule:

> Fear floods your heart and you dive to your left, cradling your head in your hands and praying that you won't land on the PR director, just after Throckmorton lunges at you with the chainsaw.

This is horrible! We've put the cause (Throckmorton's lunge) at the tail end of a long sentence in which we first show all the effects of the cause (all your reactions to Throckmorton's lunge). Nothing is more confusing to a reader.

Whenever you see the word *after* in your fiction, ask whether you've put the cause after the effect. If you have, then fix it:

> Throckmorton lunges at you with the chainsaw.

> Fear floods your heart and you dive to your left, cradling your head in your hands and praying that you won't land on the PR director.

Fixing time-scale problems

Different processes take different lengths of time. A gunshot is quicker than a wink, which is quicker than a touchdown run, which is quicker than a presidential election.

If you show two events happening at the same time, then show the fastest one first. This is a subtle issue, but it's worth fixing because it adds clarity.

In this section, we consider two common ways that time-scale problems can creep in.

Simultaneous events

Read the following sentence, which combines fast-happening and slow-happening events:

> The roar of the chainsaw cuts off just as Throckmorton lets out a long, bellowing roar while pitching forward wildly toward the floor.

An author means well when he tries to pack as much as possible into one sentence. However, your reader doesn't care if you mean well; your reader just cares whether she's immersed in the story.

The problem here is that we're trying to make two things simultaneous, but they can't be simultaneous because they have different *time scales* — one happens slowly and one happens quickly:

- ✔ **Slowly:** "Throckmorton falls to the ground while letting out a long, bellowing roar." This takes a substantial fraction of a second. (Time yourself falling, and you'll see it takes quite a while.)

- ✔ **Quickly:** "The roar of the chainsaw cuts off." This happens almost instantly when his finger slips off the trigger.

Be suspicious whenever you see two phrases connected by the words *just as* or *as* or *while*. Ask yourself whether those two actions can really happen simultaneously and for the same length of time.

Notice that Throckmorton can be bellowing the entire time he's falling, so connecting those two events with the word *while* is perfectly fine. But he can't fall nearly as fast as the chainsaw can stop roaring. Therefore, using the words *just as* is a mistake, because it implies that two things happen in the same instant.

Little things can make a big difference, even if they're so small that the reader doesn't see them. The reader may not consciously notice that two things can't happen simultaneously, but she'll feel that the passage is a little fuzzy. She'll say, "I can't quite visualize it." And she's right. You've let the action slip out of focus. The solution is to figure out what started first and show that first, even if it's still going on when the second thing happens.

In Throckmorton's case, he tripped, staggered forward, let out a long, bellowing roar, and hit the ground. Somewhere in the middle of all that, his finger slipped off the chainsaw trigger and the engine's roar cut off. So write it that way, in two sentences:

> Throckmorton lets out a long, bellowing roar while pitching forward wildly toward the floor. The roar of the chainsaw cuts off.

Special problems in private clips

The following passage mixes up the time scale inside the second private clip (the third paragraph):

> You hit the floor and feel the breath go whooshing out of you. For an instant, your vision goes dark. Forcing yourself to shake it off, you stagger blindly to your feet.
>
> Before you can turn around, Throckmorton grapples you from behind. "Time to die, you Nazi!" A strong hand closes around your throat.
>
> You remember a trick that a friend of yours demonstrated for you when you were researching your book. You stomp on Throckmorton's instep, jab an elbow in his gut and instinctively claw on the hand at your throat. A rush of fear knifes through your belly.

This passage goes fine until the third paragraph, a private clip. There we get the time scales all turned around.

Here's the time scale for feelings, instinctive actions, and rational actions and speech:

- ✔ Feelings happen fast, on the order of a few milliseconds.
- ✔ Instinctive actions happen almost as fast, on the order of tenths of a second.
- ✔ Rational actions and speech take the longest, at least half a second.

Therefore, in a private clip that contains all three elements, you need to show the feelings first, then the instinctive actions, and then the rational actions and speech. Take a look at the third paragraph of the example and see how it now makes more sense when we reorder things:

> You hit the floor and feel the breath go whooshing out of you. For an instant, your vision goes dark. Forcing yourself to shake it off, you stagger blindly to your feet.

Before you can turn around, Throckmorton grapples you from behind. "Time to die, you Nazi!" A strong hand closes around your throat.

A rush of fear knifes through your belly. You instinctively claw on the hand at your throat. Then you remember a trick that a friend of yours demonstrated for you when you were researching your book. You stomp on Throckmorton's instep and jab an elbow in his gut.

Throckmorton's hold on you weakens.

You spin around, give him a knee plant to the groin, and jab a thumb into the soft spot at the base of his throat.

That's dirty fighting, of course, but you can't afford to give Throckmorton a break. You can't afford to give your reader a break, either. She bought your book because she wanted a powerful emotional experience. If you let your scene get out of focus, even in the tiniest details, you're giving your reader less than she paid for. Whether you write the grittiest action novels or the gentlest of romances, you owe it to your reader to deliver the most powerful emotional experience you can.

Getting In and Out of Flashbacks

If a flashback is called for, then use it (we discuss how to know whether it's called for in the earlier section "Deciding Whether to Show or Tell"). The only question left is how to edit your flashback. Remember that a flashback is really nothing but a container for a sequence of clips set in the past, along with a transition at the beginning and the end. We discuss editing clips in the preceding sections. The only other thing you need to worry about is editing your transition points.

There's nothing mysterious about the transitions. They just need to make it clear that your POV character is flashing back or flashing forward. You normally do this by making an explicit reference to a memory. Here's an example of how not to do it:

"Tell us how you were able to fight off a man twice your weight," Larry King says.

Brad says, "Grab me from behind and try to choke me."

You wrap your arms around his body and reach for his neck. An instant later, pain stabs through your instep. An elbow to your gut steals every molecule of air in your lungs. A hammer shot to your groin sends an explosion of pain rocketing up your insides.

"I guess I just think fast on my feet," you say.

Whoa! The switch from Larry King to Brad to Larry is confusing. The problem is that we rush too fast into the flashback and too fast out. The reader needs cues each way to bookend the flashback, like this:

> "Tell us how you were able to fight off a man twice your weight," Larry King says.
>
> You've been trying for two years to forget the day you interviewed your ex-SEAL friend Brad on street-fighting tactics for your book.
>
> Brad says, "Grab me from behind and try to choke me."
>
> You wrap your arms around his body and reach for his neck. An instant later, pain stabs through your instep. An elbow to your gut steals every molecule of air in your lungs. A hammer shot to your groin sends an explosion of pain rocketing up your insides.
>
> That was two years ago, and you still haven't forgiven Brad. You didn't give him an acknowledgment in your book. You haven't told a soul about that interview.
>
> You blink at Larry King and give him a crooked grin. "I guess I just think fast on my feet."

Editing Telling

We hope you aren't under the impression that we hate telling — narrative summary, exposition, or static description. Far from it. These telling tools have their place in any story. If you don't believe us, read the first page of *Harry Potter and the Sorcerer's Stone.* The entire page is telling, and it's brilliant. It works. If you're going to tell, make sure that — at the very least — it works. If you can arrange to be brilliant, do that, too (see the nearby sidebar "Creating your own style" for our notes on becoming brilliant).

Here are the most common problems we see with telling and some ways to liven up these telling segments:

- ✔ **Wordiness:** Be as concise as you can.
- ✔ **Abstract language:** Be as concrete as possible. Use strong nouns and verbs and vivid details.
- ✔ **Explaining too much:** Resist the urge to explain.

We discuss these three fixes in this section.

TIP

Creating your own style

As you advance in the art and craft of writing fiction, you'll find a style that works for you. In this book, we're cautious about trying to teach you how to create your style, because it's such an intensely personal thing. You do have options — loads of them. Here are a few questions for you to think about as you develop your style:

✔ How important is style to you (as compared to the other four pillars of fiction — story world, character, plot, and theme)?

✔ Do you want a distinctive style that sets you apart from all other writers, or do you prefer to write in a style that doesn't distract the reader from the story?

✔ Do you have a particular author whose style is similar to the one you'd like to have or the one you already have? If so, how are you different from that author?

✔ Do you write in a category with a typical style that your readers will expect you to conform to? (A hard-boiled detective novel has a flavor very different from a Regency romance.)

✔ How important is it to you to avoid clichés? Must every sentence you write be fresh and original? Or has "outside the box" become the new box?

We can't tell you which style is best for you. We do encourage you to experiment with new stylistic techniques. Do they resonate with you? Do they work for your test readers? If so, then keep them. If not, then don't. Your natural style will bloom in its own time.

Tightening text and adding color

Editing often means both cutting out unneeded words and inserting words that add vividness. Here's an example of a segment of telling that needs both tightening and color:

> Walking through the airport after your interview, you realize that the near-disaster at your first book signing has been good for your career. Airports often have bookstores, because airline passengers have little to do in the air, so many of them like to read. Every bookstore you pass on the way to your gate has lots of copies of your book. You fall asleep on the flight home and have a disturbing dream that gives you an idea for your next book.

This is mostly narrative summary, with a bit of exposition. There just isn't much going on here to advance the story, so we clearly don't want to show this segment using clips. However, we don't want to cut it altogether, because it makes a nice transition from the previous scene to the next one, when you're home thinking about your next novel.

The first two sentences explain too much. If the disaster at your book signing got you on the Larry King show, then obviously it was good for your career. Most people know why airports have bookstores, and those who don't know can easily guess. Resist the urge to explain.

The last two sentences lack any color or concrete details. Even though you aren't showing the walk through the airport or the flight, you can still make them a bit more vivid.

Here's an edited version of the same segment that trims out the excess words and unnecessary explanation and puts in just a bit of color:

> Walking through the airport after your interview, you pass a Barnes & Noble with a ceiling-high display of your books. While you sit waiting at your gate, six different passengers approach you clutching copies of your book and ask for autographs. You close your eyes on the plane, hoping for some sleep. You get a little, but your dreams are disturbed by hundreds of Throckmorton clones, all bearing chainsaws, all chanting your name. As your plane descends into your home airport, the last orange rays of the dying sun reflect on the windows of the terminal building in an explosion of color. And just like that, you *know* what your next book has to be about.

Notice that the edited version is longer than the original, even though we cut out the unnecessary explanations. That's because we've inserted some concrete details, and those details add words.

Knowing when to kill a segment of telling

Sometimes you find a segment of telling that doesn't need editing; it needs killing. Here are the most common reasons you may want to cut a segment completely:

- **Telling the backstory:** Every author knows that backstory is bad — for other authors. Every author thinks that he is the lone exception and can get away with writing pages of backstory in chapter one because the reader is dying to know it. This is a lie from the pits of hell. The reader doesn't care two figs about your backstory in chapter one. Readers only start caring about a character's backstory when they start knowing the character.

  If you tell any backstory in your first five chapters, ask yourself whether you're willing to pay your editor ten dollars per word for the right to leave it in. If so, then keep it, in because it must be brilliant. Otherwise, take a chainsaw to it.

✔ **Explaining the story world:** Writers have a saying: "Resist the urge to explain." We won't bother to explain why this is true, but it is. Explain as little of your story world as possible.

✔ **Expounding on a theme:** Your reader is smart and doesn't need to have the deep meaning of your novel explained. Explaining your work makes it shallower. Resist, resist, resist the urge to explain.

For some more solid advice on editing segments of telling, see the chapters on description and exposition in *Revision & Editing,* by James Scott Bell (Writer's Digest).

Part IV
Getting Published

The 5th Wave   By Rich Tennant

"I'm pretty confident about selling my novel.
I already have an agent, a manager, and a lawyer.
It's my barber, my mechanic, and my dry cleaner."

In this part . . .

Although some people may be happy being great, unpublished novelists, for most writers, getting published is the reason they write. In this part, we take a look at what it takes to get published, including info on cleaning up your manuscript, developing a winning book proposal, finding an agent, and selling your novel to a publisher (with or without an agent).

Chapter 16

Getting Ready to Sell Your Book: Polishing and Submitting

· ·

In This Chapter

▶ Polishing your manuscript

▶ Ironing out potential legal issues

▶ Choosing between traditional publishing and self-publishing

▶ Writing a query letter

▶ Sending more information — the proposal

· ·

Selling fiction is about writing excellent fiction. That's why, in this book, we've focused on improving your writing craft — because 90 percent of marketing is having great craft.

Before you start contacting agents or editors, you need to make sure that your manuscript is as perfect as you can make it. In today's competitive market, "good enough" is just not good enough. After you complete and edit your manuscript, it still needs final polishing. In this chapter, we give you some tips on doing that.

When the manuscript is truly ready to go, you still need to make a critical decision: Will you try to sell your novel to a traditional publishing house, or will you try other options? With today's advances in technology, you have more options than ever. Does working with a traditional publisher still make sense? That depends, but most often the answer is yes. In this chapter, we discuss those ticklish "other options" and tell you when you may want to consider them and why.

If you decide to work with a traditional publisher, then selling your novel almost always begins with either a *query* or a *proposal*. A query is a concise letter designed to help you attract the attention of an agent and then an editor. A proposal is much like a query, but with much more information. Writing a good query or proposal isn't hard, and we lay out all the principles here in this chapter. You have lots of freedom to be creative, but you have to avoid certain pitfalls if you don't want an instant rejection.

If you want detailed information on dealing with agents and publishers, we recommend reading *Getting Your Book Published For Dummies* (Wiley). We discuss agents and editors a bit more in Chapter 17. For now, though, in this chapter, we give you the basics on how to make the crucial first approach.

Polishing Your Manuscript

The usual process for preparing a novel for publication goes like this:

1. Write the first draft, using whatever creative paradigm works best for you. (Chapter 4 outlines several creative paradigms. Chapters 6 to 11 discuss the various aspects of writing the first draft.)

2. Edit the manuscript at least once, and possibly several times. (Chapters 12 to 15 give you a strategy and some analytic tools for editing your manuscript.)

3. Get feedback from a serious writer or an agent or editor or some other publishing professional. (Don't ask one of your relatives or non-writer friends; they love you too much to give you the painful criticism you may need.) Use the feedback to edit the manuscript again.

4. Proofread the final manuscript, or hire a proofreader to do it for you, to eliminate any spelling errors or grammatical flaws.

Can you polish your manuscript to a high gleam all by yourself? Yes, it's possible. We've seen it done. We've done it. However, most writers edit their own manuscript until it's as good as they can make it, and then they get an outside opinion. We assume that you've completed steps 1 and 2 above, and that now you're ready for steps 3 and 4 — to get an outside opinion from a qualified person. In this section, we look at your options.

Teaming with critique buddies

A *critique buddy* is a writing friend with whom you trade critiquing favors. The usual way this works is that you trade sample chapters and critique them. The ideal critique buddy loves the category you're writing and really gets you and what you're trying to say. He or she understands you well enough to know how best to work with you. If you're sensitive and your ego is easily wounded, then your critique buddy should know how to lay on the praise for what you do well and then salt in helpful comments on your weaknesses. If you're rhino-skin tough, then your critique buddy should know how to pierce your armor and make you see the things that need fixing.

Where do you find critique buddies? Wherever you can find them. Randy has found most of his at writing conferences, usually when he wasn't looking for them. You may find your critique buddy in a writing class, in a critique group, in an online writing group, or in the frozen foods section at the supermarket. Where you find them doesn't really matter, as long as you're both agreeable to working together.

Critique buddies aren't forever. You may outgrow yours, outlast them, or outlive them. The important idea is that each of you should benefit the other. As long as you're both happy with the relationship, then let it continue. When it's not working out, let it fade away.

Joining critique groups

A *critique group* is a group of writers who meet periodically to critique each other's writing. You can meet in person or online, whichever is more convenient. Most critique groups meet at least monthly. Some meet as often as once a week, which is pretty intense. Some meet sporadically.

Typically, the quality of critique you get varies. The rank beginners in your group may not have the skills to give a good critique, but they'll learn if you take the time to train them. Having at least one published author or very strong writer who can give guidance and lay down the law when one of the members is giving bogus advice is great, but this isn't a requirement.

What a critique group may lack in consistency it makes up for in variety. If you have a group of five to ten members, you get a wide range of opinions. You need to develop some judgment to know whose opinion you trust, but you may find that even the greenest critiquer will sometimes nail you perfectly, so don't ever write off anyone's opinion as useless.

Where do you find a critique group? One common way is to join an organization that has one or more existing critique groups that you can join. If you have a local writing center or writing club, it may have some critique groups. Likewise, the local university or college may organize critique groups, or you can try craigslist (www.craigslist.org). If you have enough friends who write or want to write, you may try forming your own critique group. You need to have at least one person in the group who is good enough at organization to make sure that the group runs smoothly.

No critique group lasts forever, but they may last you a good long time. Randy was in the same group for about eight years, and that group brought him from the middle freshman-writer stage all the way to the junior level. (See Chapter 1 for a discussion of the four stages of a novelist's road to publication.)

Working with freelance editors

Every novelist needs a *substantive editor* — someone who helps critique characters, structure, plot, and theme. The longer you work in the publishing industry, the more firmly you'll believe this. When a publisher buys your novel, it assigns you a substantive editor to help you do revisions on the structure of your novel. A substantive editor doesn't fix your work. Instead, she tells you what she thinks you need to fix and why, leaving you to restructure your manuscript and rewrite things in your own unique style.

Substantive editing is different from *copy editing* — where an editor helps fix problems in formatting and style. Copy editing helps ensure that your work is clear, correct, concise, comprehensible, and consistent (the so-called "Five Cs.")

You may feel that you need a substantive edit or a copy edit before you try to sell your work. If you think so, then odds are that you do. (Even if you don't think so, you may need one.) Randy published his first novel without a freelance editor, but he wrote his next two with a co-author and discovered the value of having a strong critical eye look over the manuscript before submitting it to the publisher. Soon after that, he began working with a freelance editor, and he doesn't think he'll ever try to write a novel without one again.

Where do you find a freelance editor? You can do a search online and you'll find an enormous number of them. (If you choose one this way, ask for references and be sure you know exactly what you're getting before you sign a contract.) If you belong to a writing organization, such as Romance Writers of America (RWA) or Mystery Writers of America (MWA), you'll find a fair number of freelance editors among the members — many excellent novelists work part time as freelance editors. You may also have a writer friend who can refer you to a good editor, or you may meet one at a writing conference. Many college English and Journalism departments have postings for freelance editors.

If you decide to hire a freelance editor, consider these guidelines:

- ✔ Look for someone who understands fiction, loves your category, and gets you and your writing.

- ✔ Look for someone who knows how sensitive you are to criticism and can adjust the level of her sting to get through your armor without killing your drive to write.

- ✔ Tell the freelance editor what sort of work you want done. If you only want an analysis of your story structure, tell her. If you think only your characters need attention, tell her. If you want a complete analysis of the whole story, tell her. You're the boss, so you get to decide what work your editor will do for you.

> ✔ Make sure you understand the editor's rates in advance and get an esti-
> mate on how many hours she'll need to evaluate your work. Also, make
> clear in advance just what you expect to get out of the evaluation. Are
> you looking for someone to merely suggest changes that you'll then
> make, or do you want your editor to actually edit the manuscript to
> make the changes herself?

> ✔ Get references and ask yourself how similar you are to the person who
> gave the references. The freelance editor will give you references only
> from people who like her work, so you need to decide how likely it is
> that she'll mesh with you as well as she does with her other clients.

A good freelance editor can help push you to a level that you'd never reach
on your own. A bad freelance editor will merely waste your money.

Hiring freelance proofreaders

Some writers need a proofreader — someone to catch and fix errors in punctuation, usage, grammar, and spelling. You may find that these mechanical
aspects of writing simply escape you. This doesn't mean you're a bad writer.
Many great writers have been unable to master these mechanical skills. If
your critique buddy or critique group routinely finds typos of this type, you
may need to hire a professional proofreader to clean up your manuscript
before you try to sell it.

This isn't acceptance of a moral or intellectual failing; it's acceptance of a
mechanical weakness. A fair number of professional novelists routinely hire
proofreaders to fix up these minor issues.

A proofreader's job is not to change your writing. She won't analyze your
story structure, characters, or theme. She'll just fix those pesky commas
and spelling errors and busted syntax. If you need a proofreader, hire one.
You can find proofreaders the same way you find freelance editors (see our
suggestions in the previous section) — online, in writing organizations, by
referral from writer friends, at a writing conference, or at a college. Ask for
references and hire one who fits your budget.

One final thought — the proofreading stage should come only *after* you've
edited your manuscript, because editing usually means structural change and
always includes a lot of rewriting. If you were to edit after you proofread, you'd
probably introduce a whole new set of typos that need to be proofread again.

Looking at Three Common Legal Questions

Your manuscript is edited, polished, and ready for publishing. Before you start thinking about which type of publishing you want to pursue (see the next section), stop and make sure you've addressed some common legal issues that sometimes affect writers. These issues should be ironed out prior to working with an agent, editor, or publishing house or service.

Standard disclaimer: We aren't lawyers and nothing here should be construed as legal advice. For detailed information on contracts and the legal issues associated with getting published, contact a lawyer or refer to the book *Getting Your Book Published For Dummies* (Wiley). However, we'd like to answer some of the common questions we get about legal issues. Here's our best understanding of these issues:

- ✔ **Should you copyright your novel before submitting it to agents or editors to protect yourself from them stealing your work?** No. U.S. copyright law says that anything you write is automatically copyrighted as soon as you write it, so you don't need to protect it further by registering a copyright. Doing so is a fine way to tell the world, "I'm an amateur interested in doing business with you, but I don't trust you not to steal my idea." If and when you get your novel published, the publisher will usually pay for the copyright to be registered in your name.

- ✔ **Are you allowed to base your novel on real people and real situations?** That depends, and if you have any doubts, you should talk to an attorney about your specific case. *Libel* is a false statement, either published or broadcast, that damages a person's reputation. A dead person cannot be libeled. If you tell the truth about a public figure, then that's not libel (but you'd better be able to prove it's the truth). If you tell the truth about a living non-public figure, that's not libel, either, but it may very well be invasion of privacy, and you could be hit with a lawsuit. The living relatives of a dead person may also sue you for invasion of their privacy.

If you insist on writing fiction about people who aren't public figures, then change everything you can — names, dates, genders, ethnic backgrounds, and any specifics that make it clear who your characters actually are. Or get permission. If you base your character on a real person (like yourself or someone close to you), you risk creating a *Mary Sue* — an idealized character who's too good to be true.

- ✔ **Can you quote from books, newspaper articles, magazine articles, or songs?** This is tricky. A concept called *fair use* defines how much you can quote from copyrighted sources. It depends on a number of factors, such as how much you're quoting, what fraction of the original you're quoting, what economic impact it has on the source you're quoting, and so on. The issue is complicated, and your best bet is to get permission or consult an attorney. Lyrics from songs are especially tricky, and often you can't quote any of it without paying. You can quote anything in the *public domain* — works too old to be protected by copyright, or works intentionally released as public domain by their authors. However, you still need to tell the original source of a quotation from a public domain source so you won't be accused of plagiarism.

If you have doubts about any legal question, consult an attorney.

Deciding between Traditional Publishing and Self-Publishing

In the old days, you wrote a manuscript, mailed it off to a publisher, and hoped for the best. These days, you have other options. We explain them here.

Understanding how traditional publishers work

With a traditional royalty-paying publisher, the publishing company takes all the risk and earns most of the profits on a book. Here's how the process works, in brief:

1. You write a manuscript (or a partial manuscript if you're a published author with a good track record for meeting deadlines), and then write a query letter or proposal and send it to an agent.

   If the agent agrees to represent you and your book, she then contacts acquisitions editors at several publishing houses. Or if you decide not to work with an agent, you submit your work directly to acquisitions editors for consideration. (See later in this chapter for information on how to write a query letter or proposal.)

2. The acquisitions editor considers your work and decides whether it merits publication and whether it's likely to sell enough copies to be worth their while from a business perspective. Publishers are not in business to fulfill your ambition to get published. They're in business to make money. If they don't believe they'll make money publishing your work, they won't try.

On average, publishers want a book to sell (at the very least) eight thousand copies in three years, to offset printing costs and turn a profit (six-to-eight thousand is the minimum print run required by most major printers). The bigger the publisher, of course, the more copies they want to print and sell in that three-year period – but most publishing houses aren't very big.

Usually, the acquisitions editor needs to get agreement from a publishing committee that includes executives of the publishing company, the marketing director, the sales director, and other editors.

3. If the publisher decides to pursue your manuscript, the editor will call your agent (or you, if you don't have an agent) and make an offer.

   Along with the offer comes a lengthy written contract that spells out every detail of the agreement. You'll be offered a *royalty* — a percentage on every book sold. Normally, you'll also be offered an *advance* against royalties. This is a fixed sum that the publisher pays you before your book actually earns any money.

   If your royalties don't earn enough to cover the advance payment, you won't be asked to repay the advance. The publisher is therefore risking that advance payment, along with the money it pays its editors, marketing team, sales force, and printer.

4. You or your agent negotiate the terms of the contract with the publisher until all parties are happy.

   Then you sign the contract and work with the publisher to complete the book, revise it, launch it, and promote it. Your agent is paid a fixed percentage (traditionally 15 percent, though the number may vary) of any payments you receive from the publisher.

The above arrangement is obviously low-risk for you, the author. Only the publisher invests any money upfront. You put in some effort and time, but you don't invest a dime in the product. If the book tanks, you lose nothing but your time and effort.

With a traditional publisher, your earnings are only a small fraction of the total sales of the book. The publisher is taking most of the risk, and it therefore expects most of the reward. It provides the editorial assistance and cover design, and it pays the marketing, sales, production, and publicity costs. You're expected to help on promotion, but you aren't expected to pay for it (although you can if you think it'll benefit you).

Understanding how self-publishing works

You don't have to work with a traditional royalty-paying publisher, of course. You may well ask why you should pay somebody else to do what you could do better. You can hire a freelance editor to help you make the manuscript a polished masterpiece. You can hire a graphic designer to do the cover and interior design. You can hire someone to typeset the book, someone to print it, someone to warehouse it, someone to make deals with distributors, someone to market it and publicize it.

You can even do some or all those things yourself if you have the skills. You wouldn't get an advance, but you'd get all the profits on the book, which could be substantial.

Over the last few decades, as computer technology has invaded publishing, more and more writers have tried their hand at self-publishing — being their own publishers. A number of them have made phenomenal successes of their books. Be aware that most of the successful self-published books have been *non-fiction*. It's much harder to make a success of a self-published novel.

You have two main options if you self-publish. You can get a large number of books printed all at once, or you can make an arrangement with a print-on-demand (POD) company, which will print only as many copies as you need, as often as you need them. It's more expensive and more hassle to print thousands of copies up front, but the cost per copy is much less than it is for a POD copy. POD publishing is rapidly becoming more popular, because it's a fairly inexpensive way to get a book in print.

To add even more complexity, the market is finally opening up to electronic books (eBooks) which can be produced and distributed very cheaply. The Amazon Kindle and other eBook readers show promise of radically changing the world of publishing in the next few years. These days, any publishing contract spells out the eBook rights in detail. It's unclear what fraction of the market eBooks will claim in the future, but most people think eBooks will be an important part of the market from now on.

Why don't all writers self-publish their novels and reap the rewards? The answer is simple: Publishing is work — hard work. Editing, graphics, marketing, sales, and publicity are all highly specialized skills that take a lot of time and effort before you reach excellence. Publishing is also a risky business, and fiction is one of the riskiest categories in the industry. Most novels just don't do as well as the publisher hoped. This is true at even the very largest publishing houses, and it's especially true for self-publishers.

The biggest problem for the novelist is that marketing fiction is extremely hard. A very few authors have made enormous profits self-publishing their novels. (William Paul Young's self-published novel, *The Shack*, is one of the few self-published novels that's done well. It reportedly sold more than 6 million copies in its first two years.) However, the vast majority of self-published novelists sell only a few dozen up to a few hundred copies. You can sell only so many copies to your friends and relatives.

We believe that self-publishing can sometimes make good business sense, if you have a strong marketing platform in place. Please note that it's much harder to build a marketing platform for fiction than for nonfiction.

Should you self-publish your novel? Maybe, if any of the following are true:

✔ You know for certain that you can market a lot of copies of the book.

✔ You only want a few copies for yourself, friends, and relatives.

✔ You demand complete control and ownership of your work and the creative process that goes into it.

Beware the vanity publishers!

You may have seen ads in magazines that offer to publish your book, sight unseen, no questions asked. Have you ever wondered how these "publishers" can make money when they don't even know whether your book's any good?

The answer is that they take no risk; you do. You invest the money to pay for the production of your book. The "publisher" just takes your work and prints it. In the worst cases, they don't edit it at all. If they do edit it, you pay them for the editing. The publisher provides a cover design, but you pay for it. You pay for the printer, the paper, the warehousing. In the worst cases, you then have to buy copies from the publisher (even though you already paid for them). All too often, this sort of publisher does nothing to promote your book — no marketing, no publicity, no sales team, no deals with book distributors. These publishers are often called *vanity publishers* (especially those who will publish anything, regardless of quality) because they cater to your desire to get published at any cost. An alternative term is *subsidy publisher*. Some subsidy publishers are quite picky about what they'll publish and exercise a lot of quality control.

Bookstores usually won't place orders with vanity publishers, because there's no quality control with a vanity press. Bookstores don't want to buy something unless they can sell it. If you owned a bookstore, you wouldn't either.

If you browse around on the Web, you'll find plenty of controversy about whether vanity publishing (or subsidy publishing) is a good deal for the author. Some writers maintain that this kind of publishing is always a bad deal. Others insist that there's a broad spectrum, and that some subsidy publishers are legitimate.

Should you work with a vanity publisher or subsidy publisher? Maybe, if you want to self-publish but you want somebody else to do all of the production work that a self-publisher would normally do. (See the previous section for some reasons you might decide to self-publish.)

If you're tempted to work with a vanity publisher or subsidy publisher, be very careful and ask lots of questions. Better yet, ask some industry professionals about any company you're interested in working with. Published authors, literary agents, and editors at traditional publishers all have plenty of experience in telling the scams from the real thing. (This is also true when choosing an agent or a traditional publisher — ask around if you don't know an agent or publisher's reputation.)

Our recommendation

We believe that a novelist's best deal is *usually* to work with a traditional royalty-paying publisher who'll take the risk and will do the hard work of marketing your novel. Almost every novel by a traditional publisher will sell thousands to tens of thousands of copies. Almost every self-published novel will sell dozens to hundreds of copies. You don't need a calculator to do the math on which one is a better deal.

If you decide to work with a traditional publisher, you need to find one willing to work with you. We strongly recommend that you get an agent to help you sell your work to a publisher. (We discuss agents in Chapter 17). It is still possible these days to sell a novel without an agent, but it's much harder than it used to be. Most novels sold these days to traditional publishers are represented by an agent.

To get an agent, you usually need to write a query letter in order to make first contact. We discuss that next.

First Contact: Writing a Query Letter

When you contact an agent or editor for the first time, you usually send a *query letter* — a short introduction which tells about you and your book and asks whether they're interested in hearing more. (Chapter 17 tells you more about agents and editors. You should always check the Web site of the agency or publisher to see exactly how they prefer to be contacted. Follow their directions precisely.) It's okay to query more than one agent at a time. We highly recommend that you query several at a time, because agents often take a long time to answer queries.

The purpose of a query letter is to get the agent or editor to ask for more information. You should be as short as possible. Publishing professionals are extremely busy and they receive many queries every day. The quicker they can make a decision, the more they'll appreciate you. If they want to know more, they'll ask for more.

For a very detailed description about how to write a query letter, we recommend agent Noah Lukeman's e-book, *How to Write a Great Query Letter,* available on Amazon.com.

You can send a query either by regular mail or as an e-mail. The Web site of the agent or publisher will tell you which they prefer. Here's how to set up your query letter if you're sending a paper copy. Use one-inch margins on the sides and single-space the letter in a good readable font such as 12-point Times New Roman.

✔ **Create a letterhead at the top of the page.** It should contain your

- Name

- Mailing address

- Phone number

- E-mail address

The type size for your name can be a bit larger than the usual 12 points, whereas the type size for your contact information can be a bit smaller.

✔ **Address the letter to the agent or editor by name.** Spell his name correctly. If you're querying an editor, it's a good idea to call the main phone line of the publisher (don't call the editor) and double-check that the editor you're interested in still works for the publisher and verify her job title. Editors move around frequently, and you don't want to query someone who left two months ago.

✔ **Begin with a *hook* — a sentence that creates interest right away.** If you're querying an agent, a good hook might be that one of his other clients referred you. It might be some startling fact related to your novel. It might be your storyline. It might be something remarkable about you. Follow the hook up with a sentence or two more that develops it further.

✔ **Write a one-paragraph summary of roughly the first quarter of your manuscript that ends with the story question of your novel.** Focus on the big picture, not the details, and be as concise as possible. This will probably be an expansion of your one-sentence storyline, which we discuss in Chapters 8 and 13. Write it in present tense, just as you would for a synopsis.

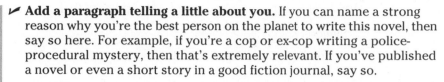

✔ **Add a paragraph telling a little about you.** If you can name a strong reason why you're the best person on the planet to write this novel, then say so here. For example, if you're a cop or ex-cop writing a police-procedural mystery, then that's extremely relevant. If you've published a novel or even a short story in a good fiction journal, say so.

Resist the urge to tell how much your mother loves your story. Say nothing about how you've been reading fiction since you were four years old. The editor assumes both of these are true, because she's already read thousands of queries from people just like you. She wants to know what makes you different from every other writer. Tell her. Don't be weird, but do be real.

✔ **Finish by asking permission to send more information.** "May I send you some sample chapters and a synopsis or a proposal?" is plenty for your closing paragraph.

When you write a query letter, make it brief, clear, and professional, and tailor it to the recipient. It's easy for authors to shotgun out zillions of queries, so if you send a query, personalize it so that the agent knows you have some reason to be querying her — other than that she's listed in *Writer's Market*. The agent or editor is looking for any sign that you failed to do your homework about her company. Nothing shouts "Reject me!" faster than a query that's obviously been sent to everyone.

Here is a sample query letter for Randy's novel *Oxygen*, which he coauthored with John B. Olson. This is a simplified version of the actual letter that Randy and John used when they submitted their work to editor Steve Laube:

Dear Mr. Laube:

Getting to Mars is easy. NASA engineers have known since the 1990s how to put humans on the Red Planet, using a mission design invented by Dr. Robert Zubrin, president of the Mars Society. The hard part is getting astronauts to Mars *alive.*

In our science-based thriller OXYGEN, four astronauts launch from Cape Canaveral in January of 2014, bound for Mars. Soon after the trans-Mars injection burn, an explosion leaves the crew without enough oxygen to get to Mars and without sufficient fuel to return to earth. To make matters worse, evidence suggests that the ship was sabotaged by one of the crew members. The only way they might reach Mars is for one astronaut to put the others into drug-induced comas. But first they have to decide whom they can trust.

Our qualifications: Randy has a Ph.D. in physics from UC-Berkeley and John has a Ph.D. in biochemistry from UW-Madison. We're members of the Mars Society and have talked with Dr. Robert Zubrin at a recent Mars Society conference. Randy is the author of a time-travel novel, *Transgression.*

May we send you some sample chapters and a synopsis or full proposal?

Sincerely,

Randy Ingermanson and John B. Olson

Piecing Together a Proposal

If an agent likes your query letter, he'll ask for more information. What sort of information? That depends on how interested he is in you and on what information he thinks he needs. It also depends on the expectations of the publishers he might submit your novel to. It's complicated, and there isn't any one set of information that fits all situations.

In this section, we describe the *maximal* amount of information that you're likely to need to send. Some agents will ask for less, but we don't think any will ask for more. The maximal package is called a *proposal* — a business plan for your novel. In it, you describe a proposed joint business venture between you and a publisher. The proposal contains all the information an agent needs to sell your novel. It contains all the information an acquisitions editor needs to make an informed decision and to sell the idea to her publishing committee. (See Chapter 17 for more information on agents and acquisitions editors.)

An agent will use this information for two purposes:

- To decide whether he wants to represent you.

- To help him sell your novel to a publisher. Some agents will pass on some or all of your information directly to editors. Other agents will repackage the information before submitting it. Every agent has his own style of selling.

Deciding what to include

There isn't any universal format or any rulebook for what goes into a proposal, but here are the main items that you might be asked for. You may be asked for only a few of these, but you'd be smart to have them all prepared and ready to go before you query:

- A cover letter
- A title page with contact info
- An executive summary page
- An analysis of your competition

- ✔ Character sketches

- ✔ A two-page synopsis of your story

- ✔ Your author bio

- ✔ Any information on how you might help market your book

- ✔ Sample chapters (typically the first three chapters or the first 30 pages, but sometimes the full polished manuscript, depending on what the agent wants to see)

Send only as much material as the agent requests. He'll tell you what he wants when he answers your query letter. If you met the agent at a conference and he requested information, he'll give you a list of things to send.

Don't create your own cover art. Don't include chocolate, granola, lingerie, or *any* other gifts. (Yes, really, all of these have been tried countless times, and all of these scream, "I'm an amateur.") If you act like an amateur, the agent will treat you like an amateur. If you act like a pro, he'll treat you like a pro. We recommend that everything you send an agent be business-like and concise.

Your cover letter: Reminding the agent who you are

Your *cover letter* reminds the agent of who you are and explains that you're enclosing information that he requested after reading your query letter or after meeting you at a conference. The cover letter is almost identical to a query letter (for details on the content of a query letter, see the earlier section titled "First Contact: Writing a Query Letter"). Start with a paragraph reminding the agent that he's asked for more information. End with a paragraph describing what's enclosed in the package.

Your title page

The title page should have your name, mailing address, phone number, and e-mail address in the upper left corner, all single-spaced and left-aligned.

Add several blank lines and write the title of your novel in large type (36-point type is a fine size if the title is short). Italicize the title and center it horizontally and vertically on the page.

The executive summary page

The executive summary page should have a centered header in a large point size that says "Executive Summary" or something similar. Keep your executive summary to one page and make it as clear and succinct as possible.

This page should be a "proposal within a proposal" that makes the best possible case for your book.

The executive summary page should contain the following information. We like to use a two-column format that shows a subheader in the left column and the corresponding information in the right column.

- ✔ **Working title:** This is the current title for your book. The publisher often believes that they can come up with a better title, so the title will probably change.

- ✔ **Category:** This is the category and subcategory of your book. Getting this right is critical, because an editor may reject your project instantly if the category isn't right for her. See Chapter 3 for a full discussion of categories.

- ✔ **High concept:** Base the high concept on your one-sentence storyline for your novel. See Chapters 8 and 13 for details on your storyline. You can use your storyline or you can adapt it slightly, but stick to one sentence and make it as short as possible.

- ✔ **Target readers:** Describe in one or two sentences your ideal readers. See Chapter 3 for a discussion of your target readers.

- ✔ **Length:** Estimate to the nearest 5,000 words the word count that your manuscript has or will have. (See Chapter 3 for a discussion of the importance of word count for certain categories and how to determine what yours should be.) In some categories, a word count that's too high or too low can be an instant show-stopper.

- ✔ **Completion date:** You should either say, "A polished manuscript is available now" or, "The polished manuscript will be complete by ___," and fill in the blank with a date that you're sure you can finish the novel before. Publishers will believe you mean this date, so don't fib.

Selling a novel without a complete manuscript is almost impossible for a first-time novelist. Writing a novel is no easy task, and many wannabe writers never finish one, so publishers almost always refuse to buy an incomplete manuscript from a first-timer. If you've already published at least one novel with a traditional, royalty-paying publisher, then most publishers will consider you a strong bet to finish another, so you can sell a novel with just a proposal and some sample chapters. Most professional novelists do so.

- **Story summary:** Write a paragraph that tells the setup for your story, describes your lead character, and ends with the story question. (See Chapters 6, 7, and 8 for a discussion of the story question.)

- **About the author:** If you have room on your executive summary page, write a paragraph about yourself. Put your best foot forward, but don't lie. Later in your proposal, you'll include a full one-page author bio, so if you don't have room for the short version on your executive summary page, then skip it. The goal here is to highlight any cool facts about you that will make it blindingly obvious that you're the perfect author for your story.

Market analysis: Analyzing your competition

On a new page, make a header that says "Market Analysis" or something similar. This section will be a half page up to a full page telling a bit about similar books.

Talk about books that are neither too famous nor too obscure. If you compare your novel to those of Fyodor Dostoevsky or Stephen King or some other monstrously famous author, then you risk either sounding horribly egotistical or else looking pretty lame by comparison. But if you compare your work to some complete unknowns, then you risk looking like an author doomed to obscurity.

Choose three to five books that are in the same category as yours. Write a paragraph about each, giving the title and author and a one-sentence summary of each. Explain how your book is similar and how it's different. Avoid slamming the other authors. Putting down other writers doesn't make you look bigger.

Your purpose in giving a list of similar books is to demonstrate that you're familiar with your category and that there's actually a market for the kind of book you wrote (or want to write). It also gives you a chance to show that you understand how to analyze a story.

Your author bio

Create a page within your proposal with the header "Author Bio." Write several paragraphs describing yourself in third person. Avoid bragging. Instead, try to describe yourself the way a journalist would if she were writing a profile of you in *Time* magazine. Be business-like and efficient, focusing on what qualifies you to write your book. If your life is similar to that of one of your characters, then say so.

Mention your writing credits, if any, without boasting. If you have a Web site or blog, mention it and give the URL. If you have any special marketing platform, such as a newspaper column, a radio show, a TV show, a speaking business, or status as a public figure, then describe it, telling roughly how many people you get in front of in a given year. Don't stretch the truth. Lies have a nasty way of kicking you in the keister, usually at the worst possible time.

Don't pad things out with fluff. The agent and editor simply don't care how many years you've been reading or what a precocious writer you were as a child. Many writers began writing between the ages of 5 and 10, and your editor has already heard every possible piece of puffery many times over. Few of your childhood accomplishments are worth mentioning here. If you graduated from high school at age 10, or won the National Spelling Bee, those would merit a sentence in your bio.

Mention any education beyond high school that bears directly on the subject of your novel. For example, if you're writing a science-based novel and hold a college degree in science, say so. If you're a lawyer or paralegal writing a legal thriller, don't keep it a secret. A college major in English literature or journalism would be worth a mention, but such majors are as common as dust bunnies and almost as valuable. An MFA degree in creative writing carries quite a bit more weight and you should mention it if you have one.

Also tell about any life experience that fits the subject of your novel. Even childhood experiences may be worth mentioning if they're powerful enough and fit your novel well enough. For example, if your parents were career diplomats with the Foreign Service, and you grew up in Paris, Rome, London, Tokyo, and Jerusalem—and routinely rubbed shoulders with heads of state— then that experience would certainly be relevant to a spy thriller that takes place in a variety of foreign capitals around the world.

An agent or editor is interested in anything about you that answers the question, "How can I get this author on radio or TV to talk about the book?" Let this be your guide in deciding what goes into your author bio.

Character sketches

We recommend that you include a few pages telling about your characters. We call these *character sketches,* and they're valuable because most editors love character-oriented fiction. Be aware that agents and editors rarely ask for character sketches. However, we consider these sketches to be a powerful selling tool and we think you might find them useful.

Create a header for this section that says "Character Sketches." Devote half a page to a full page to each major character, telling essential backstory, values, ambitions, and story goals. (See Chapters 7 and 12 for more information on these essentials of your characters.) Then tell a bit of the story as it relates to that character. If you get the editor interested in your characters, you'll radically improve your chances of selling your story.

The dreaded synopsis

Add a new section with the header "Synopsis." The *synopsis* is two pages sketching out the main story for your novel. Use present tense, and make each paragraph summarize several scenes, focusing on the main story and leaving out inessential plot threads. Virtually all agents and editors require a synopsis.

In our experience, writing a synopsis for a proposal is the single most hated task a novelist ever faces. If you don't like writing synopses, you're not alone, but you still have to write one. Yes, synopses are often boring. A synopsis uses narrative summary, which is the least vivid kind of storytelling. Get over that and just write it.

Chapter 9 explains in detail how to write a synopsis, and it isn't as horrible as many writers try to make it. If it's any comfort, many editors hate reading synopses, but no editor will buy your novel unless you provide one. It's one of those sad little ironies of life, so grit your teeth and grim it out.

Your marketing plan

Be clear about one thing: Marketing your novel is your publisher's job. Your job is to write the story. In recent years, however, publishers have come to depend more and more on authors to help with the marketing. You may feel that this is unfair, and it is, but it's a fact of life.

Anything you can do to help market your book should go in the marketing section of your proposal. You can find any number of excellent books on how authors market their work. Be aware that these books provide a vast ocean of options. No publisher expects you to choose more than a few items from this enormous marketing menu, any more than a restaurant expects you to eat more than a few choices from their menu.

You need to do some research on marketing to find out what will work well for you. Are you an extrovert who can tie the topic of your novel to some hot topic for radio or TV interviews? That's one item on the menu. Are you a blogger with hundreds or thousands of readers lapping up your daily subtle and ironic blog entries? That's another item on the menu. If you look hard, you'll discover hundreds or thousands of other ideas on that pesky menu.

Choose a few — and *only* a few — marketing ideas and talk about them in the marketing plan in your proposal. The more your publisher believes you can help in marketing your book, the more keen they'll be to stretch their own thin marketing budget to cover it, too. This is one area where the rich really do get richer. If you have a great media profile or if you're already speaking in front of hundreds of thousands of people per year, your publisher will be thrilled to throw great steaming piles of marketing money your way — whereas if you make it clear that you intend to do *nada* to market your book, your publisher will be happy to double that investment with their own contribution of *nada*. Think about that and then do some hard thinking on what you can believably say in your marketing plan.

You may feel that you just don't want to be a marketing weasel. Although we don't advocate weaselhood, we also believe that sort of attitude is going to hurt you as a writer. Marketing is not intrinsically dirty or weaselish. If you're as good of a writer as you think you are, then at least tens of thousands of people would love to read your book if only they knew who you were. What is dirty or weaselish about helping those readers find you? Good, honest marketing is about finding the people who want to read you but who don't yet know you exist. Never be shy about helping those readers find you. They'll be glad you did, and so will your publisher.

Your writing, including sample chapters (or whole manuscripts!)

A writing sample is *essential* to both agents and editors. They want to know how well you can write. When an agent responds to your query letter, he'll tell you how much of a sample he wants to see. Send him that much. Typically, an agent will request a certain number of chapters or a set number of pages. Don't annoy him by sending more. If he asks for the whole manuscript, then send it all.

We emphasize here again that if you've never yet published a novel, then you shouldn't query an agent until you have a complete, polished manuscript. If the agent loves your query letter and asks for the whole manuscript, he's going to be very annoyed to find that you only have 50 pages done.

When editors receive a proposal, they typically scan the cover letter and executive summary, and then flip to the sample chapters. If the first paragraph is good, they'll read the whole first page. If that's good, they'll read the first chapter. If that's good, they'll read all the chapters. If they're all excellent, the editor will then read the rest of the proposal in detail. If any part of the sample chapters fails to delight the editor, she'll stop reading at once and send a quick rejection.

That's how important your sample chapters are. We can't emphasize this too heavily. The most important part of your proposal package is your writing sample. The editor needs to love your sample chapters, or your query is as useless as chocolate frosting on an old shoe.

Don't place the © symbol or any other type of copyright notice on your sample chapters. Your writing is automatically protected, and including the symbol will reveal that you're an amateur (and that you don't trust the publisher or agent to know and respect copyright law).

Chapter 17

Approaching Agents and Editors

. . . .

In This Chapter

▶ Looking at the differences between agents and editors

▶ Finding an agent

▶ Finding an editor

. . . .

*W*hen you have a strong manuscript for your novel and all the elements of a solid proposal, you're ready to get it published. Publishing a novel is a high-risk, high-reward business partnership between you and a publisher. Because the publisher takes most of the risk in the deal, it also wants most of the reward. Two key types of people help you broker a deal — a literary agent and an acquisitions editor.

A *literary agent* is someone you hire to help you sell your novel to a publisher in return for a fixed percentage of your writing income. An *acquisitions editor* is an employee of a publishing house (usually in the Acquisitions department) whose job is to find authors and buy their manuscripts for publication.

In this chapter, we describe the roles of agents and editors and help you find people who are a good fit for you and your writing.

Defining the Roles of Agents and Editors

You need to understand some crucial differences between agents and editors. Note that both of them have divided loyalties:

> ✔ **Acquisitions editors:** An editor represents the publisher's interests in the deal. Her goal is to minimize the risk to her employer and maximize the reward by shifting as much risk to you and paying as little money as you'll tolerate. The editor's first loyalty is to the publisher. However, she is *not* your enemy. She likes you and she likes your writing, and she knows that if you starve to death, you won't write any more books for her.

> ✔ **Literary agents:** An agent represents your interests in the deal. His goal is to minimize your risk and maximize your reward, but not at all costs. The agent has strong incentives to be an honest broker, because he represents many writers. The agent will do best if he brings excellent writers to publishers and negotiates good deals for them. However, agents aren't out to impoverish the publisher, because tomorrow is another deal.

Finding the Best Agent for You

Agents are optional, so the first decision you need to make is whether you want one. This section explains what an agent does and why hiring an agent may be a good idea.

If you decide that you need an agent, how do you find the right one for you and then get his or her interest? If you've got an excellent manuscript, then finding an agent really isn't that hard. Finding an *appropriate* agent is a bit harder, but we give you some guidelines in this section. We also tell you how to contact that agent to pitch your novel.

Deciding whether you need an agent

Do you need an agent? That's a complicated question. An agent does tough, difficult work for you, but he costs you money. The usual fee for a literary agent is 15 percent off the top of your writing income. Here are some common tasks that an agent may do for you:

- ✔ Critique your manuscript and help you polish it (not all agents do this)
- ✔ Work with you to develop a strong proposal (see Chapter 16 for the basics on writing a proposal)
- ✔ Pitch your proposal and manuscript to editors
- ✔ Negotiate your contract
- ✔ Be the bad guy when you have bad news to bring to your publisher (if you're going to miss a deadline or you have any kind of disagreement with your editor, get your agent involved immediately — that's his job)
- ✔ Give you career advice, including help on branding yourself and developing marketing skills (not all agents do all this)
- ✔ Check your royalty statements to verify that your publisher is paying you correctly and on time

If you can do all of these things very well yourself and if you're willing to take time from your writing to do them, then you don't need an agent. If you see even one item on this list that you can't do competently, then you probably need an agent. Please remember that the major publishing houses don't accept unagented queries from authors they don't know. Many mid-sized publishers don't, either.

You can always choose to outsource certain tasks to specialists — freelance editors, contract lawyers, life coaches, branding specialists, marketing experts, or accountants. Those people will also charge you a fee. Only you can decide whether you prefer to pay an agent or a specialist to do those. The advantage of working with an agent is that one person does all the tasks, so he doesn't need to coordinate with anyone else. In addition, an agent keeps in close touch with editors — he knows what kinds of projects individual editors are looking for, and he can match prospective authors with the right editors. The disadvantage is that he can't possibly be equally good in all the tasks, and he may be less adept at the very thing you need most.

Before you start looking for an agent, make sure you're really ready for one. If you've not yet reached the senior level in your writing career (see Chapter 1 for a review of the stages of your career), then you don't really need an agent because you have nothing to sell. An agent's job is to sell your work.

Doing your homework on agents first

If you're ready for an agent, then you need to do your homework to find the right one for you. Most writers will tell you that having no agent is better than having the wrong one. When you work with an agent, you typically sign a *representation agreement* — a legal contract which spells out your relationship. Some representation agreements have very onerous clauses that make it very hard for you to leave the relationship without losing some of the rights to your work. Other agreements are much more writer-friendly. In all cases, breaking up with an agent is never fun, so it's best to find the right one for you from the start. In this section, we help you locate literary agents, research them, and make sure you hire the real deal.

Finding candidates who fit your category

Different agents prefer different kinds of writing. Some agents specialize in selling romances. Others favor mysteries. Others, suspense. Some focus completely on religious fiction or young adult or children's. Many agents are generalists who have a broad range of interests.

Focus your efforts on those agents most likely to be interested in your work. Most of our agent friends have many comical tales of books they've been pitched that are thoroughly, outrageously, stupendously inappropriate for them. These pitches usually go straight into the recycling bin.

Before you pitch to an agent, do your homework. Consult the appropriate market guide to find listings of agents. *Writer's Market* is the standard market guide, and most agents are listed there and in the subscription-based online database at WritersMarket.com. If you want to find only agents interested in fiction, see *Novel & Short Story Writer's Market*. Both of these are large annual reference works that also list publishers and magazines. If you only care about agents, a smaller reference like *Guide to Literary Agents* might be for you. If you write for a specialized market, such as children/young-adult fiction or Christian fiction, you can find specialized market guides that list agents who focus on those niches. Follow these steps to find your best prospects:

1. **Define carefully the category for your book.**

   Name the major category and any relevant subcategories that apply to your novel. (See Chapter 3 for a discussion of fiction categories.)

2. **Look through the agent listings in the appropriate market guide and circle or bookmark those that seem particularly interested in the kind of book you're writing.**

3. **Make a list of the top ten prospects and check the Web sites of each one.**

   Decide which agents looks like the best fit for you and your book.

Researching the agents can take quite a lot of time, but it's time well spent. Having no agent is far better than having the wrong agent. Your agent will be your employee and your friend for a long time. Breaking up with an agent may be only slightly less painful that breaking up a marriage, so take your time and find the right one.

Avoiding scam artists, charlatans, and other no-goodniks

Just about anybody can hang out his shingle as an agent, whether he knows anything about publishing or not. Some of these are scammers, pure and simple. Others have delusions of grandeur and make wild claims about what they can do for you, fully believing their own PR. Others are hard workers who simply don't know what they're doing.

Most well-established agents in the U.S. are members of the Association of Author Representatives (AAR) which has membership requirements designed to screen out wannabe agents. It also has a canon of ethics that's worth reading just to see what sorts of unethical practices you should be on guard against.

You're looking for an agent with the following qualities:

- ✔ He is honest

- ✔ He understands how publishing works

- ✔ He has plenty of contacts in the publishing industry

- ✔ He understands every nuance of a publishing contract, knows which parts have much room for negotiation, and can effectively negotiate the terms of the deal to benefit you

- ✔ He earns all or most of his living by being an agent, rather than being a part-timer who has a day job that pays his bills

- ✔ He isn't so busy with other clients that he has no time for you

Normally, you should be most interested in agents with a well-established record of success in selling the kind of novel you write. Should you work with a brand-new agent who has no track record? That's always risky, because he may be a scam artist, or delusional, or a rank novice, or merely not cut out for agenting. However, there are certain situations when a new agent is a good bet:

- ✔ Many agents are former editors with years of experience working for publishers. (Some of the best agents we know are former editors.) Sometimes an agent leaves a large, well-established agency to start his own business. A brand new agency, freshly started by an experienced editor or agent, has no track record, but the agent may have a long and distinguished record in the publishing world.

- ✔ When a well-established agency hires a new agent as an employee, it typically vets the new agent in advance and provides plenty of support and on-the-job training. This agent is typically young and hungry and can get advice from more experienced agents if difficult issues come up.

- ✔ Occasionally, an agent will quit to take another job in publishing and then realize that his first love is agenting. When he returns to the agent business, he'll probably hit the ground running.

No matter which agent you're interested in, you *must* research his reputation. All reputable agents will give you names of their clients as referrals. Talk to a few and find out what they like and don't like about their agent. Not every agent works equally well with every client. It never hurts to do an online search using the agent's name and the word "scam." Not everything online is golden truth, but the Web is a useful source of info that agents can't control. You may find the online "Preditors & Editors" list useful. (You can find it with any search engine, if you get the oddball spelling correct.) Talk to other writers and to editors about any agent you're interested in. Publishing is a small world, and word gets around when an agent isn't up to snuff.

Don't work with an agent who charges a "reading fee" to decide whether to work with you. That reading fee too easily becomes an easy way to milk wannabe writers for money instead of doing the hard work of selling novels. Some legitimate agents occasionally charge minor fees for photocopying or mailing expenses — especially when they're sending large batches of proposals to a variety of publishers via overnight delivery — but most of them don't. Don't pay an agent until he's earned you money.

Contacting agents to pitch your work

When you've identified the hot prospects on your list, make an action plan to pitch your work to those agents. You'll probably pitch only a single manuscript, but bear in mind that you're looking for long-term literary representation, so the agent will want to know what sort of projects you have in mind for the future.

You have two main choices in pitching your work to an agent:

- ✔ **Pitch it in person at a writing conference.** Most writing conferences provide plenty of opportunities for writers to discuss their work with agents.

- ✔ **Pitch it cold by querying the agent.** Most agents accept queries. The exceptions have full lists and don't need any more business.

We look at both options in this section.

Getting in touch with agents at writing conferences

Many writing conferences bring in agents as faculty members. Often, you can submit a sample of your work to these agents in advance. Often, you can sign up for an appointment to make a pitch in person. In many cases, you can do both. This is a golden opportunity, because you're guaranteed to get at least a little personal attention from the agent.

If you're submitting written work in advance, prepare the best writing sample or proposal you can. (See Chapter 16 for info on how to polish your sample chapter or proposal. It's wise to show your submission to a writer friend for critique before you mail it in.) Follow the conference instructions on how to submit your work and on how much to submit.

If you're planning to make a personal pitch, then you'll typically get about 15 minutes with the agent. Prepare for this carefully. We highly recommend Michael Hauge's book, *Selling Your Story in 60 Seconds* (Michael Wiese Productions), for a very complete guide to making verbal pitches for both novels and screenplays.

Approaching agents through queries

Our experience is that pitching to an agent at a conference is better than cold querying; however, that isn't always possible, because not all writers can get to a conference, and not all agents go to conferences. You have roughly three levels of contact that you can make when you approach an agent by mail or e-mail, depending on the agent's submission guidelines:

- ✔ Sending a query letter only
- ✔ Sending a query letter with sample chapters
- ✔ Sending a full manuscript

Traditionally, authors send a query letter first. The *query letter* is a short letter to an agent to introduce yourself and find out whether he's interested in hearing more about you and your work. If the query letter catches the agent's interest, he asks for more information — typically some sample chapters and a synopsis, or a full proposal, or the complete manuscript. Then if he thinks he can sell the manuscript, he offers to represent the author. In the days before e-mail, this often took months.

Luckily, writers and agents now have e-mail, but the process still usually takes months. The reason is that delivery is not the bottleneck; the agent's schedule is. Legitimate agents work long hours trying to sell the work of their clients. They don't have much time to deal with the flood of prospective clients. They get to you when they can, if they can.

There should be no mystery in how to approach an agent. The simple rule is to look at the agent's Web site to see exactly how he wants to be contacted. He'll probably tell you what information he wants and how he wants it presented. Follow the instructions precisely — the agent will be both astonished and gratified. If the agent gives you a choice between submitting by e-mail or on paper, you may have slightly better luck with paper. An actual physical piece of paper shows that you're not just shotgunning out queries to every agent on the planet.

Virtually all agents consider query letters. The few who don't look at queries are not snooty — they're just full up with clients and have all the work they can handle. Just as you don't put gas in a full tank, agents don't add clients to a full list.

Some agents do prefer to receive part or all of the manuscript (see Chapter 16) along with the query letter, either by e-mail or by mail. If that's what your target agent wants, then send it.

Agents take substantially longer to respond to a proposal or full manuscript than to a query letter. If you don't get an answer back within three or four months, you're justified in sending a quick e-mail to ask when you should expect a response. Just remember that time spent dealing with you is time your agent isn't earning money for his clients. And every agent has a lot of writers contacting him every week. He simply can't afford to spend much time on you. If and when you sign a representation agreement with him, he'll have a lot more time for you, because then you'll be his boss. But until then, he doesn't work for you and he owes you nothing. Respect that.

Don't send your manuscript to an agent unless he requests it. If he specifies on his Web site that he wants to see 30 pages with your proposal, don't send more. If and when he wants the whole manuscript, he'll tell you, and he'll specify whether it should be a paper copy or an electronic document.

Editors, the Center of Your Writing Universe

An acquisitions editor is crucial. You can't publish a book without an editor. Although an agent may be optional for some people, an editor isn't — at least not if you're working with a traditional royalty-paying publisher. Your editor will typically take a hand in all the following tasks:

- Discover you from among the great unwashed masses of writers
- Champion your manuscript to get the publishing committee to accept it
- Fight for a great cover and a great title
- Make sure that the back-cover copy tells neither too little nor too much
- Make sure your book is placed well in the publisher's catalog and that it's presented as effectively as possible
- Talk up your book to the sales team so they'll be fired up when they go sell it to the various distribution channels
- Fight to get every possible marketing dollar for your book
- Make sure you turn in your first draft on time
- Write a revision letter to you that praises what's good and points out what you need to improve in a way that motivates you to write your final revisions
- Track your manuscript through the copy-editing, line-editing, and proof-reading stages
- Make sure that *galley proofs* — printed pages of the typeset copy — are sent to you so you can verify that the copy is correct
- Give the publicity department the information they need to get you any possible TV, radio, newspaper, or magazine interviews

> ✔ Hold your hand through the process when you feel lost, discouraged, or distraught
>
> ✔ Do everything possible to make sure the publisher earns a decent return on its investment

Your editor loves great fiction and she likes you, but her first obligation is to her employer — the publisher. Of course, making you happy and successful is a very important part of making her publisher money. She walks a fine line, and if she sometimes has to get tough with you, it really isn't personal. Publishing is a business. If you act like you're in business, you'll make your editor happy and your relationship will go far more smoothly than if you act like a prima donna artiste who lives above the grungy world of filthy money.

We strongly recommend that you let your agent find the right acquisitions editor. Effective agents have more contacts than you do. However, it's still possible to sell your book directly to a publisher, especially to smaller ones. It's worth telling you how to do so, even if you don't ever do it yourself, because your agent will follow roughly the same steps as you would, and it's good for you to know what your agent is doing.

Selling a book almost always happens by persuading an acquisitions editor at a publishing house to be the champion for your novel. How do you (or preferably your agent) find the one editor best suited to champion your book? It comes down to research.

First you decide which publishing houses are appropriate for a book in your category. Then you look for the editor at each house most interested in your category.

Targeting a publishing house

You or your agent will work through the following steps to make a list of publishers that may be interested in your book:

1. **Write down the category and subcategory of your book.**

   You can't sell your book unless you know its category, so define the category as precisely as you can. In Chapter 3, we discuss the various fiction categories in depth, precisely so that you write a book you can actually sell.

2. **List a number of recent books that fall into this category and subcategory.**

3. **List the publishers that published these books.**

4. **Ask around or check any industry sources you have (such as Novel & Short Story Writer's Market and other market guides) to add other publishers who are interested in your category and subcategory.**

5. **Check the Web sites of these publishers and cross out any publishers that have gone out of business or have quit publishing in this category.**

Choosing which editor to contact

After you know which publishers may be interested, find one editor at each house who you hope will be the champion for your novel. Again, the Web site of each publisher is your best source of information, but you may also know writers, agents, or other editors who can give you the inside scoop on who loves your category and subcategory.

For each publisher on your list, add the name of the acquisitions editor who seems most appropriate. For smaller publishers, a single editor often handles all acquisitions. For larger publishers, you may find many editors, and you need to read the info on each one to figure out what they like.

Now you have a choice:

✔ You (or your agent) can contact your chosen editors by mail or e-mail.

✔ You (or your agent) can pitch your novel to the editor in person.

✔ Have an industry insider contact the editor on your behalf. (This isn't all that common, but it does happen to well-networked writers.)

If you have an agent, he'll handle this and you can just sit back and write while you wait for something to happen. If you don't have an agent, then it's up to you to make things happen. Your odds are stronger if you meet an editor at a writing conference than if you send a query directly to a publisher. We discuss querying editors in the next section.

Contacting editors directly

Many years ago, when agents and conferences were rare, writers simply mailed their manuscripts directly to publishing houses and then hoped for the best. The writer knew nothing about the editor, and the editor had no clue who the writer was. The process very rarely works like that these days, even with small publishing houses.

From orders to bargain bins: Distribution and how it works

Long before your book gets printed, your publisher creates a catalog that covers the coming new releases over a period of three to four months, along with a listing of available older titles *(backlist)*. Your publisher pays a sales team to use this catalog to present your book to the buyers for bookstores and bookstore chains. The orders come in before your book is even printed, and this helps your publisher decide how many copies to print in the first print run. They print enough to fulfill the preorders and they also print extra, because it's cheaper to print one big run of books than several small print runs. Even if cost were no issue, publishers almost always outsource their printing, and most printers require large print runs. Any books that aren't immediately ordered go into the warehouse.

Bookstores have the right to return unsold books for credit. This means that they don't take any risk when they order too many books. When they later decide they can't sell them all, they just send them back as *returns*, and the publisher is required to take them.

Ideally, bookstores *sell through* their first order of your books and then reorder. If your book continues selling well for a long time, then the bookstore may reorder many times, and eventually your publisher runs out of books in the warehouse. Then they call the printer and your novel goes into a second printing, and a third, and a fourth.

What if your book doesn't sell well? Then the publisher is stuck with unsold books in

the warehouse and with returns from the bookstores. No publisher wants to warehouse those books forever, so when your book has run its course, your publisher tries to liquidate its stock and take the book out of print. The publisher will probably offer you first dibs at the copies, usually at cost. If you don't buy them all, the publisher sells them to a liquidator at a small fraction of the original list price. If you've seen the bargain bins in bookstores, now you know why those prices are so insanely low.

Your contract has paragraphs that deal with all these issues. Most publishers hold back some of your royalties as a reserve against the inevitable returns (which are *negative sales* that you deserve no royalties for).

Your contract specifies an advance payment to you. This is not free money; it's an advance against royalties. If your book doesn't *earn out* its advance, your publisher eats the loss. If your book does earn out, then you get residual income periodically, based on the royalty rate for sales of your book.

If all this sounds complicated, that's because it is. No genius has ever figured out how to predict which books will be winners and which, losers. Publishers create contracts that try to minimize their risks and maximize their rewards. Agents negotiate hard to shift some of that risk back to the publisher and some of the reward back to you. That's why your contract is complex. That's why you probably need an agent.

Many editors (especially those working for major publishing houses that pay the big bucks) no longer take any kind of submissions from writers they don't know, not even simple query letters. In recent years, many mid-sized publishers have quit taking these kinds of submissions also. They have two main reasons for this:

- ✔ **Time:** Publishing houses often get thousands or tens of thousands of unsolicited submissions every year, mostly from amateur writers who haven't read a single book on writing and who can't be bothered to figure how to submit a manuscript correctly. Over the years, more and more publishers have simply decided not to bother with these unwanted submissions.

- ✔ **Risk:** After the anthrax mail scare following 9/11, a number of publishers decided that they didn't want to expose their mailroom staff to the hazards of opening packages from unknown sources. Furthermore, because of computer viruses, some publishers are wary of opening electronic attachments in e-mail from unknown people.

If you're going to contact an editor directly, check the publisher's Web site and find out exactly how she wants to be contacted (if she wants to be contacted). Follow the instructions to the millimeter. They'll specify whether the editor wants a query letter, a query package with sample chapters, a proposal, or the full manuscript. They'll also specify whether she wants a paper or electronic submission.

If you've already met the editor at a writing conference or elsewhere and are following up with sample chapters, a synopsis, a proposal, or a full manuscript — per the editor's request — mark your submission as "requested material." For more information, flip to Chapter 16.

Part V
The Part of Tens

The 5th Wave   By Rich Tennant

"I'd like to become a novelist. I'm just not sure I have that much prose in me."

In this part . . .

In this classic *For Dummies* part, you find a couple of quick-reference chapters to help you through the process of writing and selling compelling fiction. We cover ten steps to designing and analyzing your story and ten reasons publishers reject novels.

Chapter 18

Ten Steps to Analyzing Your Story

*G*reat fiction happens by design, not by chance. You can give your story some sense of order and purpose before you write it or after. The important thing is that at some point, you must work out the design of your story and then shape or reshape your story so your design helps you reach your main goal: giving your reader a powerful emotional experience.

In this chapter, we describe ten steps in Randy's *Snowflake method,* a popular method for analyzing the design of a story. These steps help you start simple and add complexity in stages until you have a beautiful design. The steps are in order from highest level to lowest level. Also, Randy finds it wise to alternate between character and plot development; so steps 2, 4, 6, and 8 involve plot, and steps 3, 5, and 7 involve character. This keeps the story development balanced.

You can apply the Snowflake ideas no matter which creative paradigm you use — a *creative paradigm* is just a method of getting to a first draft. The Snowflake is a method of analyzing a story. So if you use the Snowflake or outliner creative paradigms, you probably want to apply the Snowflake analysis before you write your first draft. But if you use the seat-of-the-pants or edit-as-you-go creative paradigms (see Chapter 4 for an explanation of these common creative paradigms), you write your first draft first, without any design. Then you can use the Snowflake method to analyze your story to help you edit it. (For more information on the Snowflake method, visit Randy's Web site at www.snowflake method.com.)

None of the steps in the Snowflake method are magic. None of them are required before you write your story. You can do them in any order you like. You can even do them backward from Step 10 to Step 1. The steps are just tools to help you design your story and to analyze it. Use what works for you and ignore the rest.

Step 1: Write Your Storyline

First, write out your *storyline* — a summary of your story in one sentence. (See Chapter 8 for a detailed explanation of how to write a storyline, with many examples.) You'll use your storyline to get the interest of your agent or editor. Your agent will use your storyline to sell your book to a publisher. Your editor will use your storyline to sell your idea to publishing committees and sales teams. Your storyline will be used at every point in the selling chain — right down to your readers, who'll use your storyline to explain to their friends why your book is so cool. Your storyline will even benefit you — it'll keep you focused during the editing phase, so you always know what's essential to your story and what isn't.

The storyline for Randy's first novel was, "A physicist travels back in time to kill the apostle Paul." That's only 11 words, but it sold a lot of copies for him at book signings and elsewhere.

In your storyline, focus on the central conflict. Don't name any characters; instead, tell something interesting about the one or two or three characters who are most important to your story. The storyline should be 25 words or less, and you get extra credit if you can do it in less than 15.

Step 2: Write Your Three-Act Structure

Expand your storyline to a three-act structure — a single, one-paragraph summary that describes the high-level structure of your story. (See Chapter 8 for full details on the three-act structure of a story, which is a widely-used concept in the publishing industry.) If you've already written your story, you'll find that analyzing the three-act structure helps you understand the big chunks of your story better.

We recommend that you write your one-paragraph summary using five sentences, in this simple pattern:

- **Sentence 1:** Describe the story backdrop and tell about the lead characters. (See Chapter 6 for details on the story backdrop.)

- **Sentence 2:** Describe the beginning quarter of your story, culminating in a major disaster that forces your lead character to fully commit to his story goal. (See Chapter 7 for details about characters and story goals.)

- **Sentence 3:** Describe the second quarter of the story, leading up to a second major disaster at the midpoint of the story.

- ✔ **Sentence 4:** Describe the third quarter of the story, ending in your third and worst disaster. This disaster will force your lead character to commit to a final confrontation.

- ✔ **Sentence 5:** Explain the final confrontation and how it resolves the story.

A story has a beginning, a middle, and an end, and each of these is one of the acts in your three-act structure. Act 1 (the beginning) covers roughly a quarter of your story. It ends in a disaster that leads directly to Act 2 (the middle). Act 2 is quite long — roughly half the total length of the book, and it needs a major disaster at roughly its midpoint to prevent a sagging middle in your story. Act 2 ends in a third disaster that leads directly to Act 3 (the end). In Act 3, you show a final confrontation and resolve all of the story threads.

Step 3: Define Your Characters

For each major character in your story, write down the following basic information:

- ✔ **Name:** Write the name of your character (or the character's role, such as "Hero" or "Villain," if you haven't figured out names yet).

- ✔ **Ambition:** What one abstract thing does the character want most?

- ✔ **Story goal:** What one concrete thing does your character believe will enable her to achieve her ambition?

- ✔ **Conflict:** What prevents your character from reaching her story goal?

- ✔ **Epiphany:** How will your character change or what will she learn in the course of the story?

- ✔ **One-sentence summary:** If this story were mainly about this character, what would the storyline be?

- ✔ **One-paragraph summary:** If this story were mainly about this character, what would the three-act structure be?

If you've already written your story and you can't answer all of these questions, that's a strong indicator of a weakness in your characters. Now is a *great* time to solve that weakness, before you plunge into editing scenes.

Every character in your story believes that he or she is the lead character. Write your one-sentence summary and one-paragraph summary for each character as if he or she really were the center of the universe. This is critical for creating three-dimensional characters. Never create a character who exists solely to make some other character's story work. (For more on creating characters, flip to Chapter 7.)

Step 4: Write a Short Synopsis

In Step 2, you write a one-paragraph summary that describes the three-act structure of your story. Now expand each sentence in this paragraph into a full paragraph of its own. You should get about one full page, which we call a *short synopsis.* This will be somewhat shorter than the normal two-page synopsis for your query that we describe in Chapter 9.

Your short synopsis should be in present tense, and it must summarize your story briefly. Focus on the high points here. You can't describe every scene. You can ultimately use this short synopsis to write your synopsis for your proposal, but the main purpose of the short synopsis is to help you understand your story structure better by adding detail to the paragraph of Step 2.

Step 5: Write Character Sketches

For each important character defined in Step 3, write a character sketch in one paragraph or a few paragraphs (up to a page for the most important characters). Summarize the character's backstory. Explain his values, ambitions, and story goals to show how they all fit together into the story. The character sketch is immensely valuable, mainly by focusing on back story and values, and adding details to the front story. Also, the character sketch fills in a lot of details missing from Step 3 that are critical to understanding your characters.

Notice that you are alternating between plot analysis and character analysis. We've found that by alternating between them, you make both stronger.

Editors love to read character sketches. If you write these in complete paragraphs in a way designed to arouse interest in each character, you can integrate these character sketches directly into your proposal.

Step 6: Write a Long Synopsis

In Step 4, you write a one-page short synopsis that summarizes your story briefly. Now expand each paragraph in that short synopsis into several paragraphs (up to a page) to create a *long synopsis* that now captures all the high-level details of your story. This will probably run four or five pages, so it's somewhat longer than the normal synopsis for your proposal that we describe in Chapter 9.

Again, you are adding detail in a systematic way, first on plot, and then character, and then back on plot again. This principle of alternation helps keep you engaged and keeps your story balanced between character and plot.

Your long synopsis should be in present tense, and you can afford to get a lot more detailed now. You have room for a paragraph or even two or three on all the sequences of scenes in your story. Glossing over the unimportant scenes here is okay, but you should capture the important scenes. The purpose of this synopsis is to make sure you know how your story works. You may ultimately use it to write the synopsis for your proposal, or you may never show it to a soul. Your goal is to fix those pesky logic plot problems in a simple document that you can easily scan in just a few minutes.

Step 7: Create Your Character Bible

For each important character in your story, create a bible that details everything you need to remember. (See Chapter 12 for what goes into a character bible and why you need one.) This is the place to save every bit of information that you need. Some of the obvious things that go into this bible are

- ✔ Census data, such as name, birth date, and so on
- ✔ Physical descriptions, including hair color, eye color, height, weight, and scars
- ✔ Physical and mental disabilities
- ✔ Education, work skills, and special talents
- ✔ Fears, hopes, and dreams
- ✔ Backstory (your character's history)

There's no complete list of features that you need to track for your characters. Focus on the character traits that are important for your kind of story. Remember that the purpose of your bible is to prevent you from making rookie mistakes like having a character with green eyes on page 17 and gray eyes on page 384. You need to know far more about your characters than you tell your readers.

Step 8: Make Your Scene List

Write a scene list, which gives you a short summary of every scene in your story. (See Chapter 9 for an explanation of a scene list and how to create one.) In Steps 4 and 6, you create short and long synopses of your story, but neither of these covers every scene in your story.

The purpose of a scene list is to let you rearrange your scenes and see how that affects your story. If you do this before you write your story, then the scene list helps you fill in the missing gaps in the story. If you do it after you write your story, the scene list shows you the full story in one large view, and you can make decisions about which scenes are pulling their weight and which aren't helping the story.

If you are a Snowflaker or an Outliner (see Chapter 4 if you're not sure what your creative paradigm is), then by the end of this step, you have enough information to write your book proposal. Should you do so? That depends. A published novelist almost always writes a query or proposal, sells the book, and *then* writes the manuscript. But novelists who haven't yet sold their first book almost never can do that, because agents and editors want to see proof that you can finish a novel before they'll buy it. The proof that they want is a finished, polished draft of your novel. No publisher can afford to get burned by an amateur writer who can't finish a story. (See Chapter 16 for details on writing queries.)

The bottom line is that if you're a published writer, then it makes good sense to take what you have, write a query or proposal, and start submitting it to agents or editors. Even if you're not published, writing a proposal now is good practice. You may find it useful to write a proposal and take it to a writing conference. A good proposal may get an agent excited about you and your writing. Just don't expect to make a sale until you have a polished manuscript to back up your proposal.

Many writers keep their scene lists on index cards so they can shuffle them around to find the best order. Other writers prefer to create their scene lists on a computer. Randy has long preferred using a spreadsheet for his scene lists, because a spreadsheet lets you

- ✔ Easily move scenes around, edit them, add new scenes, and delete unneeded ones

- ✔ Make copies so that you can play around with new combinations without fear of losing your work

- ✔ Easily keep track of the number of words in each scene; if your manuscript has too many words (or too few), then you can see the effect of dropping or adding scenes on your total word count

Step 9: Analyze Your Scenes

In Step 8, you create a scene list. If you don't have a first draft of your manuscript yet, you may be itching to start writing. You're free to do that. But if you want to do a bit more thinking about your scenes, or if you already have a first draft written, the next step is to analyze your scenes. For each scene in the story, write down the following:

- ✔ **Type of scene:** Is it a proactive scene or a reactive scene? (See Chapters 10 and 14 for a discussion of these two main kinds of scenes.) A proactive scene has the structure goal-conflict-setback. A reactive scene has the structure reaction-dilemma-decision.

- ✔ **POV character:** Who is the point-of-view character in the scene? Are you writing in first person, third person, objective third person, or some other viewpoint? Are you writing in past tense or present tense?

- ✔ **Setting:** Where is the scene taking place? What is the date and time? Which characters play a role in the scene?

- ✔ **Beginning:** If this is a proactive scene, what's the goal? If it's a reactive scene, what's the reaction?

- ✔ **Middle:** If this is a proactive scene, what's the conflict? If it's a reactive scene, what's the dilemma?

- ✔ **End:** If this is a proactive scene, what's the setback? If it's a reactive scene, what's the decision?

- ✔ **Other comments:** What special information do you want to remember to put into this scene (if you haven't written it yet)? What should you remember to research or fix in this scene (if you've written it already)?

You don't have to analyze your scenes before you write your story. That's perfectly fine. Get it written! But later on, after it's written, you still need to get it right. The preceding questions are precisely the ones you'll need to ask to help you get it right.

Step 10: Write and Edit Your Story

This step applies only if you don't yet have a first draft of your manuscript. If you've been using the Snowflake method to help you design your story, you're now ready to write. Go for it! Start writing whichever scene interests you most.

Remember one thing — at any instant in time, you should be in either creative mode or editing mode. Don't edit it before you write it down. That's called writer's block, and it's a perfect prescription for getting nothing done. Just write. Write fast. Write hard. Get into the skin of your POV character, become that character, and drill out some words.

The software side of story design

Knowing what to do is one thing; actually getting it done and keeping track of where you put your story is another. Randy spent many years in a day job as a computational physicist, and he's developed a software product, *Snowflake Pro*, that makes it easy to work through the ten steps of the Snowflake method. *Snowflake Pro* runs on all major computer operating systems — Windows, Mac, and Linux.

The program helps you keep track of all those pesky storylines, disasters, characters, values, ambitions, story goals, synopses, and scenes. And *Snowflake Pro* has a nice feature at the end: Press a button, and it writes a skeleton of your book proposal for you. The ten steps of the Snowflake ask you to create much of the information you need for your proposal, so *Snowflake Pro* gathers all those pieces together and writes out an RTF document that you can load into any word processor. The software leaves slots open for you to complete any missing pieces of the proposal in your word processor. You can find out more about *Snowflake Pro* on Randy's Web site at www. snowflakemethod.com.

You can edit your first draft whenever you like. Randy normally starts out each writing session by editing whatever he wrote in the previous session. This gives him some momentum — by the time he finishes editing the previous scene, he's up to speed and eager to write the next one. Peter likes to write an entire chapter and then edit it. If you're an Edit-As-You-Go writer, then you may prefer to write a single page and then edit it. That's fine. But write it first before you edit.

As you get into your story, you may find that the characters have come alive and are refusing to follow your carefully constructed plan. That's perfectly okay. You are the god of the universe you're creating, but you have the right to grant some measure of free will to your characters. When they exercise that free will, they won't do what you expected; they'll do something better. Go with that.

If your story starts diverging from your design, what do you do? The answer is simple: Redesign! Randy normally tweaks his complete Snowflake design after writing about a quarter of his manuscript. This takes only an hour or two of effort, and it's worth the time to examine the consequences of those pesky characters who insist on going their own way. Randy also does a redesign at the midpoint of his novels and another redesign just before writing the ending. You're free to redesign your story as often as you need to in order to get your first draft written.

Chapter 19

Ten Reasons Novels Are Rejected

- -

In This Chapter

▶ Targeting your book

▶ Strengthening your writing craft

▶ Delivering a powerful emotional experience

- -

*P*ublishers give many reasons they don't buy a particular book. Sometimes a book is fine, but the time just isn't right for it. If that's the case, you can't do anything but write another book while you wait for the time to be right for the one you wrote.

In other cases, the time is right but the book just isn't. That's a hard, hard thing to hear. Yet if that's the case, you don't have to wait passively for some mythical "right time" that may never come. You need to figure out what's wrong so you can fix it and resubmit it somewhere else.

If you've had your novel rejected multiple times, go ahead and take some time to lick your wounds. We've been there. Getting rejected stings. It's also perfectly normal. Jack London got rejected 600 times before he ever sold a thing. Jack scraped himself off the floor, figured out how to improve, and went on to become a pretty darn good writer.

First let's talk about who has the power to reject your work. If you've read Chapter 17, you know that your first step is usually to find an agent. Most agents get dozens to hundreds of queries each week, and must reject most of them. Once you've got an agent, he'll submit your work to acquisitions editors at publishing houses. The job of such editors is to sift hundreds of queries, proposals, and manuscripts and reject most of them. Rarely, an acquisitions editor decides to champion a project and takes it to the publishing committee. The committee has the final word, and it may reject your work, too, but your odds are actually pretty good if your project makes it to the committee.

It's clumsy and awkward to refer to "agents, acquisitions editors, and publishing committees" throughout this chapter. So we'll simply use the word "editor," and you can mentally substitute in all the others. Most rejections happen quickly, when the editor spots a show-stopper in your submission. In this chapter, we look at a number of common reasons for rejections, looking at them roughly in order of how fast the editor decides to say no.

Listen carefully when an editor rejects your work. Don't argue with her. She knows her business, which is to champion books her publishing house can sell at a profit. If she doesn't strongly believe that her house can sell your book, then she can't do much for you, because much of publishing is making a leap of faith and taking risks. That works best when the editor has loads of faith.

So listen to the words you hear in those painful rejections and see what you can take from them. (In Chapter 1, we tell Randy's story of selling his first novel. His breakthrough came when he realized that he could write a new novel that met all the objections he heard from one particular publisher. That publisher ultimately bought three of his novels.)

The Category Is Wrong

Editors normally have three reactions when you mention a particular category: They love the category, they're neutral about it, or they really hate it. (See Chapter 3 for a discussion of the many categories and subcategories in fiction.) Your novel will do best with an editor champion who absolutely, positively, deliriously loves the category you're writing. An enthusiastic editor is one of the main reasons novels succeed.

Suppose you make an appointment with an editor at a conference. You sit down and she asks about your novel. You start out by telling her you have a paranormal romance novel. She interrupts to say, "Sorry, but I don't do romance at all. I only look at thrillers." Now what do you do?

First, apologize. You just wasted her time and yours by making an appointment with the wrong editor. You should've done your homework better, and now she has a 15-minute block of unproductive time.

Second, ask her advice. You may say, "Listen, since this obviously isn't a book for you, maybe I can just get your advice on who might be interested in a story like this one." She may say no, and that's her right. However, you have nothing to lose by asking. She may say yes and then ask you to tell her a bit about the story. If she does, give her the exact same storyline that you already planned to deliver. But now she doesn't have to worry about possibly having to reject you (she's already done that); she's free to give you friendly advice as an industry professional. If the storyline is good, she just might say, "Wow, that's actually not a bad story idea," and direct you to a couple of editors who may be interested. If you don't yet have an agent, she might point you to one who's suitable.

Of course, next time you make an appointment with an editor, do your homework and choose one who likes your category. Conferences almost always tell you what categories their faculty are interested in. If you don't bother to read this information, you're hurting yourself and wasting the time of the editors or agents you make appointments with.

Bad Mechanics and Lackluster Writing

The first thing an editor actually sees is either your query letter or the cover letter on your proposal. If this has mechanical errors or is badly written, she knows she doesn't need to look further. That's an instant rejection and she can move on to the next project.

Many editors often look at the sample chapters second. If the writing is truly wretched, the editor knows it within a few words. If it's merely mediocre, that's clear within a paragraph or two. If you use too many adverbs, have weak style, write dull dialogue, or show weak action, those all show up in the first page or two. Editors have finely tuned reading instincts, and they can say no to most sample chapters they see within a very few pages.

Great craft is critical to getting published. Do yourself a huge favor and polish your work as well as possible, and then get a second opinion before you send it to an editor. This is one reason we strongly recommend getting an agent first. A good agent makes sure that your work is up to snuff before he submits it to editors. Of course, before you send your work to an agent, it's a really good idea to get it critiqued by a strong writer or a freelance editor.

The Target Reader Isn't Defined

Your proposal for your novel normally defines a target reader. If you don't include this in your proposal, then the editor may well assume you don't know. That puts the onus on her to figure out what sort of person would be interested in your book. If she doesn't think there are enough of that kind of person to justify publishing your book, then you're out of luck.

If you hear anything like this from an editor, then read Chapter 3 for info on defining your audience and your target reader. Spend some time thinking about this. Just being a good writer isn't enough; you also need to be a good writer who connects with readers. Publishers aren't in business to make you happy or to print copies of books they can't sell. They're in business to earn money in a business partnership with you. If you can show them that you mean business — enough to tell them who your customers are — then you stand a chance of forming that partnership.

The Story World Is Boring

If your personal life is dull, what do you do? Your quickest solution is to get out more — out of the house, out of your routine, maybe take a vacation. In other words, change your environment. The story world for your novel is the environment for your characters. If your story world is boring, your characters will be bored, and so will your reader. What's the solution? Change their environment.

You have two main avenues of attack for improving your story world:

- **Know it better.** You may need to do more research. If you know your story world intimately, you can't help but show the parts of it you love best to your reader. Chapter 6 covers researching your novel's story world.

- **Show it better.** If you know your story world well, then the problem may be that your descriptions of it don't shine. Do you have too little description? Then add more. Do you have enough? Then buff it up by showing it through the eyes of your POV characters, focusing on the elements that trigger a powerful emotional experience in your character. See Chapters 10 and 15 for specific tips on integrating description directly into your story.

For more advice on building your story world, read Chapter 6 and work through the exercises.

The Storyline Is Weak

Every great story can be reduced to a great *storyline* — a single sentence that hooks your target reader. (See Chapter 8 for details on storylines.)

Editors are always looking for strong storylines. Here's why:

- **A good storyline is a sign that you're a professional writer, not an amateur.** Editors prefer working with pros.

- **If you have a good storyline, then the editor knows she can sell it to her publishing committee (and to every other person in the selling chain).** If you have a weak storyline, then she's going to have to spend valuable time helping you craft one.

✔ **If you have a good storyline, the manuscript you submit is likely to be on target.** It probably won't need massive editing. The editor probably won't have to return it to you as "unacceptable." No editor ever wants to tell an author that the final draft for a contracted novel is unacceptable, but sometimes it just is.

If your storyline is weak, think hard about your story. Figure out what it's really about. Work through the exercise in Chapter 8 on creating your storyline. If you need help, recruit some of your writing buddies. Take time every few months to rethink your storyline. The more you think about it, the better you'll understand your story.

The Characters Aren't Unique and Interesting

The surest way to an editor's heart is to give her a unique, compelling, fascinating character. Remember that your reader is going to be *paying money* for the privilege of spending several hours with your characters. You wouldn't pay to hang out with boring people.

If you get any hint from an editor that your characters aren't interesting, then you have some work ahead of you:

✔ **Make sure you understand what makes a strong character.** Characters need backstories, values, ambitions, and story goals, and they shouldn't be stereotypes (read Chapters 7 and 12 for details).

✔ **Get an opinion on your characters from one of your writing buddies or from a professional freelance editor.** They'll see things you miss.

✔ **Review each scene of your novel to make sure that you've identified a point-of-view (POV) character for each scene.** Also, verify that your reader can easily tell who the POV character is.

✔ **Make sure that you're putting your reader solidly inside the heart and mind of each POV character.** For more information, read Chapter 10.

The Author Lacks a Strong Voice

Many agents and editors say that the very first thing they look for in an author is a strong voice. *Voice* has everything to do with how unique and interesting your writing is. We don't say much in this book about voice, because most authors eventually find their voice on their own without any help from books or coaches.

How do you find your voice? By writing. Writing a lot. And reading. Reading a lot. Time and experience are the most important ingredients in developing your voice. Should you try writing a whole full-length novel before your voice is fully developed? Sure, go right ahead. You don't develop your voice by just doing exercises. You develop your voice by writing — for real, without a net.

If you're hearing that your voice isn't strong enough yet, then be encouraged. This means that you have most of the ingredients for a good novel in place — good story world, characters, plot, and theme. All you're missing is that magic oomph that will make you different from every other fiction writer out there. If you're destined to be a fiction writer, then you'll find that magic oomph. Just keep writing until you sell. You may be closer than you think.

The Plot Is Predictable

When you hear that your plot is predictable, you need to identify carefully the underlying reason. A predictable plot is a *symptom;* cure the disease, and the symptom will go away. Here are the most common reasons your plot may be predictable:

- ✔ **Weak research:** If you haven't researched your story world well enough, then you'll fall back on what "everybody knows," which usually is what everybody learned from watching thousands of hours of TV. And TV is a bad way to learn about cops, or doctors, or scientists, or priests, or just about anything. TV is Cliché City. The solution? Do more research on your story world. Find out so much that you won't rely on the obvious plot twists you learned from TV. You'll come up with something new.

- ✔ **Weak values for your characters:** Your characters become unpredictable when they have a conflict in their underlying values — the core truths they believe about the world. If your characters are predictable, then you can solve this by giving them values that conflict, forcing them into tough moral dilemmas. They'll make choices that your reader can't predict, because they'll make choices that *you* can't predict. Your characters will start acting like they have a mind of their own. They do. Let them. Be surprised. (See Chapter 7 for a discussion of character values.)

- ✔ **Weak setbacks in your scenes:** When your character hits a setback, he's forced into a dilemma. This needs to be a real dilemma with no good options. If you leave him any good options, then both he and the reader are going to see it — and the reader will probably see it first. To solve this, strengthen your setbacks. Box in your character tighter. Reduce his options. (See Chapter 9 for a discussion of setbacks.)

The Theme Is Overbearing

Nobody likes a sermon in a novel. When you design a novel that's nothing but a theme sliced, diced, and spliced into a story, it's going to reek like last week's wallaby stew. Your reader doesn't want a sermon, and therefore no publisher will buy one.

If your theme is overpowering the other elements of your fiction, then you need to seriously rethink your story. Read Chapter 11 for info on what a theme is and how it emerges naturally from a story. Then do the following:

1. **Analyze each character, focusing especially on the character's values, ambitions, and goals (Chapter 12 provides some tools to help).**

    Do these seem designed specially to illustrate the theme of your novel? If so, change them. Start by giving every character values that conflict. This is often the easiest way to turn a flat character into a living one. Then see whether you can change some of your characters' ambitions and story goals so they aren't so obviously tied to your theme.

2. **Rewrite each scene so that it reflects your new and improved characters.**

    This may spiral out of control, and you may find the story getting away from you. Good! It's about time. If you had the story under your control the entire time you were writing it, then your characters were not in control. You need to give them some rein and see where they take you. If they're living, breathing, honest-to-God people, then they won't be nearly so interested in your theme as you are. They'll be too busy finding ways to satisfy their ambitions and story goals.

The Book Fails to Deliver a Powerful Emotional Experience

Writing fiction is about giving your reader a powerful emotional experience. You do this by showing your POV character having a powerful emotional experience and then convincing your reader that he or she *is* that character.

What's the solution? That depends on why things are breaking down. Here are the most likely causes of the problem:

 ✔ **Low stakes:** If your characters are playing for low stakes, the emotive level is going to be low. Raise the stakes on your story question and your characters suddenly start getting serious about the story they're in. Your reader will follow. See Chapter 6 on the story backdrop and the story question to get some ideas on raising the stakes. How important is your story question to your characters? To how many characters is it important?

✔ **Flat characters:** A character can have a powerful emotional experience only if she's real. That means she needs her own values, ambitions, and story goals — hers, not yours. If you've cooked her up just to hold a place in the plot so that your story works out the way you want it to, then she's going to be flat as paint. Read through Chapters 7 and 12 to juice her up with a life of her own.

✔ **Telling, not showing:** When you tell your reader about an emotional experience, your reader doesn't experience it. You must show that emotional experience. There's no better way to do that than by mixing action, dialogue, interior monologue, interior emotion, and description, as we explain in Chapters 10 and 15.

Index

• Y •

Business/Accounting & Bookkeeping

Bookkeeping For Dummies
978-0-7645-9848-7

eBay Business
All-in-One For Dummies,
2nd Edition
978-0-470-38536-4

Job Interviews
For Dummies,
3rd Edition
978-0-470-17748-8

Resumes For Dummies,
5th Edition
978-0-470-08037-5

Stock Investing
For Dummies,
3rd Edition
978-0-470-40114-9

Successful Time
Management
For Dummies
978-0-470-29034-7

Computer Hardware

BlackBerry For Dummies,
3rd Edition
978-0-470-45762-7

Computers For Seniors
For Dummies
978-0-470-24055-7

iPhone For Dummies,
2nd Edition
978-0-470-42342-4

Laptops For Dummies,
3rd Edition
978-0-470-27759-1

Macs For Dummies,
10th Edition
978-0-470-27817-8

Cooking & Entertaining

Cooking Basics
For Dummies,
3rd Edition
978-0-7645-7206-7

Wine For Dummies,
4th Edition
978-0-470-04579-4

Diet & Nutrition

Dieting For Dummies,
2nd Edition
978-0-7645-4149-0

Nutrition For Dummies,
4th Edition
978-0-471-79868-2

Weight Training
For Dummies,
3rd Edition
978-0-471-76845-6

Digital Photography

Digital Photography
For Dummies,
6th Edition
978-0-470-25074-7

Photoshop Elements 7
For Dummies
978-0-470-39700-8

Gardening

Gardening Basics
For Dummies
978-0-470-03749-2

Organic Gardening
For Dummies,
2nd Edition
978-0-470-43067-5

Green/Sustainable

Green Building
& Remodeling
For Dummies
978-0-470-17559-0

Green Cleaning
For Dummies
978-0-470-39106-8

Green IT For Dummies
978-0-470-38688-0

Health

Diabetes For Dummies,
3rd Edition
978-0-470-27086-8

Food Allergies
For Dummies
978-0-470-09584-3

Living Gluten-Free
For Dummies
978-0-471-77383-2

Hobbies/General

Chess For Dummies,
2nd Edition
978-0-7645-8404-6

Drawing For Dummies
978-0-7645-5476-6

Knitting For Dummies,
2nd Edition
978-0-470-28747-7

Organizing For Dummies
978-0-7645-5300-4

SuDoku For Dummies
978-0-470-01892-7

Home Improvement

Energy Efficient Homes
For Dummies
978-0-470-37602-7

Home Theater
For Dummies,
3rd Edition
978-0-470-41189-6

Living the Country Lifestyle
All-in-One For Dummies
978-0-470-43061-3

Solar Power Your Home
For Dummies
978-0-470-17569-9

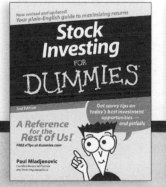

Internet

Blogging For Dummies,
2nd Edition
978-0-470-23017-6

eBay For Dummies,
6th Edition
978-0-470-49741-8

Facebook For Dummies
978-0-470-26273-3

Google Blogger
For Dummies
978-0-470-40742-4

Web Marketing
For Dummies,
2nd Edition
978-0-470-37181-7

WordPress For Dummies,
2nd Edition
978-0-470-40296-2

Language & Foreign Language

French For Dummies
978-0-7645-5193-2

Italian Phrases
For Dummies
978-0-7645-7203-6

Spanish For Dummies
978-0-7645-5194-9

Spanish For Dummies,
Audio Set
978-0-470-09585-0

Macintosh

Mac OS X Snow Leopard
For Dummies
978-0-470-43543-4

Math & Science

Algebra I For Dummies
978-0-7645-5325-7

Biology For Dummies
978-0-7645-5326-4

Calculus For Dummies
978-0-7645-2498-1

Chemistry For Dummies
978-0-7645-5430-8

Microsoft Office

Excel 2007 For Dummies
978-0-470-03737-9

Office 2007 All-in-One
Desk Reference
For Dummies
978-0-471-78279-7

Music

Guitar For Dummies,
2nd Edition
978-0-7645-9904-0

iPod & iTunes
For Dummies,
6th Edition
978-0-470-39062-7

Piano Exercises
For Dummies
978-0-470-38765-8

Parenting & Education

Parenting For Dummies,
2nd Edition
978-0-7645-5418-6

Type 1 Diabetes
For Dummies
978-0-470-17811-9

Pets

Cats For Dummies,
2nd Edition
978-0-7645-5275-5

Dog Training For Dummies,
2nd Edition
978-0-7645-8418-3

Puppies For Dummies,
2nd Edition
978-0-470-03717-1

Religion & Inspiration

The Bible For Dummies
978-0-7645-5296-0

Catholicism For Dummies
978-0-7645-5391-2

Women in the Bible
For Dummies
978-0-7645-8475-6

Self-Help & Relationship

Anger Management
For Dummies
978-0-470-03715-7

Overcoming Anxiety
For Dummies
978-0-7645-5447-6

Sports

Baseball For Dummies,
3rd Edition
978-0-7645-7537-2

Basketball For Dummies,
2nd Edition
978-0-7645-5248-9

Golf For Dummies,
3rd Edition
978-0-471-76871-5

Web Development

Web Design All-in-One
For Dummies
978-0-470-41796-6

Windows Vista

Windows Vista
For Dummies
978-0-471-75421-3

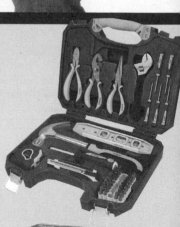

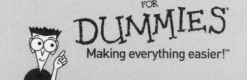